THE
Land,
ALWAYS
THE
LAND

ALSO BY MEL ELLIS

Run, Rainey, Run, 1967

Sad Song of the Coyote, 1967

Softly Roars the Lion, 1968

Ironhead, 1968

Wild Goose, Brother Goose, 1969

Ghost Dog of Killicut, 1969

Flight of the White Wolf, 1970

The Wild Runners, 1970

When Lightning Strikes, 1970

Caribou Crossing, 1971

This Mysterious River, 1972

Hurry-Up Hanson, 1972

Peg Leg Pete, 1973

No Man for Murder, 1973

Sidewalk Indian, 1974

Sermons in Stone, 1975

The Wild Horse Killers, 1976

An Eagle to the Wind, 1978

THE Land, ALWAYS THE LAND

MEL ELLIS

Illustrated by Suzanne Ellis
Edited by Ted J. Rulseh

The Cabin Bookshelf

1234 Hickory Drive
Waukesha, WI 53186

The Land, Always the Land
by Mel Ellis
Edited by Ted J. Rulseh

The Land, Always the Land
© 1997 by The Cabin Bookshelf

The Cabin Bookshelf
1234 Hickory Drive
Waukesha, WI 53186

Cover painting and illustrations
© 1997 by Suzanne Ellis, Madison, Wisconsin

Text and cover design © 1997 by Tamara L. Cook, TLC Graphics, Orangevale, CA

Publisher's Cataloging in Publication
        (Prepared by Quality Books, Inc.)

Ellis, Mel, 1912-1984
        The land, always the land/Mel Ellis. — 1st ed.
        p. cm.
        ISBN: 0-9653381-2-6
        1. Natural history — Wisconsin.   2. Human ecology.   3. Nature.
        I. Title.
        QH105.W6E56   1997   508.775
                                                    QBI97-40956

Library of Congress Catalog Number: 97-69174

contents

LITTLE LAKES
AND LOST MANUSCRIPTS

A wild honking, carried on an Indian summer breeze, drifted in the door of the small bookstore in downtown Waukesha, Wisconsin, where a book event for Mel Ellis' *Notes From Little Lakes* was just concluding. Mel's daughter Debbie and I stepped out onto the downtown sidewalk and, looking up, watched a wedge of Canada geese fly directly over the store, almost low enough so we could hear the whishing of wings. Nothing could have seemed more right.

Indeed, nothing has been more right than bringing Mel Ellis back into print for the first time since his death in 1984, at age 72. As soon as word about the new book *Notes From Little Lakes* hit the papers in fall 1996, the phone on the publishing desk in our home started ringing. We heard from a nurse who cared for Ellis during his last days; from a woman whose husband once shared a Northwoods cabin called the Boar's Nest with Ellis and eight others; from a former airman who flew with Ellis on World War II bombing runs (he said Mel always carried two cigars on missions: one for himself and one for the pilot, to be lit upon landing safely back at the base).

We heard from people who had hunted and fished with Ellis, from women who had grown up with his daughters (known as the Rebels), from writers who had profited from his advice and inspiration. Most of all, we heard from everyday people who had been touched in some way by the man's writing, be it his columns and articles in the *Milwaukee Journal* or any of his eighteen books.

Wisconsin has known many fine outdoor and nature writers — Aldo Leopold, Gordon MacQuarrie, Clay Schoenfeld, George Vukelich, August Derleth, Dion Henderson, and others — but few if any found their way into readers' hearts the way Mel Ellis did. Perhaps that was because Ellis shared his observations of nature within the familiar context of home, family and parenthood. Perhaps it was because he had a way of helping readers appreciate the beauty around them, whether in the countryside, in a suburban back lot or on a city block.

Whatever the case, those who read Ellis learned to see things in the natural world that they never noticed before, and to see the familiar in brand new ways. If not for Ellis, could we hear a humble prayer in the song of the robin after a rain? Would we watch against a full autumn moon for the shadows of migrating birds, or listen for their distant calls beneath a sky of sparkling stars? Would we brighten our day by crushing a sprig of cool-scented mint to carry around in a shirt pocket?

Probably not, and maybe that is why when *Notes From Little Lakes* appeared, people poured out their gratitude, in calls to the publisher, in cards and letters to Mel's wife Gwen and the Ellis daughters, and in attendance at programs hosted by Gwen at bookstores, nature centers and libraries — programs that included pictures of Little Lakes, the wildlife haven Mel and family created in the little Southeastern Wisconsin village of Big Bend.

People delighted in seeing on a slide screen the world they had read about for so many years. And they rejoiced upon hearing that Gwen had arranged to protect the Little Lakes property from rampant development by selling it to a private foundation (which prefers to remain anonymous). Under the terms of sale, Gwen will live at Little Lakes as long as she chooses, while getting some help with the never-ending work of maintaining fifteen acres of trees and plantings surrounding a creek and four spring-fed ponds. When she does leave, the property most likely will be used for nature study. Whatever the final arrangement, Little Lakes is destined to become an environmental landmark on par with Aldo Leopold's shack.

With the future of his Little Lakes secure, and with his literary presence restored, Mel Ellis now returns in a book that almost was — should have been — published while he was still living. *The Land, Always the Land* revolves around a series of twelve essays that capture the moods, sights, sounds and sensations of all the months of the year.

First planned as a coffee-table picture book of essays drawn from Ellis' finest writings, *The Land* was all but ready to go to the printer in fall 1977. But before it came to market, the publisher, Waukesha-based Country Beautiful, closed its doors. After that, the manuscript passed through a series of regional publishing houses, until it came to be known in publishing circles as "the lost Ellis manuscript."

The Land, Always the Land now appears some two decades after its intended release, built around the original manuscript, but also drawing from the best of "The Good Earth" and "Afield with Ellis" columns, which appeared in the *Milwaukee Journal* magazine section in the 1970s and 1980s.

This collection shows Ellis at his full maturity, both as a writer and as an observer of the natural world. Just as lovers of outdoor literature best remember Aldo Leopold for his *A Sand County Almanac*, so they will come to connect Mel Ellis with *The Land, Always the Land*.

Readers may wonder why this book of monthly reflections begins with April. Ellis intended it to begin with March. "If you're wondering why this book starts with the month of March instead of the first of the year," he wrote to one prospective publisher, "try beginning something with a month which holds as little promise as January."

With the permission and support of Gwen Ellis, we have chosen to start with April, so that the book both begins and ends on a note of renewal and awakening. We think Mel would approve, and not incidentally would be gratified by the enthusiasm that has greeted the new volumes of his work..

If there has been one disappointment so far in bringing Mel Ellis back, it is that the readers who have gravitated to him are mainly those who used to read him years ago. His appeal, and the importance of his message, are by no means limited to his own and one or two succeeding generations. They are timeless and universal, as those younger people who have just discovered him will attest.

So, for all those in that large group of long-time Mel Ellis fans, perhaps the time is right to share him with someone younger, so that his legacy may live on for generations to come.

Ted J. Rulseh
June 1997

Prologue

During half a century, its quicksands have sucked me down to within a breath of death. Its trees, trembling to the insult of my insensitive saw, have split up the middle and exploded in my face. Its rivers have bounced me from boulder to boulder, spun me through their whirlpools like a sodden leaf, and spit me writhing and retching out on the beach. Its bogs and swamps have mired me almost beyond endurance. And a riptide once sucked me seaward, and that would have been the end of that, except for the hook of a rock-strewn peninsula.

Twisted ankles, broken bones, pulled ligament, dislocated joints, shin splints, Charley horses, swollen-shut eyes, and scratches, welts and cuts as unnumbered as the rashes and lumpy swellings — marks of hornet, fly, tick and flea, of nettles and brambles and poisons of ivy and sumac.

On foot behind horse, behind plow. On knees weeding carrots. Breathless on sliding shale, one handgrasp from mountain top. Even twister-lifted like a wisp from a hay load to get spiked like some shrike's trophy in a thornapple tree. Frozen — careless tongue to axe head, lashes to lashes, fingers and feet from red to white to black. Burned crimson. Thirsty as a discarded snake skin. Hungry as a blind lion. Rendered weak as mist which my breath might part, though never enough to show the way to shore.

Then, as if all that were not enough, it has cheated me with prickly ash where I intended plum. Insulted me with burdock where I have planted trillium. Smothered my Kentucky bluegrass with crab and quack. mocked me with a white-hot bolt to splinter my burr oak, once a peaceful place of shade — shattered, smoking fragments hissing at the rain.

More than a half century of callous deceit. Fifty years of fighting, of going to bed wondering what it will do while I sleep, and getting up every morning trying to anticipate the mood, the temper of its day.

Curling my shingles. Splitting my cellar walls. Flooding my road and turning my garden to dust. Whacking out windows. Rusting the troughs beneath the eaves, even the lock against unknowns of the night. Killing and maiming friends and, my God, drowning even little children.

So, why do I love the land? Because for every vice, ten thousand virtues; for every deceit, all the truths (if I can find them); for every ugly second, a million minutes of beauty; for every hurricane, a decade of quiet nights; and for every death, a multitude of births.

So it has flailed me unmercifully and sent me whimpering and blistered to bed. Yet, after everything, to whom do I go for comfort and strength when friends and even family fail me? And who has always, in manner mysterious, calmed my tortured spirit, strengthened my dwindling resolve, restored faith, and fostered such courage as not only brings me anxious but exulting right into the face of an unpredictable tomorrow?

It is the land, always the land! My womb and my tomb.

April

I found a wild Arbutus in the dell,
The first-born blossom from the womb of Spring.
Lays hold of me, something I do not know
Unless among these blossoms once I knew
A little boy, oh, long ago.

LEW SARETT

TOMORROW IS EASTER, BUT I AM WITNESSING THE RESURRECTION TODAY. It is a task as Herculean as breaching vaginal barriers, and the rebirth as miraculous as any Christly escape from the shroud. Again and again, a barren patch of soil, which last year provided a dusting place for birds, trembles and lifts. Particles of soil, still moist from melting frost, tumble into the tangle of dead winter grass, which hems a brown border around the old dusting dish.

Finally, a mound of earth, round as a baseball, has separated and lifted itself from the soil surface. For awhile it remains inert. Then it quivers, and through twin cracks in the mud ball a pair of eyes appear. A scudding cloud lets loose a sudden spate of rain, and there, in velvet browns of many shades, a washed toad blinks once, then hops from its wintry cemetery to break its long fast, breakfast on a pale slug, slimy gastropod, itself only seconds from somnolence. No matter what the scientists say, the toad's rebirth remains as much a mystery as the Biblical version of Christ's resurrection, because if I bury myself for the winter, soon there is ice in my veins and my heart turns to stone. There is a little snow mixed with the next brief gust of rain, and

*There is
no stopping
April,
even if
the winter
wind plans
one more
assault.*

I cross the tension line, which is the top of the hill. The south side where I had been sitting is greening, and trees are budding. But on the north side of the hill, there are no green grass spears and the branches hold no leafy promise. But beside a scarf of gray snow close to a spruce skirt, already spearing from the ground to grow a pulpit for a priest, is the Indian turnip the colonists came to call Jack-in-the-pulpit. Pilgrim come in haste to preach — green his surplice, green his bands, erect and reverent beneath penciled canopy of black, brown and green. Once poultice for injured eyes of the Menominees, once starch for the ruffs of Queen Elizabeth's courtiers, once memory root for child fooled into biting its bitter bulb, today mostly red berries for pheasants during the waning days of summer. Eager pilgrim, anxious to be in vestments before the white trilliums crowd around to:

Within days, the snow turns to tears on tree branches, and rising mists put ethereal halos on the hills until the sun burns through.

> Come, hear what his Reverence
> Rises to say
> On his low painted pulpit
> This calm Sabbath day.

But if the earth is restless with white, yellow and purple violets, brightening the entrance to the den from which the woodchuck emerges after its long sleep, and if the turtle, frog and salamander are up from the mud to see that water lilies are already lifting to spread green pads on the water, and if the garter snakes untangle in their common cave to go separately and silently among great masses of anemones, which have whitened the brown earth, then the airways also are alive, vibrant with whistling and wing. It all started weak as a whisper in March. Then, during these warming days of April, came the sounds of insects. Survivors and the newly hatched swarm from ground and water, from beneath the bark of trees and cracks in houses, until the air hums. And dragonflies slowly climb last year's dead brown reeds to dry their iridescent wings in the sun. All are food for the feathered millions.

Then, while crow, raven and buzzard still count the winter toll of carcasses, up from the ice to rot even before they can be eaten, or before the burial beetle has done with its macabre job, the incredible millions that spent winter in the south crowd north in what is likely an unparalleled phenomenon. At least one, the arctic tern, flies from the bottom to the top of the world, from an Antarctic winter resort to a summer nesting home on the edge of the Arctic circle. The jeweled thimble of a hummingbird crosses the ocean from Cuba. The robin heads from Louisiana to the very same apple tree that last year held its Wisconsin nest. They come singly and in gangs, nonstop or loafing along the way. They move forward only to sometimes retreat again in the face of a boisterous blizzard. Some fly by night and, if there is a full moon, I lie on the damp grass to watch their shadows cross its gleaming face.

Heron, grebe, duck, swallow, oriole, wren, thrasher, flicker, eagle, tanager — some early, some late, but always pushing winter a foot, a mile, a thousand miles northward. The restlessness becomes an eruption. Screaming robin chases robin. Blackbird power dives another blackbird. Territory is the name of the game, and survival of a species the goal. Flamboyant drake ducks corral drab hens and fight off any tempted to cuckold them. Above it all, the hawks, seemingly serene, ride the thermal updrafts, dipping in occasional sizzling swoops to select a victim from the blizzard of birds below.

Working their way north, too, are the storms, the tornadoes. For every gentle April rain, storm clouds gather, and there may be a deluge goaded by thunder, lashed by lightning. Rivers turn brown, batter angrily at boulders, crest and spill from their basins back into the fields. But the fish are not dismayed, and trout and salmon, leaping waterfalls, torpedo upstream; bronze carp turn from the current to swim in pastures among last year's cow pies; pike thread their way among last year's cattails to thrash a back bay into a frenzy of foam. They will honeymoon come high water, even if the river is Styx, waterway to whatever hell.

And now the fox kills two cottontails instead of one, because already there are denned kids to be fed. And the coyote, cousin to the wolf, forages days as well as nights, and if her udders swell and are splendidly fat, beneath her winter coat, scraggly now and patching out for a summery suit, there are only winter-lean sinews, rubber bands that keep her running like a marionette.

April is not always kind. Sometimes crusted snow still lacerates the slender forelegs of a deer, and it goes down, a hapless bundle of bones within sight and scent of fresh forage, its strength left behind on the packed snow of an ancestral wintering yard. But the deer did not die in vain, because come another April and a bush will have taken enough sustenance from the pale marrow of the dead one's bones to rise higher, and some other refugee from the death camp, finding strength in this meager browse, may make it across the tension line over to where there are buds and branch tips to gorge on.

Even the horned owl has troubles, because hares turning from winter white to summer brown are mottled and less distinct in spotty camouflage, at precisely the time owlets, already hatched and having shed their down for feathers, are ravenous. But there is no stopping April, even if winter plans one more assault, and swallows die on the wing because there are no insects in the air. Within days, the snow turns to tears on tree branches, and rising mists put ethereal halos on the hills until the sun burns through. Then birds sing again and even the two-legged ones smile, because spring is a thing of the heart, instinctive just as it was so long ago, when any who survived winter knew they were among the favored few upon whom fate and fortune had smiled.

Dragonflies slowly climb last year's dead brown reeds to dry their iridescent wings in the sun.

≫≫ *Lightweight Winter* ≪≪

Victory is never so sweet as when the fight has been long and difficult. A crucial part of the human experience is the enjoyment of that exceedingly refreshing drink we had to hike half a day to get. So despite whatever lingering backlash may yet be in store, winter has blown it. Even though it will be lush and beautiful, spring will not be as welcome, nor as appreciated, as last year, when we were left on the doorstep of the vernal equinox, shivering and shattered.

Since we have been reared to find a satisfying sense of accomplishment only in things that have been the fruit of self-denial and hard work, we should all feel just a little guilty enjoying the rewards of a spring that has not been paid for with frosted brows, chapped lips and icy feet and fingers. Perhaps you consider this puritanical nonsense, and are asking where it is written that a sunset may not be enjoyed when we have spent the day loafing instead of sweating at honest toil. It is written in the Bible, of course, which is replete with admonitions such as: "The Lord reward him according to his work." But rewards aside, what red-blooded Wisconsin man, woman or child does not welcome the challenge of a winter storm? Who among us does not feel a primeval tingle when, with a preliminary roar, we gun the engine before hurtling the car forward through wave after wave in that vast sea of snow?

Pioneer stock, right? Whether our ancestors came over on the Mayflower or in steerage, on a Concorde or up from the South in a truck, our residency in Wisconsin says to the world, "We are tough. We can take it."

In Wisconsin, getting ready for winter is like girding for war. Come November, excitement ripples through the state as the first winds hit us with spates of snow. We condition our cars to accept anything winter can throw at them. We prepare our dwellings and ourselves with all manner of insulation. We thrill with anticipation as we stiffen our attitudes, toughen our minds, strengthen our resolves. Then, at last, we are ready. We have dug in, fortified our positions, not only to withstand but to fight back against the most violent forces nature can assemble.

We anticipate that it will be a trying but exciting time. Each night we go to bed with an ear cocked for the first warning — the eerie moaning of a searching wind. Each morning we part the curtains and peer out to see if we missed the first skirmish, or if winter came while we slept. If it did, there, in carved drifts, are her battlements. Winter always has been big with me. I was born during that other winter — the year of the Titanic — when weather records went flying like shingles off the roof. The doctor summoned to deliver me never got closer than the cheese factory two miles down the hill. My screams of indignation at being so rudely ousted from the warm, watery haven where I had been floating were a fitting accompaniment to the angry howling of the wind. Weather history was being made, and I was a part of it!

My first lullaby was sung by a banshee. My first enemy already was slamming doors, rattling windows and shutters and threatening to move the house south. Little wonder, after such a turbulent entry into the world, that the winter now winding down, though it had its moments, is a disappointment. It has been a soggy, foggy, simpering season without enough backbone to decently stiffen a dead blade of grass. But there is hope, a promise for next year.

⁂ *Spring Fever* ⁂

Spring fever is a sickness that reaches epidemic proportions in April, when unseasonably warm weather triggers mass hysteria among the afflicted. Physicians once thought spring fever was caused by a sudden thickening of the blood, and even today I gag at the vile remembrance of sulfur and molasses. So I am more than usually delighted to announce that it has at least been discovered that the eyes become glazed and the pulse rate quickens only because the wishing gland has secreted more than its usual amount of fluid to the brain.

Neither youngsters nor adults are immune. In severe cases, the patient seems to take leave of his senses, and goes golfing in a snowstorm, gardening in frosty ground, driving in the rain with the top down, staring glassy-eyed at passing girls, and doing all manner of things insane and unpredictable. The disease is rarely if ever fatal, and the only known cure is to go sloshing through icy mud and water, so the sharp wind may reduce the fever. Except for the likes of me, teetering now on the edge of old age. The mud, water and wind aggravate such war and other wounds of life as keep me from rushing down through the wet grass to count coon tracks, kneel by a flower, and stand like a statue to see if the fish are yet running the creek.

Sometimes, then, I feel a profound sadness, until I look to where the lake begins, and I see a child kneeling to peer into the water, and another watching a crow add a twig to its nest of sticks. The sadness leaves me, and I can sit in a kind of cottony contentment, seeing in my mind's eye the new crayfish chimneys, the coon tracks, crow's nest and arrowing fish, remembering how I found them first. Now it is their turn, except that I must never tell them that I found them first, because they are sure, as is every generation, that they are the discoverers and it would be cruel to tell them otherwise.

⪼ *Grand Courtships* ⪻

I would like to discuss, somewhat blushingly, a subject that has been exhaustively examined in thousands of books ranging from the somewhat sinful to the scientific. It is sex. My abiding obsession in matters sexual is my objection to the description of an aggressively lustful man or woman as an animal. The inference is that animals mate with passionate abandon bordering on brutality. It is a libel; nothing could be further from the truth. The courtship and joining of the wild ones is a ceremonial ritual of beauty and grace.

If television has done nothing else, it has pictured the courtship of some wild ones in a way that makes the mating a mutual celebration, not a passionately brutal capture. I am no bluenose, and I admit my frailties, so I admire the males of a wolf pack, who acquiesce without a fight when the dominant female selects the most physically sound male as her mate. Then the rejected suitors, instead of going off to sulk, stay to feed, protect and curry the progeny of the male that won the prize.

It is a wonderment to come each spring to the south bog at evening and hear the beautiful twittering courtship song of the woodcock. He is so high I cannot see him. He dives and dives. His song filters down. But, just as the shadows begin to lift, he slides, silent as a shadow, down to where his hen has been watching and waiting.

Some birds mate in mid-air after a winged ballet. The encounter is so brief the mated pair lose virtually no altitude. Even the antlered animals do little while collecting a harem except an exercise in mock combat. Stallions of wild herds rarely use their heels on anything except predators. A mare leads the band of wild horses while the stallion never presses his case, but waits peaceably until a mare comes to season. There is no brutal taking, no assault. Even the penguin, dullard that he seems, makes his intentions known by presenting his love with a stone.

Some jungle cocks first build ornate nests to show to their prospective mates, each hoping she will be pleased and accept him. The cardinal offers the most succulent seeds during courtship, weeks before the union. Even a bull bass prepares the nest, often cutting himself while fanning it clear of stones, and then waits patiently for the bride to make the overture. Squirrel courtship is a long-time, gentle, caressing, tumbling affair, which begins even in mid-winter, months before there will be mating. If there is quarreling, it is hardly more than a swift chase, a quick nip to send a rival suitor scooting. No squirrel wife winds up weeping.

Courtship antics of the cranes may seem hilarious to us. The dance of the red fox, forepaws to forepaws, is hardly believable. The grebes have such stylized courtship maneuvers that we are moved to laughter. But they conform in their best tradition to give significance to an event that is more important than any other in their lives. Perhaps men and women once also understood the necessity of making love a celebration. Maybe many still do. Whatever, they will be hard-put to match the courtship finesse of the wild ones.

⫸ *Many Faces* ⫷

As character is indelibly stamped on the faces of old people, the good and bad years are recorded as a tree grows, and even a small child can learn to read such chapters as tell of a lightning strike, a fire, an insect invasion, a drought, a wind, a disastrous winter or a careless cut, as well as chapters telling of mild Januaries, and warm, wet, delightful springs. So it pains me sometimes to see people pass through a forest heedless of the many faces of trees. Likely they are the same people who see only death in an old man's face, instead of such nobility as life sometimes sculpts with practiced hand on the countenances of those who may have been bowed but never broken by the storms. If adversity ensures strength in most people, so too are the scars on a tree's limbs and trunks tougher than such bark as has gone unscathed. Each tree covers old wounds with scabrous fibers so it can never twice be wounded in the same way, in the same place.

Just as the human community has more good than bad people, so trees are members of a friendly community, and if you, looking through a magnificent forest, are not convinced, just ask any squirrel, raccoon, blue jay or warbler, and they can tell you. Then, if you have seen a tree jump from four to forty feet, count yourself luckier than most, because we restless Americans do not often stay in one place long enough to see the forest lift its crown high enough to look down on the morning mists. During a lifetime associating with countless trees, I have made thousands of friends. Some were real characters, and their stories rival those of any of the two-legged eccentrics it has been my luck to love. Maybe you have your own tree friends. If you do not, perhaps you might like to make some acre of any park or public forest your own, by visiting it regularly so that over the years you may see how your friends, the trees, are responding to life.

Of one thing I am sure. You will become convinced that the ancient cliche, "As a tree is bent so it grows," is an absolute falsehood. No tree grows as it is bent. It always strives to straighten out, and mostly it is successful. Then maybe, having your own private forest friends, you, too, will notice how trees are remarkably like people, and how this or that old oak has been indelibly stamped by such years of living as have made grandfather's face so interesting.

⇒⇒ *Miracle Songs* ⇐⇐

I am on the side of poets who insist that a bird's song is a celebration, not merely, as many scientists claim, a territorial scream saying: "Get out! This property belongs to me." Certainly a bird's airspace is marked by many rituals, including song. But then, are not some of our most inspiring marches really territorial songs born of pride and love and the necessity to protect our land of the free and home of the brave? Were not some of our most stirring hymns born of battle? Great music often springs from great travail, and though we varnish those songs with a veneer of sophistication, deep down they throb with the heartbeat of hearth and home.

No matter how you cut it, our great love songs have their roots in the joining of people in sadness and happiness to celebrate the mysterious ritual of procreation. Basically, it would seem, in all great music, creation is the theme, day-to-day living carries the beat, and the rhythm is the eternal ebb and flow of generations reaching for some star. So in what way, then, is our music so different from that of the birds? Is it because we must invent our music, while birds are born with ready-made songs? Or because we insist on analyzing, providing a rationale, not only for our music, but for bird songs as well?

Of course, the robin intuitively knows that one backyard will produce just so many earthworms. The chickadees can come up with a reasonable estimate of the number of ant eggs that the stumps on a given range will produce. The bobolink and meadowlark can make a pretty good guess as to the number of acres of meadow necessary to raise their broods. Even the tree swallow knows approximately the number of square yards of water required for the fly-over territory to collect the airborne insects it needs. And, if you put twenty swallow houses on a pond large enough for only four tree swallow couples, sixteen houses will stand vacant.

Even as there is no accounting for our taste in music, so there is no accounting for musical tastes in the bird world. The tiny nuthatch sounds like the turning of a rusty wagon wheel. The flicker, not satisfied with its raucous, strident war cry, also hammers dead trees, roof shingles or the downspout next to your bedroom window. The kingfisher's song is a rattling saber-thrust of sound, issued while winging patrol. The heron croaks, the gull screams, the raven gargles, big owls hoot and little owls whimper. The chickadee has no song. It has a wolf whistle so human I have seen it stop a woman in her tracks. Another whistler to turn your head is not a friend seeking attention, but that spot of flame on a topmost bough, the cardinal.

Want to carry bird-song variations further? Well, the ruffed grouse sings with his wings. Perched on a fallen log, the cock grouse does a drumroll by fanning its wings so swiftly the bird becomes a blur of feathers. Likewise the woodcock. The little timberdoodle climbs high, then dives precipitously and with such speed that the wind winnowing through its wing feathers produces an eerie keening. The jacksnipe does likewise, except it spreads stiff tail feathers as a foil for the air. The prairie grouse cock comes to ancestral mating grounds and, inflating air sacs on the sides of its neck, struts in front of admiring hens and expels the air with a low, bass, booming sound.

The dove, voice of the turtle, coos. The goose sends down a clarion call. The eagle, carried on a staff even into our battles, screams. The wren repeats and repeats its bright little litany. The whip-poor-will whistles in the gloaming and the oriole trills under the sun. The mockingbird turns the night rapturous with a surprisingly varied repertoire.

Protecting territory? Of course. But a celebration, too. With woodwinds. Drums. Strings. A brass section. Even the flute-clear song of the white-throated sparrow is calculated to turn a heart of granite into a marshmallow. A celebration of life! New life in the home nest. And songs about the continuing cycle of life, the only eternity for which there has never been any doubt.

⋙ *The Year Spring Got Lost* ⋘

There was an April when winter, long on its deathbed without dying, had spring reluctant to embarrass the Old Man by flaunting her freshness. So she kept her flowers in last year's fodder, her spinning spiders in dark crannies, brilliant butterflies in drab cocoons, eager birds south of the cold line, exasperated children in overheated schoolrooms even during recess. Then, as I, too, turned from the damp wind and retired to my thinking chair, it occurred to me that many can never escape into the out-of-doors.

The thought made me feel guilty, because I was privileged to forget the trials and tribulations of the world by immersing myself in the semi-wilderness that always surrounds me. Perhaps it is not fair that I am able to relegate war and poverty to some out-of-the-way cubicle of my brain by merely contemplating the new, green leaves of spring. I suppose there is little justice in shrugging off the burdens of the whole world by immersing oneself in a sunset. Yet, that's the way it is, and I placate my conscience by assuming the afflicted may also forget their cares by looking through a window at a robin tugging at a worm or clouds scudding to cover the sun.

That same year, the year spring got lost, April fell from the calendar, and we all went marching into May, and when winter persisted, I became so mentally depressed it also occurred to me that a general worsening of our environment might affect the mind more than the body. What I mean is, perhaps there is greater danger in the mental depression a polluted atmosphere may cause than in the cancer it might induce. It reminded me of the time I had to spend in a large city, where street lights were my only stars. I was almost a basket case by the time I got back to the country to seek solace from the soil.

Remembering, I wonder what is happening to people who do not even have a window box for petunias. Or, more to the point, maybe if there were more cracks in the concrete where the grass might grow, our prison walls would not have to be so high. But, being neither psychiatrist, psychologist nor even philosopher, it could be that I am only a victim of an overly active imagination. And so, I can only tell how I felt the year spring got lost, and there is danger in speculating that others may have felt the same.

⫸ *Resting Places* ⫷

Last spring, my octogenarian neighbor, Jerome Washicheck Sr., a vibrant, white-haired man of the soil, went to his rest on a green hillside looking down on the river that winds through our village. I did not send flowers, but only a check on which I wrote: "For one small tree for his final resting place."

Hardly a month later, a young man named Tom Guyant, whom I especially requested to be my assistant while I was still a staff writer for the *Milwaukee Journal*, died at the age of thirty-six. Once again, I did not send flowers. I handed his mother a check bearing the same request. A few weeks ago, I read in the paper that a prominent brewery family was planning to spend ten thousand dollars to repair its million-pound marble mausoleum, and I tried to calculate how many trees that money might have meant.

Then, in my mind's eye, I saw the graves of my mother, father, brother and a wife, mostly sterile tracts surrounded by a cold forest of sometimes-ugly gravestones. I thought of other cemeteries, old and new, and then my mind moved to that white waste of crosses that is Arlington. But would I dare? At the risk of what wrath might I presume to dictate to the dead? How could I ask their anonymity, an unmarked grave in a wild place where deer might browse or a wren sing — never a requiem, but a sweet song of joy?

And what about the living? Could a wife find solace if she came only to a forest of young trees and never knew beneath which her husband lay? What about a mother still mourning a child? Would she consider it a desecration to see other children playing, and perhaps picnicking, upon the very soil beneath which her loved one was buried? So how would I dare suggest that, acre by acre, as the soil reclaimed its own, new forests be started, never as a memorial to the dead, but as a gift from them to the living?

Well, of course, I could suggest it. Not memorial parks, you understand, but tens of thousands of acres filled with wildlife, sparkling with ponds, running with the silver of creeks. I could suggest it, and if it came to pass, the dead would be making one really lasting contribution to the living. But of course, some will argue, in this crowded world, the day is not far off when burial will be forbidden, when ashes to ashes and dust to dust will be a matter not for the centuries, but for a flash of fire.

Likely true, but why should all the burial places now extant lie unused until the day they are old enough, and long enough forgotten, to be sold for building sites? Would it not be better, acre by acre, year by year, steadily as the dead come, to make them into parks and wild places where the living might come to find some semblance of the peace that has finally been visited upon the deceased?

But how? Some cemeteries are owned by churches. Some by communities. Others are privately owned. States have some. The federal government has national cemeteries all across the country, not to mention the Congressional Cemetery in Washington, D.C. There are big city cemeteries and tiny family cemeteries. There are cemeteries grown to weeds with crumbling tombstones. There are modern cemeteries with ornate walk-in sanctuaries. There are Indian burial grounds. There are military cemeteries.

Well, how about a National Cemetery Act providing that all burial grounds ultimately, acre by acre, be put into a bank of public parklands and wildlife areas? Then, perhaps, instead of a Grant's Tomb we would have a Grant's Forest; instead of an Arlington Cemetery, an Arlington Arboretum. A small bronze plaque could mark each year's addition to the wildlands. Then anyone who needed to be close could stand in the forest marked 1972, or the acre marked 1985, and know that it was in fact the very special gift of a loved one. Then, if you would come to pay your respects to the dead, there might be other hundreds there, too, never praying for the dead, but rejoicing that even such a thing as death made possible one more bright green place in this world. Wouldn't that be a real resurrection?

⫸ *Simple Joys* ⫷

When the vicissitudes of life loom disappointing on every horizon, perhaps it is time to lower your eyes and look at your feet. It works for me. Sometimes when money seems to be going out faster than it is coming in, or when the aches of ailments have me feeling sorry for myself, it is easy to forget how good chicken soup tastes, or how magical is the brilliance of a sunset, or how soft feels the caress of a loving wife.

I suppose it is just plain un-American not to keep one's eyes on the horizon. It is drummed into us from the days when we, as life's Little Leaguers, were taught that a home run was more important than the fun of playing baseball. One of the most vicious phrases in today's lexicon of careless expressions is: "He (or she) is a loser." We use those careless words indiscriminately. Someone's hair length may trigger it. Or we use it to dismiss the Little Leaguers warming the bench, especially if our son just hit a home run. We are sometimes even guilty of using it to describe a close friend, only because he or she chooses not to travel in the fast lane.

Success is, of course, laudable. But if it must be paid for in such coin as is minted from the simple joys of life, savoring an invigorating spring morning or a lazy summer afternoon, it may as well be counterfeit. To go careening down life's highway intent on being first at every finish line is a sure way of cracking up without ever having smelled the flowers. Every time I see a plane that can fly faster than sound or a proposed high-speed train, I wonder what can be important enough to justify this mania for speed, especially when it takes longer to get out of the train station or airport than it does to make the trip.

So I am a stick-in-the-mud. And if this be heresy, then truly I am a heretic. Not that I condone indolence over industry. And, of course, ambition is laudable, energy necessary, initiative praiseworthy, work as necessary as eating. But even our moon travelers, having soared beyond worldly horizons, came back to praise the simple delights of Earth.

Americans worship success. But ask a truly successful person, one who apparently has moved all the way to the horizon, and likely you will hear that no one ever really reaches the horizon. If you do not believe it, start walking and watch the horizon recede. Aesop wrote many a fable extolling the value of the simple joys and rewards that we often bypass for a chance to grab the brass ring. Witness the fox obsessed by the grapes just beyond reach. Though there was food in abundance, the fox worked himself into a lather trying to reach the grapes. When he could not, he told himself they were sour, anyway.

Wise men have blamed wars on greed — the greed for power and possessions. Perhaps, but I am inclined to believe that wars are started by people who cannot take their eyes from the horizon to see the devastation of battle at their feet. But, then, who am I to say — I, an Earth-scratching old man? Except that, like most of you, I have had many horizons in my life. And now that I could not travel in the fast lane, even if I wanted to, I find comfort in paraphrasing the Bible: "What profit a man if he gain the whole world but lose the ability to enjoy it?"

⋙ Sterile Streams ⋘

I am annually impressed by the television portrayals of a volunteer group that each spring cleans up the portion of the little river that winds through their semi-rural community. It is heartening to see young and old, ditch digger and doctor, shoulder to shoulder in the stream, dragging an old bedspring to where trucks wait to haul the junk to a recycling center or such oblivion as it deserves.

Then I get a shock. After the bedspring has been disposed of, the muddy volunteers put a rope around the roots and stump of an ancient river snag, and that, too, comes grudgingly from the river bottom. In turn, then, I am encouraged to see beer cans come ashore, and then discouraged when I see weeds — coontail, pencil reeds, rushes — getting the same treatment.

In the end, I am sure these volunteers will have themselves a clean river sparkling over white stones, a sight to delight the eye. Except, where will be the snails, the gamerus and the nymphs, and where will be the darting minnows that speed lance-like toward the shallows to avoid the jaws of a charging bass? And where will be the bass? And where will be the redwing when the blackbird's home of rushes has come down because it traps algae, which sometimes stinks when the weather warms? And to what other home will the kingfisher move after the minnows have migrated? And will the heron stop now that the frog has lost its home? And where will be the iridescent dragonfly now that its prey, the bluebottle fly and cousins, have nary an overripe fish to feed on?

A river is a delicate ecosystem, fragile as a spider's tapestry. So even as I exult that so many, many good people sacrifice their Saturdays and Sundays to clean up their river, I am sad, like the man who built his house of glass and discovered too late that the contrasting shadows were really what made the sunlight so beautiful. More bluntly, to a woman with a pair of nylons, a snag is a disaster. But to a fisherman, a snag is a blessing.

Forgive me, but I honestly and actually once threw a kitchen sink into my own little Watercress Creek. The current dug a hole beneath it to make a hiding place for fish, and all manner of minute creatures attached themselves as the sink became green and slimy. I have since removed the sink, as well as an old wagon wheel, half a car hood and other objects, to be replaced by rocks, logs and other current deflectors and food factories that blended in with the surroundings and did not shock the pants off some of my visitors.

Unfortunately, beauty and fertility are not always woven from the same cloth. I know some Canadian rivers far beyond road's end that are picture-postcard perfect. They run clear, cold and sparkling above immaculate bottoms of glistening stones. But they are lifeless, dead as a glassful of

chlorinated tap water. I also know some southern rivers, almost impass-
able because of snags and vegetation, which sometimes stink to high
heaven, but have such a varied wildlife community that to visit them is as
breathtaking as a country bumpkin's first bewildering visit to the streets
of Manhattan.

Cleaning a river is a very specialized business. Even a trained biolo-
gist may be puzzled at times. No matter what the interest and enthusiasm of volunteers, they must continue to remind themselves that what
appears to be beautiful in their eyes becomes a desert of death for the
turtles, fish, frogs, snails and all the furred and feathered creatures that
once lived there.

⋙ *Born Again* ⋘

If you are among those who consider themselves born-again
Christians, or born-again Jews, or born-again Moslems, do not scoff
when I say I have been born again, hundreds of times. It has been a rare
springtime when I have not come at least once to the river when a soft,
warm wind was nudging birds north, and for a mystifying moment
glimpsed eternity in the simple unfolding of a fragile leaf. Indeed, I was
born again.

Even as a child, having despaired only as youngsters can, I have been
lifted with gentle hands from the mire of despondency to the fragrance
of my mother s breast, and my heart stopped shivering in the warmth of
a love beyond reckoning. Indeed, I was born again.

In Salt Lake City, in Madison, in Chicago, as a derelict of the
Depression, confused, hungry, frightened and cold in body and soul, I
have felt suddenly safe and profoundly content alone in the Tabernacle,
alone in an Episcopal church, alone in a Rescue Mission chapel. Each
time, I was born again.

Returning from an especially perilous mission over wartime Berlin
through squadrons of enemy fighter planes and across acres of flak, I sat
under the wing of our bomber while my crew went through the ritual of
kneeling to kiss the earth. Less than twenty feet away, unperturbed by the
roar of engines, a large hare went about its business, contentedly nibbling
grass stems. My eyes filled with tears. I was born again.

A faltering heart, one beat away from good-bye. A wailing siren and
then only voices, voices, voices. Back from the void, and a woman in
white whispering: "You'll be all right now." Indeed, I was born again.

No Bible thumping. No resounding amens. No oratory. No church. Only a tent. And there, through the open tent flap, I watched from my sleeping bag as the sun thrust back the night and, burning away the valley mist, revealed the grandeur of mountain peaks. I was born again.

Stifling hours of theological rhetoric, days of conflicting doctrine, nights of meaningless prayer, and then, by chance, a glimpse through the trees of a disciple celebrating in the cold waters of a creek, stripped of all except his shorts. I was born again.

A strange land. A strange language. Strange faces. A crush of frightening figures. No place to run. No place to hide. No mercy, little hope. Then, one smile. One outstretched hand. A slow and careful walk to the safety of an adobe home. There, born again.

A grave. A silent house. Sleepless nights. Meaningless days. Loneliness in every room. Ghosts of the past in every dim corner. Dust gathering on the shelves and the soul until a kindred spirit, flowers wilted in her heart and on another grave, came through the door. Born again? Indeed, two people, born again.

Perhaps some of us need moving music to be born again. Perhaps we need the evangelical fervor of a self-appointed professional savior of souls. Perhaps we need the surging emotional lift of a crowd pressing forward toward salvation. Perhaps we need, even depend on, the pomp and ceremony, the necessity of giving vocal witness, the assurance that if we get on God's side, He will always be on ours. Perhaps some of us even need the Good Book as a ready reference to be able to distinguish right from wrong. Perhaps each morning, on awakening, we need to recite all the reasons for being good to ourselves and others.

I will not quarrel with that. Just so I can have the breeze through the curtains, a bird's song through the window, and, so long as it is possible, my sweetheart at my side. Born again? A smile. A kind word. An outstretched hand. Sometimes that is all it really takes to be truly born again.

⋙ *A Model T and Manhood* ⋘

I was thirteen. She was thirty-three. I adored her. So, when she asked if I would give her a ride in my Model T, which was held together as much by hairpins as anything else, I suppose I was the proudest boy in Juneau, the State of Wisconsin or maybe the world. That Model T was a junkyard mongrel of parts cannibalized from rusting derelicts. It had no top, no windshield, and a door on only one side. It ran on kerosene, if I could come by enough gasoline to get the motor sufficiently hot so it would accept the less volatile fuel.

Strapped to a wooden platform bolted to the frame in the rear were four spare tires. Even then, some trips ended in a humpity-bumpity ride home. But I loved that car, maybe almost as much as I loved her. That she should require its services (few others would risk riding in it) put upon me the stamp of a man, thirteen and already a driver. She needed the car to travel the four miles from town to the river, where she would begin the spring ritual of opening a cottage. I loaded boxes of bedding, towels, dishes and curtains on the backseat. Then I started the car on gasoline and, when the engine was warm, added enough kerosene for the trip. Getting behind the wheel, I squeezed the bulb of an old horn that once had decorated an Oldsmobile of pre-World War I vintage. At the sound of the horn, she stepped out onto the front porch, a vision in white with a crown of hair truly as black and shiny as a raven's wing. Beside me in the front seat, she put a silk scarf over her head. So, including shoes and stockings, she was clothed completely in white.

If I was apprehensive, I do not remember it. All I remember is that I was proud, and that I kept taking side glances to see if any of my friends were watching as I drove down Main Street, turned south at the offices of the weekly *Independent*, then east again at Griffith's lumberyard, and headed for the river road. Except for the cloud of white kerosene smoke trailing us, the first two miles were uneventful. The car rolled along at a respectable seventeen miles per hour, and fields with grazing cows and butter-breasted meadowlarks slipped gently past. Then ahead, where the river road angled off the main highway, loomed a flagman waving me off from a half-dozen men pouring tar into the potholes left by winter.

I pushed up the gas lever on the steering wheel, put in the clutch and depressed the brake pedal. The pedal sank to the floorboards and nothing happened. I had no emergency brake, so I began squeezing the rubber bulb that honked the horn. *A-hooga! A-hooga! A-hooga!*

Her hand touched my knee as though to steady me. I saw the men scatter. I could see their angry faces, their shouting mouths. I saw buckets in the air and tar splattering on the hood. I felt tar hit my face. And then we were on the river road. As we coasted to a halt, I dared to look at her. Her white dress, her scarf, her cheeks were speckled with tar. Sliding through the door to the ground, I lifted one side of the car hood, reached down and, with a length of wire, repaired the broken linkage — the reason for the brake failure.

The rest of the trip was uneventful. We spoke little, and we did not walk down to look at the water after we had locked the household items inside the cottage. All the way back home, it seemed my heart grew harder and heavier until I was ready to believe it might truly turn to stone. At the house, she got out of the car and, without saying a word, started across the lawn. I sat still, gripping the wheel. She was halfway to the house before she turned to look at me. Then she said: "Thank you. Thank you for the ride."

When she was as far as the steps of the house, she turned again. "And just think of it," she said. "Not a single flat tire!" To this day I am proud of her, my mother.

≫ *April Shower* ≪

Quicksilver against a gray day, an April shower. The rain puts the iridescent green tree swallow patrol low to the water. Robin under bough, shaking beaded rain from its feathers, anticipates a glut of worms. Along the creek, fuzzy willow catkins turn to glass beads. Grass blades collect diamonds. Rain speckles ponds until they look like old gray barn boards, shot through with insect tunnels. Buds are crusted in crystal. Pines washed green. Stones rinsed white. Brown fingers mark a clear creek where water trickles from a bank.

Currents quicken, but crocuses close. Smoke flattens and spreads to hang like mist. Frogs come up onto the lawn. A sparrow is surprised to see itself reflected in a puddle. The cat steps gingerly, shaking a wet paw, and waits at the kitchen door. Quarreling grackles call a truce. Raucous carpenter, the flicker, waits half in and half out of its yet-unfinished home.

The earth drinks greedily. It absorbs the rain, relishes the soft caress. Pregnant with millions of seeds, shoots, roots and spores, it swells nigh unto bursting. It can birth now that the womb has been softened and the way made slick. All night, water softly on the roof, dripping from eaves, and in the morning it is difficult to convince a child that rain is colorless. They believe, or they want to believe, that the gift from the sky is a special spring dye come to repaint the winter landscape, even as they do their Easter eggs. After the rain they see the grass greened, the willow turned a translucent yellow, the marsh gilded with golden marigolds. So who am I to argue that the rain is not a mixture of nature's own special formula, calculated to transform the barren, wintry waste into a stunning fairyland?

May

MAY, AND THE RESURRECTION BECOMES AN
ERUPTION. With so little time, every living thing
keeps crowding creation into a few vibrant
months, so nature may sit back for June to take
the census. While my back is turned, wild onion
puts up green spears. Overnight, mushrooms put
crimson shelves to rotting stumps, open umbrellas, build spheres, form cones and fairy rings.
And while I basket a morel, a flower opens where
the mushroom grew.

Then, as I have watched the April toad arise as
from the dead, I sit on a sandy bank where last
September I saw a tardy turtle drop eggs, white
and round as ping-pong balls, into a hollow she
gouged into the sand with the strong claws of
her powerful hind legs. Surely winter must have
frozen those leathery eggs solid as rocks but, now
that they are warmed, I discover once again that
cold is not always the killer. One by one, eight
painted turtles, the size and roundness of quarters, struggle into the sun, blink, and unerringly
head for the open water of the shining pond.

May, birth month of trillions. Sixty-thousand
from the white pebbles of a single bluegill nest.
Another four thousand from the rock crib of the
trout, which has vivid rainbow slashes down each
side. A million mosquitoes from wigglers in a
single, tiny swamp. Eight bare, blind cottontails
from a single doe already eyeing an impatient
buck, with a penchant for doing things in tripli-
cate.

Gob of jelly, a tan swarm of tadpoles.
Crayfish eggs, glued beneath the curving tail,

*If there
be nothing
so rare as a
day in June,
it is May that is
the Month of
Miracles.*

suddenly and miraculously replicas of the blue-pincered, bronze-armored mother. Eight or a dozen embryonic possums at last detached from nipples to peer wide-eyed from the furry flap of the grizzly female's pouch. Young mourning doves on the wing, and already two more white eggs on the fragile platform nest of twigs. Rookeries ganged with herons craning long necks from tier upon tier of nests. Islands almost completely white with gulls incubating eggs. Deer dropping twins, triplets in sheltered thickets. Gangling moose, spraddle-legged to clean the birthing lubricant from a wobbly youngster.

Blackbirds, thrushes, grackles, stuffing tens of thousands of outstretched, red, gaping throats. Tiny wren singing in the sun to a hen who boards in a darkened man-made house. Oriole, dropping like a fireflake from a hanging, intricately woven nest. Starlings, shimmering in sequins, flying any edible thing to waiting kids. Olive, brown, white, speckled, blue. Tiny as peas, big as cherries, huge as baseballs. Kingfisher eggs at the end of a long, underground tunnel. Mallard eggs in a downy nest in a hayfield. Coot clutch on a floating island of rushes. Crow's eggs on sticks in a tree.

Quail, killdeer and ruffed grouse kids running even before their feathers dry. Muskellunge kids, egg sacs absorbed, rising and scattering so their mother cannot catch and eat them. Snowshoe hares born open-eyed and fully furred, and knowing without being told where to hide and when to run. Bear warily to fish, twin cubs trailing. Squirrel, youngster by the throat, back to the high den from which it fell. A single, undulating file of black-and-white-striped skunk youngsters mimicking, step for step, tail posture for tail posture, the mother who leads the parade. A raccoon gets slapped, and four masked brothers and sisters back away from the creek bank, lest they get slapped, too.

May! How many trillion insects? You count them or, better still, try to find a square foot under or on the ground or in the water that does not have its colony. The south wind has kept its promise and May becomes the

The south wind has kept its promise and May becomes the month of flowers.

month of flowers. Already brilliant, brash summer colors in the south diminish along the trail north to pastels. Virginia bluebell, wake-robin, periwinkle, pepperroot, bellwort; four, six, eight shades of violets; pink, white and stormy purple lilacs. Ivy, wild cucumber, grape, already halfway up a tree whose leaves are only now unfurling. Hawthorns, a cumulus white; multiflora rose, a bridal archway of blossoms. Trillions of blooms destined to become seed, nut, fruit.

May, the month of burgeoning beauty. Teeming, prolific, fruitful. Too much. Hand me some adjectives. None at my command are adequate, because how describe gold fields of buttercup? How describe the monarch, crumpled royal butterfly, trembling from chrysalis, soon sailing on smooth wings? Such imperfect talent can only feel but never sing the song.

If only we might hoard the wealth of May. Cherry blossom snow. Fragile ferns from drift of spore. Candles of new growth gleaming on pines. Spears of wild asparagus, three where you picked two, four where you picked three, startling progression right on into June. Watercress in emerald mounds, and golden dandelion coins with roots just as succulent in salad as the cress.

May. Old men put their coats on the ground to sit upon, and watch children playing in shorts. Human migrants straggle back north from Texas, California, Mexico and Florida. South on the Mississippi above New Orleans, boys plunge fearlessly into the water. At St. Louis, they wade in slowly. In Minnesota, where the great river is born, they test water temperature tentatively with a toe. So also, Florida bass have already forgotten the honeymoon. Arkansas bass are still protecting eggs. Ontario bass, with powerful tail sweeps, are only getting around to making their white pebble nests. And while southern hyacinth is already lush and nigh impenetrable, Wisconsin wild rice, still flat on the water, is first trying to rise so stems may grow strong enough to hold the head spray of seed.

Then, while the southern frog chorus is already holding nightly concerts, their northern cousins are first tuning up, until the nighttime rhythm, at first a solemn beat, turns into a wild cacophony of birdsong when dawn first streaks the east. The sun always rises to keep its eternal promise, and May gets on with its job as the architect of June. And then, if there be nothing so rare as a day in June, it is May that is the Month of Miracles.

≫≫ *Wildlife Watching* ≪≪

I sit often these days, especially during the waning hours, and mark the minutes by squirrel traffic through the treetops. It seems squirrels follow rigid schedules, and I know it is 8 p.m. when a gray matron comes from a soft maple across into a chestnut, on into a red cedar and leaps to the basswood where it dens. I know it is 8:30 p.m. when a mourning dove perches for several minutes on a limb among the leaves of a white birch before disappearing among the branches of a Douglas fir, where it has a nest of little sticks. These same doves, once housekeeping chores are over, tell me the sun has slipped below the horizon when they come from the fields to the high, dead branches of a willow for a last minute of sunshine before diving into the spruce to roost.

The schedules of these wild ones change slowly as the seasons shorten or lengthen daylight hours, but knowing the date it is possible to tell time without looking at your watch. I think if I were to lose my sight, I could say with some accuracy that the blue jays have found a cat among the ferns or an owl in the burr oak. Their raucous harassment varies not only in intensity, but in tone and frequency, depending upon the victim. If I am on a bank of Fish Pond, without looking I can differentiate between the watery sounds of a bass snatching a bluegill, a green sunfish slashing through a school of bluegill fry, a startled muskrat diving for concealment or a big trout sucking down a mayfly. If there is a nearby cone of silence where I should be hearing crickets, I can be reasonably sure a green heron is proceeding in measured strides that take it five minutes to travel five feet.

This is not something to be learned quickly. Rather, it is knowledge you absorb little by little over many years. Usually, the only talent required is the ability to sit, look and listen. In the beginning, only the more obvious messages will be readable. For instance, a sudden dearth of songbirds where minutes ago there had been dozens, and you will put a hawk off his perch if you hunt long enough. Likewise, if birds along the road suddenly scatter, or ducks in the marsh paddle for cattail cover, you know company is coming up the road or up the stream. Furthermore, if the birds or waterfowl are but lightly perturbed, you will know your visitor is coming by horse, boat or car. If they beat a hasty and somewhat frantic retreat, you will know company is coming afoot.

Depending on the time of year, crows will tell you if it is a cat among the ferns, an owl in an oak, or a fox in the canary grass they are pestering. But once their eggs are laid, the crows may nest within yards of the back door and you will get but few glimpses of the pair as they use all available leaf cover to slip swiftly and silently into and out of the nest tree. If a Baltimore oriole sings only his half-song, likely he is near the nest. If he gives out with a full-throated warble, he is announcing territorial rights on the far edge of the territory he has laid claim to.

Should you hear a bird song you cannot identify, write down "starling." If ever a bird starts barking like a dog, it is likely to be this sequined highwayman of the aerial crossroads. I am sure the robin predicts rain with its rain song, because my old and aching bones concur. Then if, on a clear and sunny day, the swallows come down from the sky-high places to skim low to earth, watch the west for storm clouds. Halt if gophers, more correctly ground squirrels, stand straight and motionless as sticks, because something is coming. If you hear the half-angry, half-frightened squeal of a chipmunk, you are late, because something has already come and gone and the chippie has gone below.

A catbird meowing might mean a snake. A catbird singing, all is well at home. A great blue or black-capped night-heron squawking at quick, excited intervals means an invasion. Same squawk, more tentative and coming at long intervals, means somebody is inquiring about roosting accommodations from those already settled in for the night.

Oddly, wildlife will tolerate closer observation if you are mounted on a horse or riding in a boat or auto. Of course, never present a silhouette on a ridge or forest clearing, and wear mottled clothes of nondescript colors. On entering a clearing, remain in the edge brush for at least fifteen minutes and perhaps some wild one will enter the clearing ahead of you. Never take a step at any time until you have looked high, low and all about to see if there are any wild ones watching you. Of course, always walk with the wind in your face. It is fun. Your librarian can recommend books on how to watch birds, mammals or insects. But except for specific information on habits of wild ones, only through a process similar to osmosis will you instinctively learn to do it properly. Remember, you, too, are an animal. So do not let your overdeveloped brain get in the way.

⇛ *Front Row Seats* ⇚

I suspect that to those charged with guiding the destiny of the world, I qualify as a wastrel. If I have added anything to the eternal efforts to civilize society, it has been accidental — a by-product of my enthusiasm for self-gratification. This is in no way an apology. I am merely sweeping the doorsteps of my mind of any residual guilt, so I may be done with this task of writing and go outside.

There are no sky streaks to the east yet, and except for a single robin, I hear only the distant, soft and throaty throbbing of doves among the spruce. There is nothing — unless, of course, I look at the clock — to indicate that if I were five miles up, I might already be able to see the sun. I am at the kitchen table. I have had coffee. Though two rooms removed, I can hear Gwen purring in her sleep. And I am scribbling with a ball-point pen, doing my penance. It is penance because I do not want to be here at the kitchen table. Already I should be moving, softly, as the years have taught me, along the footpath to the bridge, so I may be sitting with my back to a big willow, indistinguishable (I hope) when, in the first light, the wood duck hen pops from her house and drops to the water of the creek to say good morning to her drake in waiting.

If I am not there at the precise moment, I will not see the hen. Nor the drake, unless I have the unlikely good luck to catch him sneaking out from his forest of last year's brown cattails to a bait of corn that I replenish daily. If I am lucky, and if she is in the mood for it, I may see a little lovemaking. Then, old as I am, I will thrill a little, and although callused by the years, feel a twinge of guilt at playing the role of a peeping Tom. The wood duck interlude will be brief. She will dip to run beads of water over her back, then eat sparingly. The drake will act out his role by swimming a nervous circle around her. Then, poof! There will be a soft sound of feathers, and she will be back on her eggs in the tree house. He, sensing my presence, will try to appear nonchalant as he swims back into his cattail forest, but a nervous turning of his brilliantly crested head will give him away. It will be light then, although the sun will be awhile yet. So what shall it be next?

Woodcock? I think so. I hurry, because now there is no need for stealth — the blue jays, crows and grackles pass the word that I am coming. There are sun shafts in the east by the time I get to the spring bog, where a woodcock couple almost always nest. I back in, and sit beneath the skirts of a spruce to watch, but more important, to listen. Then if I hear an eerie sound, I will know he is up there and is sizzling earthward in his courtship dive. The woodcock does not know it, but during the winter I cut a small tunnel through willow and ninebark to the area where the nest is likely to be. I might, therefore, even get a telescopic view of the old bug-eyed, hammer-headed boy landing and looking important. But then the sun comes up, and although a half-dozen times I am sure I heard the thin, sharp whistle of wind in his wings, it must have been a quivering reed, or maybe my imagination. Well, maybe this evening.

So I rise, but now there is too much. The airways are crisscrossed with birds, and their voices rise in a bewildering cacophony. But there will be other mornings. I have arranged seats in the front row where a couple of mallard nests will be sprouting ducklings. And I have marked, with tiny stakes, four cottontail nests, holes in the ground the size of billiard balls where youngsters will come popping out.

Once (once in an entire lifetime!) I saw wood duck youngsters come tumbling twenty feet to land on their downy breasts and go scurrying for water. Twice I have been present at the birth of killdeer. I saw a whitetail doe give life to two fawns. But this is enough atonement, enough paper scratching for one morning. I hear Gwen's cough, a not-so-subtle signal that she is ready for coffee, and then it is outside to continue my progress report on all manner of things. So you see what a wastrel of precious time I really am, because none of it is important, except to Gwen and me, as each evening we make our surprise announcements about some new resident, flora or fauna.

⇒ *The Family* ⇐

The family has formed the bedrock of all civilizations, and it is when the world's adults start working primarily for themselves, instead of their children, that society seems threatened. Few men or women have the capacity for a lifetime of excellence unless motivated by what seems some inherent need to build a better world, not for themselves, but for posterity. Countries have tried and failed to establish a society of communes in which children are wards of the state.

Now, perhaps I might go to the wise men of the world to gather supporting evidence for the above conclusions. But for just this once, let this little old country boy poke around in the briar patches of the earth to see what he can come up with. Starting with the mink, a nomad if there ever was one, family life, except for the brief interval during which the kids are dependent on the mother, is nonexistent. There is, therefore, no mink society. There are only individuals traveling independently. Population levels, even under the best or worst of conditions, rarely fluctuate. What is more, the animal exhibits cold and calculating instincts, killing often only for the sake of killing, and, except for captive animals and the very young, displays no affectionate gestures that might be interpreted as play. A mink lives for itself, not for its children or a society of minks.

Then there is the wolf, with a family style most resembling humans. A female keeps house and cares for the kids with aunts, uncles and cousins helping. There is much cooperation among pack members. There is considerable play and even teasing, which passes for high jinks as animals assume the almost human roles of the clown, or the wise or the timid, or even, sometimes, the treacherous one. He, in the end, may be driven from the pack to become the lone wolf. Before humans pushed the wolf to the edge of extinction, these wolf families often combined into a society of larger packs when that became necessary to fulfill a survival need. The wolf, living for its children, is one of the best examples of the family role in the wild society.

In the bird world, the common grebe, also known as the helldiver, is the lonely one. Like the mink, it is a nomad, and once mating and parental demands have been satisfied, it goes its solitary way, never seeming to increase or decrease in numbers, and never forming flocks, belonging to no society. During a half-century of observation, while watching ducks play and sport about on the water, while watching coots bicker and assume roles, I have never seen a helldiver do anything except feed and then sit by himself like a sad old man, a wild recluse.

At the other end of the wild bird society is the Canada goose. Often mating for life, they are fiercely protective, not only while their goslings are helpless, but even after they are airborne and until it is time for another egg-laying spring. The Canada goose even waits for the maturity of the second year before mating. Once the northern nesting grounds are vacated, the goose family forms flock societies to better wedge through obstinate air currents while aloft, and so that there may be adequate sentinels for ground duty while feeding or sleeping.

Even among the hoofed wild ones such as elk and deer, where the bull and the buck seemingly share no part of a fawn or calf's life once the rut has burned itself out, there is a return to herd society in which, in emergencies, all have a part in survival. There are scores of other animals and birds — baboons, chimpanzees, prairie dogs, crows, grackles — that might serve as examples of the importance of the family to the well-being of the wild society.

In fact, it would seem that such social advantages as contentment, play, safety and survival accrue more often to those of the wild society that lead the good family life. Of course, there are exceptions. But what about the highly organized, almost computerized and obviously efficient societies of ants and bees, with their single queen mothers, their drones, workers and soldiers? Don't these insects comprise the most efficient, best organized and highly disciplined societies in the world? Perhaps. And that is precisely the kind of world humans might have to settle for if we decide to abandon the family unit for a society where the young are shuttled at birth into communal nurseries.

⇛ *A Gift of Hope* ⇚

Borgese (there must have been more to his name though I never heard it) was a great (or was it a great-great?) uncle. I was very young and he always arrived without warning and at rare intervals. With him came romantic stories of Alaskan goldfields, tropical seas, windswept deserts and craggy mountains, exotic tales of faraway places. An angular man with cut-stone features that seemed ageless, he did magical things with a deck of cards, a silver dollar, a silken handkerchief, an apple, a walnut, even my own jackknife, which time and again mysteriously left my pocket for his. No matter the season or the familial mood, he brought sunshine into our home during his regulation two-day stays, after which he would pick up what he called his ditty bag and head down the street for the railroad depot.

Then there was the final visit. It was October, and already mornings were bitterly cold. World War I had ended nearly a year ago. With the country well into the postwar depression, the once-a-week pint of Sunday ice cream had been scratched from the grocery list, and we were looking toward many wintertime meals of fried dough made palatable with wild plum jam, currant jelly or sauce from the apple slices drying in the attic.

That October, Borgese did not come jauntily walking up the road, but came seated beside the driver of the dray wagon that delivered goods from the railroad depot to the dry goods store, the funeral and furniture parlor, and the old yellow brick hotel. What is more, he did not have his ditty bag, but a black teakwood steamer trunk, bound sturdily in brass, with a lock the size of a dog collar dangling from a sturdy iron hasp. It took much grunting and groaning from both Borgese and the drayman to get the chest onto the porch. Instead of his usual gusty, "Say there mates, how've we all been?" he smiled, I thought sadly, and said instead, "Well, now, hello." That evening, as soon as he and Dad had wrestled the trunk up the winding staircase to the attic, he went to the spare room.

Then, when mother knocked to say supper was ready, he said through the closed door, "You just all go ahead. I'm not hungry tonight."

Next morning, when he failed to answer my knock, I dared open the door an inch to peek in. His head, on the pillow with eyes closed, was as blue-white as carved marble. Dad was summoned from work. He opened the envelope on the washstand. There was money and an address to which his body was to be shipped, and in another envelope on the bureau was the key to the steamer trunk, along with instructions not to open it until the following May I. The undertaker came with the drayman to prepare and box his body for shipment, and when we went to the depot to see him off there was not a tear, perhaps because this leave-taking was really not much stranger than his previous, mysterious and unexplained visits.

As we had anticipated, and as the Farmer's Almanac had predicted, it was a cold, ice-hard, frightening winter, with frost sometimes creeping nearly a foot along the floor from beneath all except the kitchen door where the cooking range roared until it was a blistering red. In retrospect, it was the kind of winter that might have splintered family solidarity, a winter of bickering and backbiting, a winter such as might have sent a lesser father packing, a lesser mother to bed with any of a dozen convenient ailments, a winter that might have turned a clutch of caring kids into a rebellious, hate-filled gang.

But remember, there was the brassbound teakwood trunk. At first, none spoke of it, though each, finding a chance, crept into the icy attic to see if the trunk was still there, to touch it and sit on it, wondering what manner of treasures might be locked inside. Christmas came with a snarl of wind, turning what might have been a beautiful fall of snow into a raging blizzard. There was an orange for each, a small bag of hard candy, mittens for all, a tablet and pencil for each child, and popcorn to be eaten when it came off the small spruce Christmas tree destined to become fuel for the kitchen range.

Bleak might have been the word to describe that Christmas, except for the steamer trunk, which we had bounced down the attic steps to a place of honor beside the tree. Then, when the tree candles were lit, the trunk, its brass rubbed to a high gold finish, the dark brown teakwood rubbed with lard until it appeared to have been varnished, was our star of Bethlehem, the treasure at the rainbow's end, all the gifts of the Magi kept preciously secret and secure by the enormous lock that sometimes seemed to scream: "Do not open until May!"

The trunk never got back to the attic. It found a place where any in the house would have to walk around it a dozen times a day. Magically, frozen fingers ceased to pain. Chilblains hardly itched at all. The absence of meat on the table was no big thing. And no matter how weary or cold, all on arriving home looked each time to make sure the trunk was still there before hurrying to the kitchen's comforting warmth. Magically, too, the days seemed to speed down the weeks of each month as the sun rose earlier and set later. Even business began to pick up. I got a part-time job, as did one other in that clutch of kids. There were checkers and cards and good talk and laughing in the kitchen before bedtime. And always there was the trunk, filled with mysterious promise.

Of course, no one thought of going to bed when April 30 arrived. It was unusually warm, and after dark we drifted quietly in and out of the house to count the stars and watch the clock. Before the clock began to strike, we all had gathered around. As the clock struck the final second away for all time, father inserted the huge key, the lock grated, and we all waited breathlessly as the heavy lid lifted and the trunk creaked open.

As one, we leaned forward, and it seemed like forever before father said: "Nothing. There's nothing. Nothing except stones."

Mother bent closer and reached down. "There's an envelope."

She handed it to father, and his hand shook while opening it to bring out a single sheet of paper. Father read it, then handed it to Mother. I leaned closer to see her face more clearly. A tiny smile was starting to curl the corners of her lips. Then she read, "Many happy springtimes!"

"That's all?" we asked, almost in unison.

"That's all," Mother said.

Stunned, we went to bed. And yet, we felt no residual resentment or grief the next morning, because all the sweet smells of spring were coming through the open windows. Brothers were laughing about the great joke Borgese had played on us, and how typical it was of him. It was not until many years later that I realized that Borgese had intended this, and I could appreciate how hope moves any through a winter or a life to many happy springtimes.

Nighttime Illusion

Each May we came at night to catch bullheads, because daytimes the whiskery horned pouts refuse to venture from their dark corners and swim in full sight in the crystal-clear water. And we caught bullheads, seventeen before it was so dark we could not see the bobbers bobbing on the water. But we came away with infinitely more than a meal of fish. There was a frog right at our feet. It tried a tune, and then frogs all along the shore and in the marshes beyond chimed in. The choir kept a better beat than trained musicians; you could snap your fingers to the rhythm and hum an accompaniment. It was that precise.

In the air, formations of banded nighthawks came cruising to see what insects were hatching off the water. They maneuvered with such dexterity as only a leaf slipping on and off the currents of a capricious wind can duplicate. When the nighthawks moved to other hunting grounds, there were the bats going over in roller-coaster swoops, and when the stars came out, one fell in a quick finger of white fire, tracing a curve across the sky.

A swift shadow, but no sound. In minutes a quavering question from the oak, so we knew it had been an owl. A rippling vee right between the bobbers, and then a splash right beneath the dock. The muskrat had at last scented us. Anxious quacking. A duck startled, by what? Mink? Coon? Nightmare?

As darkness deepened, it pulled our world tighter and closer. We fished on what seemed an uninhabited island until, from afar, there was the sound of soft tires sucking at hard concrete, and a car door banging, and an impatient voice. Then we were forced to acknowledge that ours was not just some tight little sequestered island of frogs, bats and bullheads, but a vast and sometimes frightening world full of strange places and faces.

⇒⇒ *The Rocking Chair* ⇐⇐

Both snakes and toads are a nice steadying influence in this hectic world, where a man, to amount to anything, must always be going places. Mostly snakes and toads, and you might include frogs, only wait, and eventually what they are waiting for comes to them. If it is only a grasshopper or a fly, it suffices, because they have no greater needs.

Though I cannot always hold with Thoreau, it seems to me he won the ultimate victory by conquering greed. Once that happens, and a man realizes he can sleep in only one bed at a time, eat but one steak at a time, drive but a single auto at one time, he has made great strides toward inner contentment. It is no easy thing. Any man who sits by the side of the road in this day is labeled lazy. And, since we judge ourselves by what others say and think of us, we strive mightily to drive by in a shining new car, open the door to an ultramodern home, and wear suits and dresses so expensive we must buy them on credit.

Not all people, however, join the rat race. Interviewing some of my rocking chair friends, I have discovered they have a common reverence for the earth and are among the world's happiest. They can come at even eighty to smell the freshness after a spring rain with as much relish as though they had never smelled anything so delicious before.

One other trait, common to all these of the happy clan, is a faculty for being humble in the face of thousands of yearly miracles the rest of us have come to accept as routine and even boring. They are as delighted with the last violet as they were with the first. They still kneel to look into the grass cavern for the song sparrow's nest, or pause in the night to stare at the stars, though they have seen them so many times.

So, I sit also and try for a while. Then I try a second time, and a third, and a fourth. Gradually, contentment comes like the air I breathe, and without knowing it I separate myself from a world doing its damnedest to beat somebody wherever.

⇒ *Shattered Dream* ⇐

During my youth I envied the turtle, because it represented the somnolence of summer, and because I considered its shell an impregnable fortress, impervious to attack; I thought it without enemies. Being one of a shelf of sun-worshipping turtles, comfortably covering a partially submerged log, seemed the sublime way of watching the world go by. Add to this life of complacency the turtle's role as sanitary engineer, quite satisfied with its omnivorous appetite, programmed to whatever the throwaway world floated its way, and it all added up to an idyllic existence. Now I know better, and I feel somehow betrayed that even grackles, their chisel bills including a razor ridge riveted right down the middle of their upper beaks, find small turtles easy prey.

Others, too are adept at finding the hinge that holds turtle's upper and lower shell in place. One summer we counted upwards of a hundred snapping turtle half-shells beneath the nesting site of a pair of red-shouldered hawks. Otters are expert at killing and eating turtles, and some mink and raccoons get good at it, too. I have never seen it, but an old trapper I once knew claimed that eagles swoop down and, carrying turtles high, drop them on the rocks where they fragment so the birds may eat at their leisure.

Now I suppose I am some smarter, having discovered that the turtle's life is not really one of summer somnolence, but I would rather I had not discovered the chinks in the reptile's armor. As a boy, it was infinitely more satisfying to lean back in a boat, float downstream and, contemplating the sleepy-eyed turtles, dream that as blood brothers, we were always safe in the sunshine of our warm world.

⇛ *Special Talents* ⇚

Each square foot, each acre, each square mile of good earth has talents peculiar to itself. We must respect these talents and try not to pervert them. We may help nature, but we must be patient, because years are often required to grow an oak grove, to create a rolling prairie of multicolored flowers and sweet grasses, to fill up a semi-tropical bottom land with cabbage palms, towering cypress, and lakes of golden saw grass.

Nowhere is this more evident than on acres that have been burned, farmed to death, strip-mined, or contaminated by airborne or waterborne pollutants. Many times the damage seems irreparable, and though the land comes back, it never attains the heights of production that its original talents intended. In many northern states, where lumber barons once clear-cut virgin pine from doorstep to horizon, nothing grows now but crowded, stunted poplars. Areas of the Great Plains, left to their own devices after many years of gouging by the plow, have rarely come back as true prairie, but instead have produced a succession of coarse weed growths of small beauty and little value to man or beast.

A land's talents must be protected and nurtured and encouraged. And if we do abuse some tract, it is our obligation to try very hard and deliberately to set things right again. Of course, it is not always so easy. Looking out the window from the chair in which I sit, I can see a thick stand of white cedar. Twenty-five years ago, this was a sterile patch of land growing little more than burdock and bootjack. What happened was that I wanted a pond. So, I directed the dragline operator to dig it. I was naive. I made no provisions for setting aside the good, black topsoil full of nutrients and teeming with bacteria. Instead, topsoil and subsoil of sterile gravel, sand, clay and peat moss, were mixed indiscriminately. Then, when the bulldozer came to level the piles of spoil cast up by the dragline, I ended up with a mixture not good for growing anything except successions of coarse weeds.

But it was dirt (so I reasoned), and I never imagined that it would not come back to trees, to flowers, to ferns. So I waited, and when in five years it was still largely a sterile tract, a scientist friend suggested that I put it to white cedar. The cedar grew, dropped fronds, shaded out the coarse weeds, and now, after twenty years, the sun and the rain, the frost and the wind, the bacteria, have finally mellowed the land. Once more, along the fringe areas, I am getting bloodroot, Dutchman's breeches, ferns and an assortment of grasses and shrubs.

Similarly, some owners of clear-cut forest lands taken over by poplar are burning or cutting these soft, weed-type, pulp-producing trees and putting the acres back to pine. The results are amazing. Likewise, mother swatches of prairie sod have been planted on some stretches of plains worn out by poor farming practices, and now, slowly but surely, true prairie is being restored.

As I started to say, land has many talents, but they must not be perverted. Where we have abused prairie by strip-mining or reckless farming, we should not try to grow pine forests, but, remembering the virgin earth's real talent, should attempt to bring back prairie. Some of man's most futile and costly errors take decades, even centuries, to correct. Horicon Marsh, the seventeen-mile-long watershed along which I spent my boyhood, was in turn unsuccessfully used as a lake for shipping, then drained and farmed, then mined for peat, and then cropped for the coarse grasses, which were used for packing bric-a-brac. Decade after decade, people tried to turn the great marsh away from its one and only talent. Then, in the end, it became a sterile place of coarse grasses that were host to great annual fires that sent their stink sixty miles to Milwaukee and, when the wind was right, a hundred sixty miles to Chicago. Finally, back in the 1930s, the conservationists prevailed. Water was once more permitted to back up over the area.

Gradually, then, some of the old marsh plants once again began to take hold. Ducks, and especially geese, returned, until today, Horicon Marsh is one of the most famous stopping over places for Canada honkers, with countless thousands gathering to stay for weeks on their treks north in spring and south in fall. But the marsh has by no means returned to its original fertility. Abused so often, it came back with dense stands of cat-tails that provide little other than cover for wildlife. Still, the day may come when, as each succeeding crop of cattails dies and rots, the abused marsh bottom may become so fertile that even wild rice may make a comeback.

And so it goes with our good earth. Each square foot, each acre, each square mile has its own peculiar talents. And if we would recognize these talents — plant duck potato where duck potato belongs, pine where pine belongs, cranberries in bogs talented in producing cranberries — we could begin to correct our centuries of mistakes.

⇛ *A Grudging Salute* ⇚

Undoubtedly it will strike many as unreasonable, unforgivable and barbaric that for more than a half-century I have waged unrelenting war against the street sparrow. Since I could reach the eaves by standing on the rain barrel, I have broken its eggs and fed its fledglings to the cats. The sparrow was the first living target for my first BB gun. I sharpened my shooting eye with my first .22 caliber rifle by learning to aim the front sight at a sparrow's feathered breast. In winter, when the bird came in gangs seeking bird-feeder relief, I pulled the string that sprung the trap.

With a flashlight, I roamed lumberyards at night, collecting heads redeemable at a penny apiece from the property owner. I risked the towering heights of many a haymow to get a bird or three against the panes of a window in the barn's pinnacle. I lay in ambush in corncribs, park pavilions and abandoned buildings. Even this past spring, I made the rounds of the bluebird and tree swallow nesting boxes at Little Lakes to oust the sparrows so the elite of the Little Lakes bird world might use the houses I had made available for them. In the beginning, it made sense. My parents, members of the volunteer fire department, the Village Board of Health, my schoolteachers, all assured me I was doing a public service. They made mine a holy war from the likes of which bigots are born.

Nests beneath eaves were considered a fire hazard. Sparrows in haymows, they claimed, contaminated the hay. Sparrows, so they said without being specific, spread disease. They claimed the birds short-circuited wiring.

Gradually, though I did not forgive the sparrow for wanting to stay alive, I began to admire its tenacity. No matter how many birds I or anyone else killed, there were always replacements. I also began to respect the bird as a worthy adversary. If I pointed my finger at a robin, it would go on about its business. Point my finger at a sparrow and in the flick of an eyelash it would be in full flight. During periods of stress, the sparrow seemed more intelligent than other birds. If a drought turned lawns brown, each robin would have three or four sparrows orbiting about it, and the moment the larger bird found a worm, the sparrows would dash in to steal it.

The street sparrow, officially called the house sparrow by the Audubon Society, was once called the English sparrow by most. The bird came to America in the 1850s. Within less than a century, the original few thousand increased to millions, and now its population holds steady, proof of the automatic checks and balances that over the long haul control wildlife populations. Originally, the sparrow was native to Europe, Asia and North Africa. Now it lives in every temperate climate around the world.

Except for being an untidy nest builder, using trash of all kinds, the street sparrow is a clean and truly beautiful bird of many soft shades of brown, gray, white and even red. It feeds on insects and weed seeds, seldom taking more than the portion of the harvest that falls to the ground as the reaper passes. One day I am sure the street sparrow will be admired. As other bird species whose survival depends upon specific habitat begin to disappear, the sparrow will be at home among factory smokestacks, shacks, cathedral spires and the green countryside. So, perhaps it is time the bird and I declare a truce. After all, while I was alone and lonely in an English hospital, a sparrow came to my windowsill for bread crumbs and to show me a shining eye — my only visitor.

⋙ *Holy Grails* ⋘

Holy Grail. What does that mean to you? The presidency of the United States? A simple home, all your own? Scholastic honors? Holding the yardstick of life to a difficult code of ethics? Whatever, the search for your Holy Grail can strike sparks to the fires of determination and even, perhaps, transform a lackadaisical life into one of adventure. I have had my Holy Grails. Dozens. Many eluded me. Some did not. Some were laudable. Some were foolish. But all gave purpose to tomorrow. Among the more meaningful was my determination to write something good enough that a magazine editor would purchase it. I collected countless rejection slips.

Then one day: "Dear Mr. Ellis: We think your story is delightful, and we are sure our readers will agree. Enclosed please find a check ..." The drab corner of the lonely room where I did my writing became a precious, glowing place. Candles had been lighted along the trail that had led some writers to the Nobel pinnacle.

Most of my Holy Grails were considerably less meritorious, though nonetheless consuming. There was, for instance, a German brown trout of some fifteen pounds that lived in Waushara County's Mecan River. I saw the fish, and at once became obsessed. He would be mine. I fished for him at every opportunity. I fished at midnight and at midday. I tried every artificial fly in my folder. I tried worms, grasshoppers, crickets, frogs, minnows. I even rigged a small harness with hooks to float a wriggling mouse across the pool where the trout lived. Twice I hooked him. Twice he broke off. I began to neglect my wife and my work. Hollows appeared in my cheeks and beneath my eyes. Then, three years after I began my campaign, I walked into a bar at Dakota, and there, on a slab of ice, was my fish. A banker from my own hometown had caught the trout on a cane pole using a piece of cheese for bait. In retrospect, it is difficult to believe that a potbellied, slimy, finny curmudgeon of doubtful gustatory delicacy had diverted my life from more worthwhile pursuits. Ah, me, the Holy Grail.

More than a quarter-century ago, we moved to our present home, Little Lakes. These semi-wild acres produced Holy Grails by the dozens. With dedication, perseverance and copious quantities of sweat, we found most if not all of our Holy Grails. Among our accomplishments, we nurtured spruce and pine trees to the point where they began to reseed themselves. But, despite the ideal habitat we have provided, to this day no bluebird stays to nest in the houses on our fenceposts. However, our neighbor, less than a quarter-mile away, always has a breeding pair, and without putting forth any extra effort.

Still, we are not giving up, because another Holy Grail that eluded us for as long as the bluebirds at last has been found. I will not forget the first time I went in search of this Holy Grail. I began my campaign in the lakes that beautify the outskirts of Mukwonago. I rented a boat and went overboard in the stinking muck of the back bays to bring up white water lily tubers as long and thick as my arm. I took them home and planted them in Fish Pond. Result? Nothing. Over the next three years I went to many other lakes to try their tubers. Nothing. I sent to an Oshkosh nursery for tiny tubers, weighted them with nails and tossed them into the pond. They produced a scattering of anemic pads, which muskrats soon disposed of.

Sometimes I would skip a year, but then I would resume the search when the river of my youth would flow gently through my mind and I would see acres and acres of white water lilies bordering the coppery stream. As recently as two years ago, I resumed the search and planted more tubers from Oshkosh. Last year, as expected, there was a scattering of somewhat sickly pads. I purchased no more. Then, this spring, almost magically, those thin, tiny pads lifted, and grew, and grew. And now, where the horses once drank, eight huge water lily blossoms are shining like white stars in a green carpet of gently undulating pads.

⇛ *Liquid Mirror* ⇚

When the leaves on the oaks on the knoll where I sit are no larger than squirrels' ears, I can look through the branches and see three spring-fed ponds. This is where I come, especially on windless days, to see this corner of Little Lakes, not as it is, but as the calm pond waters reflect it. Now, of course, I know about the gall on the milkweed stem, about the dragonfly that made it halfway up a burr reed and then died, stuck there, now only wings and a hollow fuselage. I know about the scars on the trees, about the broken branches waiting for a wind to dislodge them. I see ruts and ugly indentations on an otherwise green slope, and a thousand other imperfections. But when I lower my eyes from pond banks to enjoy reflections in the water, all imperfections disappear. It is as though someone has touched up the reflection as an artist might a painting, leaving out or glossing over all the little uglies.

There is something truly magical about reflections in water. Fifty years ago, as a young hunter, I learned that on dark days, especially during the half-hour before sunrise, the water was the place to watch if I wanted to see ducks approaching the decoys. Long before my eyes could pick up the incoming ducks in the air, I could see them mirrored on the surface of the lake, and the reflections were always larger than life.

Of course, there are scientific reasons why clear, calm water, being able to trap light, mirrors everything better than the human eye. Still, I hesitate to dwell on light refraction or the water's shining capability of reflection, other than to note that a towering cedar seen in the water is infinitely more beautiful than the same tree viewed with the naked eye. I have no talent with the brush, but if I did paint, it would be reflections. My finished canvas likely would not qualify as art, since none of the imperfections would be there to contrast and highlight the beauty.

Years ago, one of my youngsters, who sometimes sat on the knoll with me, said, "The water's smiling."

"Yes, of course," I would agree, and then sagely add, "and when the water smiles, the whole world smiles."

That is not true, of course, not any truer than the cliché, "Smile and the world smiles with you." Matter of fact, I have received a few fat lips for smiling at the wrong time. But there is no doubt that a warm smile, like a watery reflection, transforms the face. An old woman's wrinkles seem to dissolve in the warmth of a smile. A teenager's pimples melt into insignificance and the young face becomes beautiful and brilliant when a smile starts at the eyes, then runs like sweet honey to soften an otherwise blemished countenance. Harsh lines become sculpted contours when, upon reflection, an old man's face relaxes.

Just as the smile belongs to the face, so the reflections in the pond belong to the pond. The trees, birds, grasses and flowers would be there, pond or no pond. Reflections are indeed versatile — though they may disappear, they cannot be destroyed. Cut the trees, destroy the grasses, fill the ruts, and their resurrection may take years. But throw a stone to shatter a reflection and, even as the picture falls into bits and pieces, like parts of a magnetized jigsaw puzzle, they quickly draw back together, fitting precisely into place.

Not being a preacher, I hesitate to point out any lessons in life, except that it seems I can never see the facial erosions carved by a harsh life, or the blemishes accompanying puberty — not when a face is transformed by a smile. It must be a reflection, a reflection of some inner beauty that can work such miracles.

June

JUNE, THE MONTH DURING WHICH SPRING
RAMS HEAD-ON INTO SUMMER, AND THE CLASH
OF SEASONS RESULTS IN A COLLISION OF COLOR.
Timid tints — whites, pinks and pastels —
slowly give way to more brazen blooms: metallic
blue of chicory, sparks of columbine, sun-gold
petals dripping from the bronze hearts of cone-
flowers, flamboyant deep-orange daylilies and
tigers escaped from gardens to run wild along
roadsides. But at the moment this June I am
thinking of April, and how every year a northbound loon has tarried on a home pond for two
weeks. Each night then, during its brief April
tenure, it wails like some other-worldly creature,
making it pure pleasure to come closer beneath
the blankets, delighted to shiver just a little
while, sharing one of the wildest, most primitive
and haunting voices of any wilderness.

I think of that loon this June, because we are
sitting nearly a thousand miles north on a ridge
of sand, looking down on a springhole we have
wanted to fish each of four succeeding days. But
there is a loon nesting in the trail close to the
shore, and we have had to opt for other waters.
Each morning, however, we stop by, hoping, and
on the fifth morning our patience pays off.
When we arrive, one egg has already hatched,
and the fledgling is flopping to dry itself. And
the other egg is cracked, and even as we and the
mother loon wait, the second fledgling, with
incredible strength, wrestles free. Before noon
the sun and a gentle breeze have turned the wet
black chicks fluffy with down, and all afternoon

Peace is so precious.
If only each and every one
might find a corner of
contentment.

we catch crimson-bellied trout while the newborns ride nonchalantly on their mother's back, even when our lines are cast within a few feet from where she paddles. To say it is our April loon, of course, is preposterous. But we would have it that way, and that is the miracle of imagining, our certain and unassailable right to live beyond the stringent boundaries of reality.

But June is like that, almost a dream world. End of imprisonment as children burst shouting through school doors, and cecropia moths, splitting tough brown cocoons, come free to unfold fragile, crumpled wings until they are as smooth as silk, nearly a full six-inch spread of dusty shades of pink, peach, gold, buff, gray, brown, black. But be not deceived by your own or the poet's declaration that there is nothing so rare as a day in June. If we find time to tarry and see beyond the superficial facade of brilliance, it is apparent that now every wild one is taxed to the limit of its endurance, just hustling groceries to satisfy the insatiable appetites of such multitudes as are beyond our ability to enumerate or even really imagine. The owl born in March, dove in April, robin in May, oriole in June — plus mammals, reptiles, amphibians, fishes, insects, arachnids, invertebrates — dominate earth, air and water. If all survived, human life would perish, and so they feed upon each other, and combine to reduce in numbers such a multitude as, we laughingly exaggerate, might be capable of shifting even the earth on its axis.

The plant world is no exception. So the oak dooms its own seedlings by shading them from the sun. For twenty linden saplings sharing one square foot of earth, lucky if one survives the struggle for living space. Wild grape strangles ivy. A high rise of daisies dwarfs ferns until, one June, the ferns give up the fight. Prickly ash spreads stubborn, thorny barricades against any plant invasion. Canary reed grass mats down and smothers Canada lily, black-eyed Susan, blue dayflower — all except a milkweed here, a joe-pye weed there, or a mullein, stubborn and rigid and straight, ancient phallic symbol, all plan-

Man's battles become picayune forays compared to nature's never-ending wars.

ning late summer or early autumn ascendancy. Graceful as palms of the tropics, some Solomon's seal arch six and eight feet over horsetails, and the diminutive horsetails, plants that once grew to heights of fifty feet, become even less significant, perhaps because they likely are destined to disappear like the gigantic animals that once roamed beneath their whorls of needle-shaped leaves millions of years ago.

So June in reality becomes a battle ground. It becomes the time for no-quarter combat. Compassion is not in its dictionary. The creatures of the earth are as relentless as the seemingly fragile moss. Worms cultivate the earth so grass may grow to feed rabbits for the fox, which in turn fertilizes and feeds, in an eternal cycle, the earthworm. Poets may rejoice, sing the praises of June, and I join the choir, but for every Menander frolic, there is a Melpomene echo, sad song by the Greek Muse of tragedy.

So I cannot stroll with the dreamy-eyed philosophers, who hold nature up as an example of how to live in harmony. Man's battles become picayune forays compared to nature's never-ending wars. Perhaps man, seeing the end result — perhaps a field solid with black-eyed Susans — sings a rhapsody about them, never knowing of the hundreds of flowers and grasses that succumbed to their invasion. At what cost to all plants and animals does a pine forest rise to such cathedral but sterile proportions? And where the white water lilies my children wrote poems about? Down the muskrat's gullet. Balance of nature? Pure fabrication. June is the month when the battles are won or lost, because when the horned owl has harvested from my place all except a few swift cottontails for brood stock, he moves to yours. So, when you write an ode to a purple carpet of violets, include an obituary for the May flowers that once owned that land.

The pendulum swings back and forth, and if winter is the time for easy counting to reckon the costs, June is the fulcrum on which the scales are balanced. But I watch without bitterness, only a profound respect, because this has always been the way. And from the blood-letting comes a more perfect buck deer with brighter eyes, wider antlers and broader chest. And flowers which, having been tried and proven, can rise from grit on an eye-dropper of water. Surely we all sometime wish it were not so. Peace is so precious. If only each and every one might find a corner of contentment, instead of putting forth greedy tendrils, thorns, rapacious roots and strangles of vines.

But civilization flourishes only in gardens where dictatorial requirements are strictly enforced by blade, rake and poison. But enough. There will be time when we are dying to take the morbid tack. It is time now in June to exult in the victory of the teal clutch, which has escaped turtle's jaws and hawk's talons; time to rejoice that shooting stars, routed by canary grass, have started another colony across the valley; time to give thanks that wild rice, suffocated a half-century, rises once more where creeks change course, leaving fertile back bays.

That is a balance of sorts, and it is enough, because even if, in time, the crane loses some length of leg, because eutrophication has made his lake a shallow pond, he is, under that circumstance, perhaps a better bird because on shorter legs he need not stretch so far. Wars are abominable. And if it is heresy to write that we may never have emerged from the Dark Ages without them, it is not heretical to conclude that the sugar maple alongside my drive is a better tree for having survived adversity. Forgive me, I come back to June, and there the emerald swallow, with sweeping grace, vacuums the sky, while the Garden Galahad never so much as blinks while lancing with lightning-swift tongue the same lacy-winged fare the swallow eats.

Frenetic month. The mayfly dances, drops her eggs and dies on the same day. Bees literally work themselves to death, and if you never noticed, it is because there already are other generations on the wing to perpetuate the colonies with gifts of honey. Country or city, swamps or forests, mountains or deserts, north or south, June is the fertile, fecund month of abundance beyond belief.

The mayfly dances, drops her eggs and dies on the same day.

Fishing With Susie

Where the Schnitzler road dead-ends in the farmyard, Muscovy ducks stood in the roadway, chickens scratched alongside in the loam, a shaggy black dog rumbled a greeting, and down the slope, Spring Lake glistened like a windowpane in the slanting sun. The kitchen door slammed and we were shaking hands. "Yes, the fishing has been fairly good. One man had a walleye right up to the boat and then lost it."

"You mean," I asked, "fishermen are now catching the walleyes planted in here many years ago?"

"Well, no," Schnitzler said. "It is the first I've heard of, but it shows they are still there."

A car up from the lake drive stopped.

"Catch anything?" I asked.

"Some small bass," the man said.

Since bass were what I had come for, I went to where the green oars still leaned against the shack, and then drove down to the graveled beach. Across the lake, where neat cottages perch on the wooded knolls, some nuns were picnicking, since it was a church holy day. Up in the bay, several blue herons came off the marshy shores and flapped ponderously away into the wind. In the first clump of rushes, a bass followed my pork chunk bait right to the boat, and at the last minute tried to slurp it off the surface. Minutes later, another mouthed the wavering chunk and took off on an end run, but dropped the lure when I put the pressure on. Out in the clear, a pound bass came out of the water on the strike and sent my spinner sparkling like a drop of spray.

Then, there were no more fish, not up in the flats, not on the reedy bars, nor where the water is blue and deep. It did not matter. There was Susie, sitting on the bow, and if you have a daughter like Susie in your family, you will know what I mean. Once again I really heard the blackbirds, watched the hawks, recognized the castles the clouds were building and then tearing down to build again. Even as the man living alongside the railroad tracks soon fails to hear the trains go by, so in my work the sounds of frogs and crickets, and the songs and the flight of birds, are things taken for granted and therefore go unnoticed.

Spring Lake is a better than average bass lake, and I should have been perturbed that I did not create more of a stir with my offerings. But it did not really matter, with Susie up front, pointing out the familiar things in such a way as to give them new meaning.

⇛ *Sleepy River* ⇚

There must be thousands of what I call no-account rivers, rarely explored, except by occasional bridge fishermen. These slow streams are often too shallow for outboard motors. Boaters, fishermen, campers, hikers and hunters hie on to the more publicized watering holes of the country. There, elbowing one another for room to maneuver, they shatter the solitude and their own peace of mind while the little river at their back door slips along sleepily, undisturbed. We have one such, the Fox, making a great bend to flow past our little village park.

Or, at least it was ignored until my twenty-one-year-old Waukesha daughter called my sixteen-year-old Big Bend daughter and said, "Let's float the Fox." So it was, early on the following Sunday morning, that I was heading toward a riverside park in Bumpy, our ancient pickup truck, loaded with a duck skiff, pup tent, food, water, Mary and Dianne, and a huge, lion-headed Chesapeake Bay retriever. When they shoved off, a mouse would have had it hard to find a seat. The road between Big Bend and Waukesha is ten miles long and straight as a string. But the river connecting the communities takes off on such absurdly drunken tangents that fifty miles is perhaps a conservative estimate of the distance the girls would have to row.

Boat launched, I quickly got Bumpy off the park grass and raced a few minutes south to watch as, big dog perched in the bow, they went talking and giggling between railroad bridge trestles on the only stretch of fast water anywhere on the river. For a moment, I thought of spending Sunday on intersecting bridges watching their progress. Not that they were in any danger. Mostly, I guess, I was just envious, not of their river, since I have floated most of the major waterways of our continent, but because I wanted to recapture that adventurous spirit that time and too many rivers had eroded in me.

They got back Monday, and if I were to tell you that it was an idyllic journey filled with moonlight, flowery perfumes, exciting wildlife and lazy lunches beneath peninsula oaks, I would be a damned liar. Mostly, it was hot and monotonous, and always it was backbreaking as they took hour-by-hour turns at the oars. They were even sick from sun, and when they staggered in after it was all over, they looked like two limp, red licorice sticks someone had dropped on a burning-hot sidewalk.

A veteran of hundreds of river trips, I knew that a bath, food and a nap have a way of changing perspective, putting an almost tingling tinge to what might have seemed a tour of drudgery. And, sure enough, by suppertime they were talking about the hundreds of ducks, the herons, the meadowlarks, bobolinks, marsh wrens, rails and coots, and laughing at the antics of Eekim, the Chesapeake who, tempted by schooling minnows, went diving off the bow. They were especially thrilled by having felt worldly detachment as the river took them through a sea of grasses that stretched unbroken on all sides, on and on to hills far away and vague.

Still, they had to sleep on it one more night before talking about a rerun. But next time, maybe Eekim will have to stay home, because a third daughter is lobbying for her place in the boat. So, give a glance. Maybe there is a no-account river in your backyard, waiting sleepily for someone to make it tremble with ripples of excitement.

⇛ *War of the Fishes* ⇚

A pond is a world unto itself, in which there is a lot of living and dying. It is a no static world in which nature keeps some sort of miraculous balance, but an ever-changing place where one fish species is forever trying to dominate. June is a good month for assessment, because the clouds of fry, haunted by larger fishes, by bird, mink, raccoon and even frog, swim in clouds that explode in every direction at the moment of attack.

In a pond special to us, the bluegills had it all their own way fifteen years ago. There were thousands, and they ate their own and every other fish's eggs, and in the end became so plentiful that they starved themselves out of all the deep pools and shallow places. Green sunfish took over, and they were so tough it is likely they would have stayed in power for more years than they did, except that children carrying fish poles intervened, and were ruthless in their harvest, necessary to feed their stables of turtles, aviaries of seagulls and kingfishers, mud puddles of ducks, sundry raccoons and one fish-eating fox.

But the bluegills were too few to take advantage of the situation and stage a comeback. Instead, black bass took over, and shortly the pond was teeming with bass of all ages, and cannibalism was the rule instead of the exception. Seeking to give the pond more variety, the children brought in a couple hundred rainbow-hued sunfish ("punkin seeds") anticipating they might eat enough bass eggs to stall the bass population explosion and give the pond a better balance.

But the sunfish, a gypsy breed, instead of fighting, gathered into ghettos and posed no threat to the bass. Meanwhile, however, the bluegills were beginning to take over an inlet here, a bay there. Bass, having decimated their primary food source, the crayfish, and having thinned their own ranks in cannibalistic orgies, were losing ground. In the end, after having maintained but token forces among the shadowy corridors of coontail moss, the bluegills are once more venturing forth to raid bass nests, and a census taken this June indicates that the cycle started more than fifteen years ago is likely to repeat itself.

⫸ *After the Pigtails* ⫷

There was a breeze last night, and Gwen and I lay close in a house strangely silent. It had been a hectic weekend with the children running, laughing and shouting along trails they will never forget, stopping only to quietly count the memory beads on their rosaries of time. A weeping willow, now so huge, still grasps a toy gun, left carelessly in a crotch, now buried in its heart. The girl who left the gun there twenty years ago pauses to touch the trunk where it has grown to engulf the gun. The freckles, the pigtails are gone. Only the little girl heart remains, quickening as she fingers the rough bark.

The children argue briefly about which of them set a certain seedling to soil. Then, standing back and looking up, they view the high, green spires and become suddenly silent in this cathedral of trees they planted. They touch a horseshoe, still nailed to a stall that now stables only mice, and identify it as one worn by the fiery Tequila.

They look up at a single board, once one of twenty nailed to a tree, ladder to a leafy hideaway in an old oak. They pause by the flat rock that stored the sun's warmth for their small, cold bottoms, a rock that now serves only as a sun deck for the turtles of Fish Pond. There is the handle of an old rake still bracing a rusting length of wire; a knothole where they eyeballed generations of flickers; hoof picks and curry combs still on dusty shelves. They remember, and they pause in awe beneath the tortured oak, twisted by Indians to mark a trail to the mound effigies a mile away on Maney's hill. The trunk of the tree completes a tight, full-fisted circle so branches finger the way.

A tremendous, iron-hard stump reminds them of the one hundred seventy elms beneath which they played and napped, now gone, all killed by Dutch elm disease, and then sacrificed again in a wintertime fireplace. Fish Pond, Clear Pool, New Pool, Blue Pool — all changed, yet never changing. Places where they learned to swim, row a boat, angle for fish, snare turtles, catch crayfish, count ducks, dream dreams and dodge darning needles, even though they knew the iridescent flying dragons never really did sew children's mouths shut.

On the front lawn, they pause for root beer and apples and to talk about red leaves and brown chestnuts. Moving again, they climb the hill for a panoramic view of our wooded spread. Sitting on tremendous elm logs, which defied the saw and now appear petrified, they speak softly of the mother who died and the mother who came to carry on. Then, if their hearts are saddened, their faces still shine as they once did in the sun.

Again they are silent, perhaps remembering how the dogs' water steamed in winter, how ice hung pendants from the eaves across their bedroom windows, how sunrises and sunsets were red fire. Perhaps they hear the long-ago ring of an axe, the coo of the dove. Maybe they feel again the mud oozing up between their toes, and sweat stinging their eyes before a cool plunge after a hard day hauling wood.

How tender, how tough. How banal, how sublime. How joyous, how sad. And so it was that I could have wept last night, but edged close to Gwen instead, in that silent house after the children had all left to go back to homes of their own.

⇛ *The Quiet Time* ⇚

Evening sunset. Snarling motors have been silenced. Fisherman rests on his oars. Even the wind, which has worked so hard all day, comes to rest. It is the bewitching hour, a sort of holy time. There is gold in the June sky and the forest seems afire. For a brief time, even the insects wait on day's ending. It is the interlude between today and tomorrow. The world, its trees and its waters almost seem to sigh their relief. It is the time of in-between. Daytime creatures are going to their roosts, their dens, their night camps. Nighttime creatures are up and stretching, but not yet about. The hawk, hunting done for this day, sits watching. The owl, hunting time arriving, sits waiting. Incredibly, even the fish wait before dimpling the water in a last-minute flurry of feeding.

Time has run out for this June day, but has not yet started for this night. The whole meaning, perhaps even the reason, is wrapped in this eternity when a day beyond the horizon is beginning, while this day is ending. Who has not at least felt it — the mystery of this moment? What man, what woman, what child has not paused to wonder, perhaps to ponder? People fish for many things. Day's end, however, in all its glory, seems to be the ultimate for which we have been searching. And evening, that quiet time, is when we resign ourselves to the peace that comes at night.

≫ *What Have We Done?* ≪

An opossum, suddenly being accosted by a wolf, fell down and played dead. The wolf, a great, gray, rangy specimen, pawed the inert possum and then backed off to sit down. Twisting and turning his head, the wolf, ears erect, wondered about this strange animal, which had fallen into what appeared to be a faint. Not needing to feed, the wolf pretended to leave, but hid behind a rock outcropping to watch. In time, the possum opened its eyes, closed its gaping jaws, righted itself and began industriously to search the turf for grubs.

"Just a minute," the wolf called, and then quickly added, "and don't go taking a dive on me again, or I'll make sure next time that you don't get up."

The possum crouched and asked, "Oh yes, Great One, and what can I do for you?"

"First off," the wolf asked, "what manner of creature are you, and from where did you come?"

The grizzled, gray marsupial grinned, and then said, "Well, men call me opossum, possum for short. My native land is the deep South. But in recent years my numbers have so increased that some of us have had to move north to find living room."

The wolf's eyes widened in disbelief. "But how can that be? How can your kind have multiplied, while we, the great wolves, are a vanishing breed, driven to the brink of extinction?"

The possum, sensing he now had nothing to fear from the wolf, made himself more comfortable by curling his naked tail around to one side. "I can't be sure," the possum said, "but my guess would be that somehow, in some way, you have offended man."

The wolf thought on that and then said, "Well, I suppose so. Once man came out of the caves and began to herd goats and cattle, we did, from time to time, borrow a calf or a kid."

"No, it has got to be more than that," the possum said. "Many others, from time to time, have taken pigeons from their roosts or hens from barnyards, and the great cats have even taken some of the men themselves and carried them off to their lairs."

The wolf nodded. "But the great cats are in trouble, too. Man has all but eliminated them."

"But for different reasons. The women like to wear the great cats' coats."

With a touch of pride, the wolf said, "Sometimes they wear our coats, too."

"But only rarely," the possum said. "It is something else. Now, let me think."

The wolf waited, and finally the possum said, "It's got to be that you want something that man also wants."

"You're right there," the wolf said, "because we've always wanted moose, elk, deer and caribou, and so, of course, has man. Now, you know two predators of different species both wanting to harvest the same thing cannot occupy the same territory. One or the other has got to go. Do you suppose that is why man so hates us?"

"You've hit on something," the possum said. "It is true the lion cannot hunt in the leopard's territory, nor can the cheetah live where he would be in direct competition with either. Still, it is nothing so simple. Because man kills the big cats, but he does not hate them. He admires them."

The wolf raised a hind paw to scratch his head thoughtfully. "Yes, I suppose that's not the whole answer, because I've heard man has translated our name into many meanings, all hateful. Yet the lion's name is a proud one."

"That's the point," the possum said. "There is something more."

Once again, the wolf wrinkled his brow and narrowed his gray-green eyes. "Let's come at it from another angle," he said. "Why, for instance, are your numbers increasing while ours are diminishing?"

"That's simple," the possum said, "because for millions of years, any time we were accosted, we merely played dead. We never took what man wanted beyond a few peanuts and persimmons. And if here and there one of us got roasted along with some yams, it was only a small leak in the overflowing bucket of possums."

"In other words," the wolf replied, "you just never made waves."

"That's about it."

"So the hunters rarely pursued you?"

"Who would want to shoot an animal that lies there already looking like death?"

"Yes, who would?" the wolf replied. "And it surely explains why for millions of years you have not had any trouble. But I don't think it sheds any light on my troubles."

"But maybe it does," the possum declared. "As far as man is concerned, we are beneath contempt. We offer neither threat nor are we agile prey, only bumbling, stumbling fools who go into shock at the first sign of danger. You, meanwhile, are a threat, even if only in the minds of men, because you covet some of the meat he considers his."

"But you just said ... " the wolf interrupted.

The possum raised his chin, "In addition to the threat, you brag about it by scaring men out of their wits with your nightly howling."

"But they are only territorial, mating calls, only communication."

"But do men know that?"

"Some do."

"But too few. Still, it is even more than that. You have, above every other creature on this continent, put together such a family society as most resembles man's. You, above even the great bears or the lumbering moose, are wise almost beyond the ways of animals."

"Sure, sure," the wolf interrupted, "but what has all that got to do with man?"

"Everything," the possum said, "because, don't you see, of all creatures around the world, only man believes he was made in the image of some god. And so, in his conceit, he imagines himself godlike, and you may never challenge that image without exciting his wrath."

"Maybe that's why," the wolf mused, "men even war among themselves."

"I know it sounds pretty far-fetched, but think on it anyway," the possum said. Then he quickly asked, "And now may I go?"

"Yes. Yes," the wolf said. "Go in peace."

≫ Queen of the Flowers ≪

Eighteen years is a long time to mourn the passing of a tiny flower colony, especially when surrounding swales and slopes display, in season, upwards of a hundred different blooms, many certainly more beautiful, and a few as quaint and rare, as the yellow lady's slipper. But a June never passes that we do not come to the island, intended especially for them, to wonder what happened.

It is nearly a quarter-century since we discovered the golden lode, nuggets among more ordinary leafy species. Guarding our discovery like some long-lost mine, we told only family and a few friends, lest the flowers be trampled by careless boots. Once it was one of our more common flowers. Pioneer children plucked the lips from the blossoms and, launching them on meadow brooks, called them Noah's Arks. And when there were no creeks for sailing, they called them ducks, Indian shoes and moccasin flowers.

But as with the timber wolf, even the proximity of people seemed to inhibit the spread of what many have come to call the queen of the wildflowers. So it was with considerable trepidation that we planned a trout rearing pond where the yellow flowers grew. And when the big dragline began biting chunks out of the surrounding terrain, we stood guard to see that it followed the circle of stakes, so an island was left in hopes it would become a lady's slipper refuge.

The first year then, when trout broke water to inhale the lacy-winged Mayflies, there was a yellow glint in the fishes' glassy eyes where nodding blooms put reflections of gold on the water. The second June, the flowers had backed so far from the water there were no reflections. And year after year then, the lady's slippers tightened their circle until one June, but a single flower remained. Though we brought in reinforcements from other acres, none flourished, and now, each June, when I cast a dry fly, I never feel as good when I creel the trout as during those first few years when I could look across the water to the island where the lady's slippers grew.

⋙ *Friends* ⋘

Trees remind me of people. I think of them as friends, especially now when I know they soon will be greening. Greening is a time for census of a sort. The newborn can be counted before they are hidden among growing grasses. The winter casualties can be counted before their surviving cousins shroud these naked dead with a verdant screen. Even more than the ponds, more than the seasonal succession of wildflowers, more than the communities of water, shore and upland birds, more than the coons, muskrats, mice, foxes and mink, Little Lakes is foremost a community of trees.

They are the true permanent residents, and though visitors see them with the same casual indifference as they watch a passing throng on Milwaukee's Wisconsin Avenue, I know each as an individual, even though there be thousands. And I know most of their secrets. So if a stranger is moved to remark on how a weeping willow billows tier on tier like the hoop skirt of a Gay Nineties dancer, I say to myself: "But you should see the old gal's feet. She's got her toes curled in a drain, and soon the basement toilet will back up again."

Sure, I could kill the willow, but would I kill a friend because his head is among the stars as he unwittingly bulls a pathway through my precious field of fragile jewelweed? My reverence for trees was a long time maturing. Just as with real people, I suppose you have to live intimately together for a very long time, and even then, it is not until your friend dies that you begin to fully understand how you have lost not only a truly marvelous living thing, but a vital part of your own being. Nearly thirty years ago, I was put to a terrible test. We had just bought Little Lakes when, one day, the agent of a wealthy Chicago financier said he would give me one thousand dollars for each of the forty-three Colorado blue spruce on the place. Forty-three thousand dollars! And me with an enormous mortgage, plus a frightening land contract. Still, I said, "No." And to this day I am not sure why.

For a long time after turning down the agent, I could not summon the courage to tell my wife. A hundred and one nights I cursed myself when the house was quiet, except for my typewriter, as I supplemented my newspaper income with checks from magazines. For a hundred and one days, when I walked to view the Colorado blues, all I could see were dollar signs. Fool! I told myself. And perhaps I was. Except, now I don't think so. Those blues have grown so high that low clouds, scudding up from the Fox River Valley, sometimes leave drops of diamond water on their towering spires. Hundreds of red birds have been bright sparks on the snow-wrapped spruce boughs, bringing warmth to my heart. Oh, I might have taken the money and planted seedlings to replace the trees, but I would never have lived long enough to see and be awed by their towering majesty.

There was another crucial test. A beetle brought it. The pestilence attacked the elms, umbrella trees towering so high that the chemical stream from the fire department hoses fell far short of reaching the top. There were no tears, only anger. The anger became a daily snarl of chain saws. The anger was unremitting and dangerous as the trees, fat around as a hippo's tummy, crashed to the earth, hurling splintered branches like jagged shrapnel. Now, what might I say for my precious trees? More than a hundred seventy, smoke up the fireplace chimney. It was my holocaust. A betrayal. My friends? Never! Not anymore. It remained a bitterness for a long time. Then, one day, a coppice of young elms sprouted from a stump grave. Here, there, more and more. It was a resurrection. Today, there are umbrella American elms more than a foot in diameter. I touch them almost in awe.

So the love affair resumes. I have names for the majestic, the weak, the crooked, the straight, the strong. I know which are ailing and which are jousting for living space. I interfere but rarely now, letting them work things out in their way and in their own time. Now sometimes, when I am home alone and there is no one to scold, I climb the hard maple that has limbs thicker than my body. I use the limbs as steps. Sometimes I manage to get halfway up a burr oak to sit. Or I puff up the hill and sit in a linden that is also home to raccoons. Always, day or night, good weather or bad, winter or summer, I am surrounded by my friends, and I forgive them for breaking and sometimes killing things, and I hope they will not blame me for resenting the fact that they are mortal, too. You see, now I know. The earth is truth. Why had I doubted?

⋙ *Things Could Be Worse* ⋘

A world crackling with brush-fire wars threatening a global conflagration. A job market so unstable that it threatened industrial chaos. That was the frightening prospect for those millions in the Class of 1980 as they left the structural society of college. The youngest, the last of my five daughters, was one of them, and in assessing her prospects I searched for words of solace or encouragement or advice that I might give her. Nothing came. I strained for a nugget of wisdom, but ended up with cliches.

I tired, gave up and toyed with a pencil. My eyes wandered to the ceiling, the walls, the floor, as if I might find some answers there. But there was nothing. All those years of living, all those years of failure, and all those years of success, and now, nothing. Nothing to give my daughter, nothing to give to the Class of 1980. I looked at the pictures on my desk. There were my father, my mother, Old Dog. There was a picture of three young men riding a railroad freight car.

My eyes studied the three young men. I was the one on the left. Incongruously, we were wearing the cap and gown of graduates down there in the freight yard. But there was a reason. It was a gag picture. When the afternoon graduation ceremonies had ended, we wandered from the stadium to a railroad siding that carried the trains bringing sports fans, athletic teams, food and books to the campus. We climbed the iron rungs of the freight car ladder and, with the wind billowing our graduation gowns, wore smiles of defiance for a world already crippled by the Depression. How was it we were not afraid? Or were we frightened, and was this our way of showing our derision for a world that seemed destined to self-destruct?

It was 1933. The Depression had lowered the boom on our country four years earlier while we were freshmen. By 1933, the men in the long bread lines had been gathered to form the ranks of the WPA and the CCC as men became letters in the alphabet of Franklin Delano Roosevelt's soup. And if we had escaped for four years by hanging on to familial apron strings, now came the reckoning. So why were we smiling? Was it a gesture of bravado? The condemned man puffing jauntily on a final cigarette before the trapdoor on the gallows is sprung? Well, if I did not know it then, there in the freight yard on campus, I knew it was for real four months later when I hopped a freight headed West, and stopped at a bakery to beg, for the first time, for stale bread. The smile was gone. Home was far away. My associates were hollow-eyed men in bum jungles, or overnight companions in jails.

My goals in life, once lofty, had become a reasonably full stomach and a place warm enough to flop for the night. I was disillusioned, bitter. I was terribly frightened. I blamed God and the government. I wallowed in self-pity and complained incessantly about being a failure at twenty-one. Then, one dark night, beside a tiny fire on the outskirts of a small California town, while sipping cheap wine from a milk bottle, I got my comeuppance. I was with an old man, a professional hobo to whom the Depression meant nothing because bum jungles were his home, stale bread a staple, freight cars his usual vehicle, cheap wine a luxury.

After listening to me cry in the wine for a while, he lifted his head so the firelight sparkled in his eyes and turned the white hairs of his salt-and-pepper beard to slivers of silver. "Listen, sonny," he said, "you make me sick. You'd think you were the first man in the world to be hit with a low blow." Then, beginning with the first settlers who were obliterated by starvation and disease, he took me on a trip through history. His words, which rose and fell like the flames of the little fire, carried on through the war of revolution waged by the thirteen colonies against England.

Sometimes his voice was scornful. "Sonny, if you think you've got it tough, you should have been around when the Civil War ripped the guts right out of this country!" He spoke of the westward-bound pioneers who died beside their wagon trails. He spoke of the homesteaders who battled rocks and stumps and wild animals and Indians, only to be defeated by starvation. He told of the millions of immigrants who arrived at Ellis Island with one change of socks and nothing more; of the children in sweatshops and mines slaving twelve and fourteen hours a day, seven days a week, for pennies.

Then, with tears on his cheeks, he counted the thousands of victims of the influenza epidemic that swept our country after World War I, his family among the victims. "You think you've got it tough," he said, kicking the fire so the embers scattered. "You make me sick." And he lay back, pillowing his head on an arm to wait for sleep.

⇛ *June Moon* ⇚

The moon is a barren, desolate planet. Yet, on reflecting the glory of the sun, it not only becomes a thing of beauty in its own right, but brightens our nights and softens the harsh edges of reality. It is amazing how reflected glory sometimes works wonders. In battle, the gallantry of a few has made the timid brave. Along the street of sorrow, the optimism of a buoyant beggar has turned companions from the brink of despair. Men of little talent have risen to great heights, inspired by the accomplishments of others. The naked sun can be harsh, too brilliant. But, when it is mirrored by a June moon, we may bask in its reflection without fear of being burned.

So venture out when the moonlight is on the mist, and see how trees appear to be growing out of a white sea. Note how the sharp, jagged contours of the cliff have softened, and the steep trail among the trees is a dappled invitation to climb as high as you like. Then, though you have walked the same trail under the sun, now it seems an easier, more inviting route where poplar leaves are silver-plated, and the creek flowing beneath the walking log is a wind-ripple of white linen. Even the skeleton of the dead tree wears a shroud, and the rocks look soft enough to shape.

So, though you have never felt the need to take strength from the reflection of another's glory, sit anyway among the bridal birch, where the moon has laid a bright bridge of beams clear across a lake. No one is immune, unless of stone, to the moon's magic, and when you return home, it will follow you to put a path across your bedroom rug and gild even your dreams.

⇛ *Boondoggle?* ⇚

One day soon, I must go back to a tiny river that rises from springs in what used to be called the great dead heart of Wisconsin. I must start early so that I am in the water by sunup and have the entire day to wade downstream through riffles and holes, between high banks holding birch, and through long, low stretches where the delicate green of tamarack hides deer. Ostensibly, I will be fishing. I will be carrying a tiny, three-ounce fly rod; there will be a creel over my shoulder, a sandwich in my pocket, a canteen on my hip. When finally, at sundown, I come out of the water at the first bridge, my wife will be waiting, and there may even be a trout or two to fry. But it is not the trout nor nostalgic euphoria I will be seeking. I will be primarily concerned about the riprapped banks, and whether they are holding. Have current deflectors withstood the ravages of flood and time? Do stone flumes still stand to put a rush of oxygenated water over the white wedding stones of the brown trout's spawning beds?

Where quiet inlets are tickled by passing currents, are there still log and wire wildernesses into which a tiny trout may dart to escape otter or mink, heron's stiletto, sharp bill of the arrowing blue kingfisher, toothed jaws of a red-spotted uncle bent on cannibalism? They were all intact the last time I visited, monuments to what has been described by some as part of the greatest boondoggle in American history. Others described the boondoggle as the eleven-billion-dollar miracle that gave nine-and-a-half million Americans not only employment, but a vestige of hope at a time when the bottom seemed ready to drop forever out of the Great American Dream.

I am talking, of course, of the Works Progress Administration (WPA), which from 1935 to 1943, in addition to providing employment for Americans from laborers to actors, is credited with changing the face of the nation. Just for beginners, count 651,000 miles of new roads, 78,000 bridges, 125,000 buildings, nearly 600 airports, plus building or improving 8,000 parks, 12,500 playgrounds, 1,000 libraries and 5,900 schools. Add theater groups taking shows from Broadway to the boondocks; writers salvaging history from the crossroads to the cities; artists recording in mural, on canvas and in bound volumes the color, character, flavor of a nation.

But let someone else assess the nationwide impact of the WPA. My concern at this moment is for this little river, which is not likely to appear on most maps. It is twenty years since I waded it. The WPA stream improvements were then already twenty years old, strong and holding. Now I want to go back to see how these improvements have fared during the last twenty years. I can barely believe that time and the river have not at last erased them. But perhaps not. Perhaps they still stand, because whoever engineered the project and supervised the workers was smart enough to make the water work with, instead of against, his miles of structures. Then, if having waded from dawn to dusk, and discovering that the river has, during some days of watery rage, torn out the riprapping, tunneled under and dislodged the deflectors, washed the tiny trout's hideouts far back into some marsh, and reverted to its old, sluggish unproductive self, then I would like to come home to do some talking.

I would like to visit the bars, the backyard hammocks, the beaches, to see if any who have elected to wait out their unemployment benefits before looking for work might like a northwoods vacation. I would like to tap the healthiest and strongest in the relief lines and mention how cool the water is, how well the birds sing, and how pure the air is where my river flows.

But maybe I am putting the cart before the horse. Last time I looked, those WPA stream improvements seemed as though they would last forever. Then I will not have to bother anybody. And, just incidentally, that great dead heart of Wisconsin, where my river is born, once a waste of sand and scrub oak, is green with pine and spruce. Yes, the oldest trees are now just about forty years old. They were planted by the WPA.

≫ *Adapt or Die* ≪

People are not the only displaced creatures forced to move, as progress pours concrete to thrust freeways over the land that once held their homes. Birds and animals are daily victims of suburban sprawl, but just as humans do not up and die because they have been driven from the hearth, so also the wilder ones often make such adjustments as are necessary for survival. Unfortunately, construction cranks into high gear during the warming days of June, and a park mallard leaves her nest to build another on the pilings of a downtown bridge. A street is widened, and when a den tree falls, the squirrel opts for somebody's attic. The nighthawk, which used the high, hot cliffs and ridges on which a city has been built, now lays eggs on the tarred roofs of skyscrapers. A deer finds a deep ravine that still defies builders, and learns to live surrounded by homes and roads and the rush and roar of traffic.

Adaptation by the wild ones to the changing scene takes peculiar turns, and so the cardinal, victim or victor (depending on your assessment) of charity, no longer goes south because, unencumbered by a conscience, it perceives no shame in depending on bird-feeder relief. Geese by the hundreds of thousands eyeball people across a refuge ditch, and the gray fox dens beneath a back stoop. Their rock pile gone, bees find a chink in the fireplace mortar. People, especially those who have been forced in the name of progress to move, should especially appreciate the wild society's predilection to adapt rather than succumb either to flight or oblivion. It is a plus to have even an attic squirrel, when the new road has wiped out the last vestige of greenery where curbs now crowd the sidewalks.

Perhaps I am wrong, but more and more it seems there is a deep-seated inclination to identify with the earth. I see it in the crush of traffic northbound to places of tall trees, and in the vacationing sidewalk child, breathless as the foal first turned to pasture. This need to identify with the source of life can be a terrible, debilitating hunger, and if, as psychiatrists say, the lack of contact with the natural world impoverishes all of us, well then, kudos to the birds and animals that have elected to adapt and make homes even on high, sterile rooftops.

⋙ *Endless Beauty* ⋘

Wood has been described as nature's masterpiece. In 1682, Nehmiah Grew wrote, "The staple of the stuff is so exquisitely fine that no silkworm is able to draw anywhere near so fine a thread. So that one who walks about with the meanest stick holds a piece of nature's handicraft which far surpasses the most elaborate woof or needlework in the world."

We, of course, cannot see with the naked eye the intricate structure of a stick. But a cross section of a common alder branch, smaller than a man's little finger, when magnified forty times becomes a filigree of fibers more delicately woven than the finest lace.

Aside from a few cultures that venerated trees, most civilizations have used and abused wood with callous disregard. What point was there in pausing to admire the wood when the roof had to be raised before the first snow and logs brought to the hearth before the first bad freeze? Just like the man who has forty cows to milk, there is little time to admire the strength of hock and breadth of chest, much less the smoldering autumnal colors of the cows' eyes.

Still, for designers, simple and intricate patterns beautiful beyond belief are hidden in the trees. And all that is needed to discover them is a small saw and a powerful microscope. The fibrous structure of each tree species is different. Some, seen under glass, have almost straight lines, like the furrows of a practiced plowman. Others, like the red oak, have broad rays radiating from the core over rippling rings resembling ocean waves, one pursuing the other toward the beach.

Growing seasons may alter the design in cross sections of the same species. Hard years of little rain produce tight-knit patterns. Good years of rain on good soil open the patterns and provide wide, sweeping designs. The wood pattern is set in the heartwood, or the tree's dead center, which is surrounded by the sapwood, where life not only adds girth but provides a capillary network to get sap to the crown, so the tree may grow higher. A fallen tree may rot away to the heartwood, and then, for many trees like the cypress or redwood, resist corruption for a thousand years or more.

Tree species are so numerous there is an endless variety of patterns to be sketched, photographed or merely marveled at. To perceive wood designs, it is not necessary to cut down a tree. A branch or limb will usually suffice. Just understanding the structure of wood should give humans new insights into the trees that shade them from the summer sun. During a long writing career, one of my greater satisfactions was an announcement last summer by a New York book editor, born and raised on concrete. "I wouldn't have believed it," she said, "but you've taught me to love a tree."

I do not suppose it is easy to learn to love a tree. Sometimes it is tough enough to love family members during crises, much less get sentimental about the old box elder in the backyard. It probably isn't even possible to love a tree, though they can become great friends. During one of the lonelier times of my life, as a Depression youngster, I used to haunt the parks and got to know certain trees very well. I even named some of the trees and, after making the employment booths every morning, would visit my leafy friends in the afternoon. It is easy to talk to a tree and, if you are sad and lonely and a little lost in life, you can even imagine they are consoling you when a breeze makes comforting sighs and soft songs among the leaves.

⇒ *River of Time* ⇐

"Daddy, what was the river like when you were little?"

"Just glorious, Honey! Just glorious!"

"More beautiful than now?"

In twenty-five years, during successive annual fishing visits to the Wisconsin river of my boyhood, five daughters in turn asked the same questions. The bottom line, "More beautiful than now?" always stopped me cold in my conversational tracks. Instinctively, I have wanted to rhapsodize about the flocks of fishing terns keeping constant conversation as they dipped and lifted to send schools of silver-sided minnows skittering. I have wanted to tell about the water lilies, the white flanking of flowers that marked the river's flow, and about the purple gallinules, on pencil legs and spatulate toes, shivering the round, green pads as they moved, heads cocked, bright eyes alert for snail or leech or small, floundering fish. I wanted to tell about the pike, as long as a small boy, and the black-capped night-herons' solemn evening procession as, single file, they followed from fishing grounds to island roosts at the river's widening.

I wanted to speak of all the quiet inlets into which a girl or boy might slide a boat over golden nuggets of spatterdock to where berry brambles hung with fruit almost out over the water. I wanted to tell about the teal and mallards, wing feathers lost in the molt, sneaking back among the pencil reeds, and about broad sword rushes like bashful boys caught swimming around a river bend sans suits.

I would have liked to tell, too, how garbed anew, and with children also fully feathered, the ducks returned boldly to the sky and moved like swiftly penciled marks across the pale dawn, and then against the crimson canvas of evening. That was my river: hawks on high, wrens almost hidden, popping in and out of woven, hanging nests. That was my river: a blue-armored crayfish under every rock, big black colonies of corrugated clams stuck for life in the clay of every watery bend. Then, blackbirds flocked in such endless procession that at last a boy gave up waiting and went over the hill to see how many small painted and tub-sized snapping turtles had come to special egg-laying places on sandy slopes.

Oh yes, my river was indeed glorious, so glorious that as a boy I never really believed it when my father told me that already by then it was merely a shadow of its former self; how, sometimes when he was a boy, the coots would be rafted so solidly the current put a rime of foam where it bucked up against the black flotilla of bobbing white bills; how muskrats were so plentiful that trappers had to skin along the way, lest the catch of carcasses swamp their skiffs; how then there were even prairie chickens, true yellow legs, where swales came down to the water. He would point across the cultivated fields and say, "All trees, straight up the hill," or wave a hand as we rowed between pastured banks, "A mile of wild plums right here."

And so I suppose it must have been, because why would he lie about a thing like that? And so indeed it might have made no difference if I had rhapsodized about my boyhood Eden in front of my daughters, because didn't a blue heron still stilt to fish across from where we sat? And didn't a muskrat still trail cattail roots across the current to where some kits were waiting? And wasn't there a hawk, and sometimes two? And weren't there fish in the pail, even if most were bullheads?

There still was a night-heron squawking for landing instructions as in the dusk we packed our gear. Fireflies came out, too, if not in profusion, then in numbers enough. And had the diamonds on the water been any less shining, or the sunset any less red? And was not the blackbird just as melodious as ever, even though the symphony had diminished to an orchestra of somewhat fewer chairs? And there was even an owl quavering, and the quick shadow of a raccoon in our headlights, and childish sighs of satisfaction quite as thankful, I am sure, as any I or my father might ever have breathed.

So with blessings, maybe it is a mistake to count, since it seems that even little miracles are more than enough to shine an eye and fill a heart to overflowing.

July

THERE WERE THUNDERCLOUDS OUT OVER THE LAKE AT SUNSET. In the first darkness, flashes of lightning brightened the far horizon, and we heard the distant, muted mutter of thunder. But the rain did not come, and by midnight the bedroom became intolerable. Lace curtains hung limp. Once-crisp sheets and pillowcases were wilted and damp with sweat. Gwen and I lay apart, our minds hazy with heat and hypnotized by the hum of the refrigerator motor.

Summer had put a hot hand on the land to bronze leaves and squeeze grass stems until they were tough and dry, so rabbits gravitated to the greenery of our watered garden. Crucial month, July. Fate of millions in the balance. Birds watch berries shrivel on the vine. A world of hungry children see corn leaves curl, wheat stalks wither.

Two o'clock. Up from bed and outside. We walk the trail and the stones are still hot. Surprisingly, even crickets are silent. At the lake, not a single frog voices its willingness. In fact, all the world, it seems, is silent.

The shallows are tepid, so together we walk until the water touches our chins. Gradually, like lizards, we are cooled, but by the time we are halfway back to the house, sweat is already mingling with lake water dripping from our chins. We sit on lawn chairs hoping for a breeze. Not even mosquitoes come. Back to the bedroom to sleep fitfully until the sun comes to keep the world cooking.

But rarely does July renege on all the promises spring has made. And in the course of a

In fruitful
succession
now,
berries,
apples and
pumpkins
take their
turns.

normal summer, July marks the time when blooms are blown and spring's splendor has become summer's promise for the autumnal harvest. In fruitful succession now, berries, apples and pumpkins take their turns until, months later, the hickory nuts, like white stones, are the last to hide in the frozen brown grass of October.

Children, brown bags over their heads to ward off the mosquitoes, which rise in clouds from briars and bracken, look through eye-holes to fill discarded coffee cans, hung from their necks with strings, with raspberries, blackberries, gooseberries, mulberries and chokecherries. They sample as they harvest. Lips and blouses, fingers and shirts are inked in purple by the time they trot their treasures through the back door.

Now for every white flower fallen from the steeple of blooms on the horse chestnut, a green nutlet is swelling. Break the spiked sheath to see the white nut inside, smooth as frog's skin, still silky, but ready to ripen to a glowing bronze, toy for a boy, amulet for the pocket of an old man with rheumatism.

Maple seeds are growing wings so they may helicopter on fall winds to pioneer new colonies. Ironwood drops its green whorls. Acorns fatten beneath round, curly hats. Spruce and pine cones swell until boughs bend with their burden. And tiny red squirrels, few bird nests left to rob, shop from tree to tree, like berserk brides in a supermarket on a first payday. There are brash, flamboyant colors, such as the cardinal flower, tall and scarlet as the bird it is named for. Oliver Wendell Holmes was moved to write:

> *As if some wounded eagle's breast*
> *Slow throbbing o'er the plain,*
> *Had left its air path impressed*
> *In drops of scarlet rain.*

And sometimes, illegal on a hillside, an oriental bloom, the poppy, which brings dreams, emblem of July, summer's lethargy. Cattails too, simmering and browning, like hot dogs in the heat. Armed barley beards, milky

The hot days have been beaten back. The roots of life are watered.

kernels hardening. Elderberry blooms, greening into platters, which will purple for the robins when the hot days have dried up the worm supply. Corn, golden as the dripping butter that garnishes it. Tawny melons to the kitchen counter. Banded green watermelons, so icy hard the rind snaps sharply under the knife. Washed cherries glowing on brown towel. Lettuce, third cutting, green curls in a white bowl of ice water.

Buck deer, carefully carrying velvet antlers, wearing his sleek suit of summer red, tight-fitting over fat from fine feeding. Coyote pups, falling over one another, quarreling about a mouse no one really wants because all bellies are bulging. Ambitious dragonfly, taking after a hummingbird, changing its mind lest the bird turn hunter instead of hunted.

Swallows fly high, and an old graybeard points and shakes his head. "One more day of sweat," he says. "Wait and see how the sun lights fire before it sets." The owl never bothers to hunt except at dusk and dawn, such is the clutter of cottontails. Hawk, wings akimbo and beak agape, forsakes its watchtower atop a high dead pine for a shadowy glen where it can come to a watery place and splash until it is soaked, and must settle for a grassy hummock until its feathers dry.

Fish forsake the shallows for cooler depths. It takes an unusually fat cricket or chunky chub to tempt them, and fishermen fry hamburger. Ponds dry up, and a teal, kids still in pinfeathers, begins the death march. Muskrats follow, leaving kits for the turtles. But the turtles, having buried themselves in mud, never see the crayfish crawl over the tiny carcasses, eating until there is nothing but skin, thin parchment over toothpick bones. Quickly from the banquet, the crayfish disappear down clay chimneys to subterranean homes still filled with water.

In the scheme of things, the teal kids and the muskrat kits are less than as many water drops in a deluge, because the world is looking to a harvest that must be measured by the shipload — corn, wheat, barley, oats, food for billions. So it is a thing of minuscule consequence that a spring stops flowing, and low water forces the beavers overland, and their unattended dam breaks, so ravens come to eat the speckled trout, beached to die on mud flats. Not even the ravens seem especially elated, because these days their crops are always bulging.

July. Crucial. Fortunes made. Fortunes lost. Bronze men with furrowed brows snap a wheat stalk and try the kernels with their teeth, and when they shake their heads, men in white shirts and ties sweat, even in air-conditioned offices, as the bottom drops out of the stock market. That's the way it is sometimes in July. Then the turning leaves show red veins, and man, animals, plants, insects, even birds look to the west, hoping to see storm clouds building castles.

Then the day. We smell the rain and sit on the parched lawn watching, as always, the west. Once again, there are thunderclouds out over the lake at sunset. Again there are lightning flashes and a far-off roll of thunder. But this night we do not go back to the intolerable heat of the bedroom. We have smelled the rain, and we wait in silence. We hear it before we feel its distinct splat, which sends a leaf twisting to earth. Another drop, and then another, evaporating instantly on the hot earth. A lightning flash brightens the treetops. A crash of close thunder. A slight breeze. Then the deluge.

We sit soaking it up. The downpour slows, slacks off to a steady rain. We get up and go to the bedroom. The curtains billow. We lie down. There will be a miracle of rejuvenation. The dry brown grass will green. Frogs will rejoice. Crayfish will build new chimneys. Insects will revive to beat a triumphant tattoo on screens. All nature will lift. The hot days have been beaten back. The roots of life are watered. Still wet, we lie close. The earth is refreshed; we are refreshed, and ready now for the hot hand of August.

Spruce and pine cones swell until boughs bend with their burden.

⋙ *One Morning* ⋘

One morning last summer: Out the back door by 6 a.m.. Hazy, humid, already hot. Short walk to the garage where my electric tractor, the Gray Ghost, spent the night with its umbilical cord plugged into an electrical outlet. A gauge shows that, just as sleep has renewed my energy, a mysterious force has recharged the vehicle's batteries, and it is ready to roam.

We skirt the sunburnt lawn, buzz through a plantation of young spruce, wheel across another clearing, and then coast down a slope into a green tunnel. On one side there is a solid wall of cedars and on the other an almost impenetrable tangle of sumac, honeysuckle, dogwood and briars, shaded by a second story of sugar maple, poplar, basswood, an incredible assortment of deciduous trees and bushes. Though, by this time, the sun has dissolved the haze, its rays cannot penetrate this place we call the Bush Pantry. Here, I experience the illusion of being in a cool, green cocoon, and so I rest with my arms braced against the Gray Ghost's steering wheel.

Usually, birds sing here. But not this morning, and at first I neither see nor hear any signs of life. Then gradually, two tufts of grass become a cottontail's ears. A knot on a limb becomes a robin, beak agape as though gasping for air. A blob beside the trail becomes a woodcock, and in the instant that I recognize it the bird lifts and zigzags without brushing leaf or twig through the dense cover.

Now there is a tiny ticking. I recognize it as the sound of bluegills snapping insects off the undersides of lily pads in Fish Pond, which is just beyond the orderly ranks of soldier-straight cedars. Otherwise it seems silent, though I know if I had the gifted ears of some prehistoric cousin, I might hear grasshoppers chewing, beetles lumbering, worms crawling.

I straighten in the seat, and with a low whine the Gray Ghost follows tire tracks it has molded into familiar ruts. Though I see no living thing, I know many eyes are on me. Mostly, these are the eyes of old acquaintances, feathered and furred, but when I break out of the tunnel's shadows into the sunlight, there is a furious flurry and flapping of wings. Startled, I lean back, and the Gray Ghost veers off the trail.

Now, these are visitors! Birds with a wingspread of nearly three feet. Brown birds squawking their alarm. Each lets go a load of whitewash and then, collecting themselves, all eight come back together in a ragged formation, and fly clumsily toward the Fox River. Night-herons. The evidence on the ground below tells me they roosted in the spreading oak at the end of the tunnel.

Turning, I pass the Indian mounds and come up onto the dike. Fish Pond spreads in front of me, glassy and unblinking. I head for shade. Now Queen Anne's lace is a white border to my left, and the other side of the trail is guarded by golden, head-high canary grass. There are no mosquitoes, but deer flies attack, and one draws blood from a forearm.

By the time I have traversed the dike and am resting in the shade of a weeping willow alongside Blue Pool, the fly bite has swollen to a sizeable welt. I suck it, leaving plenty of saliva behind. Then, from a carrying box back of the tractor seat, I take a shaker and sprinkle salt on the bite. I rub it in vigorously, knowing that within a few minutes the swelling and itching will subside.

The sky looks white-hot now, so I hurry on to New Pool, where bluegill-green sunfish hybrids churn the surface to collect the pellets I have thrown for them. I do not wait to watch, and the trail takes me out to the entry road. Instead of turning toward the house, I head to where the trail crosses Watercress Creek. A black-and-white duck, escapee from someone's flock, brings her two kids out onto the road to beg for corn. They will get it, but not here. Turning around, I backtrack, and they follow, quacking and peeping. Turning off the road, I head down a trail to where waters of Clear Pool cascade over a dam. I throw corn into the water below the dam, and the ducklings, in their haste, tumble down the bank.

Once there were six ducklings. My neighbor saw a snapping turtle pull one down, and we assume it got the other three. But out here, ducklings have other predators to make living hazardous. Just yesterday, while I sat in this same place watching fish broach the current below the dam, a long, svelte and slinky black mink came up out of the creek to smell the Gray Ghost's bumper before sliding silently off into the underbrush. Ducklings are favorites on a mink's menu.

Now the wild ones, mallards about ready to try their wings for the first time, begin sliding silently out from the solid stand of high, green bullrushes. I am not sure, of course, but I estimate somewhere close to one hundred mallards grew up in the two-acre spread of rushes. Having about four pecks of corn left in the tractor box, I throw it into the water for the wild ones. Now the heat bugs — cicadas — sound their sizzling warnings: It is going to get hotter. So, we head for home, the Gray Ghost and I.

⇶ *Why I Miss Winter* ⇷

It was a savage season, and now the bones of winter are white, and only the mice know about them as they tunnel among the roots of summer-sweet grasses. It was a treacherous time of dangerous days, though the trees now hide their wind and ice scars behind green leaves, and creeping moss softens the jagged cracks along concrete foundations. It was a season of violence, but already most lake and river piers tilted askew have been righted.

It was a cruel winter, scattering autos and people as it bludgeoned its way across America. Some say it was the worst winter in a hundred years, but my neighbor's dog will not remember it. Thirsty from bucking drifts, he tested the ice toward the open water of the aerator hole in Fish Pond, and plunged through, bellowing a protest at such an unseemly, watery death.

Roofs, chimneys and roads wear patches not yet weather-worn. More than the usual number of old autos, their radiators and engine blocks cracked, wait behind link fences for their turn in the crusher. Many young evergreens bent to the ground under the weight of the snow have almost, but not quite, recovered. Along roadways, animals and birds driven up from white wastelands died beneath autos, and a gray fox looking for anything to chew on was shot by a man who poked a rifle through his car window.

Of the many ducks floating on the open water of Watercress Creek, those who never learned to come to the corn died and were encased in ice by morning. And, in many human cemeteries, there are more than the usual number of new tombstones marking the graves of old men and women who might have come to this summer if the winter had been more temperate.

April finally came, and some of us breathed with relief. Then the backlash! Time and again, winter returned to rip the flowery dress of spring. They said the robins got drunk on berries that had dried to ferment on the vines, but they were wrong. The robins died by the thousands because they were not programmed to come to feeders, and what little was scattered on the ground for them went mostly into squirrel stomachs. We picked up Wilson snipe. We picked up tree swallows. Robins, because there were so many, were just pushed beneath last year's leaves. It was a cunning winter, and sometimes I felt sure it had designs on my life. It put my tractor off the trail, and there it stayed, stuck for a week. A storm swallowed my truck in one of its drifts. It had me down, crawling to get home.

So, now that the sun is hot and the nights soft and serene, why do I miss winter? Is it because of such pleasant surprises as the gangs of redpolls that visited to escape more vicious weather to the north? Is it because of the goldfinches, their buttery yellow faded to crispy brown, ganged at the tube feeders for thistle seeds? Is it because the cardinals came in scarlet bunches to wait for a turn at the sunflower seeds? Or is it because of the comic relief offered by the starlings quarrelling for seats on chimneys breathing heat?

I do not think so. I think what I miss is the drama, the excitement. I miss the mystery of going to bed never knowing what wild things will happen while I sleep. I miss waking in the night to listen to the naked tree limbs clashing like swords. I miss the many wild battle songs played by the wind. I miss the unknown, the world beyond the yard light's white circle, where birds, animals and my favorites, the trees, struggle for survival.

It is as if I have a center aisle, front-row seat at Armageddon. It is like being on the edge of the arena during a Roman holiday. It is like never knowing at what moment I might be swept on stage by a gusty wind to play the most fascinating of all roles: leading man in the battle for life. Maybe that is why I miss winter on these lazy summer days.

⇶ *City Cousin* ⇇

Among the most persistent fables is one about how the country boy romping through Elysian fields is thrice blessed, as compared to his city cousin. Throughout history, advocates of rural living have been quick to extol the virtues of rail splitting, but forget the nice timing a boy learns in making bus connections.

So, this July, while our city cousin visits, and while his country cousin makes life miserable for him, I will put my money on the boy who dodges trucks instead of bumblebees, because he has his life on the line. There is no sweat for him when death comes close again and again, though I am sure it would drive his country cousin up a wall. The city cousin builds his own world, and it is in his mind, and you cannot come in unless you are specifically necessary to the ball game in progress. He flows with the crush of people as easily and smoothly as a wood chip on a riotous river current.

The city cousin might get lost in a two-acre wood lot, yet find his way from one end of a teeming city to the other with speed and precision. If he cannot identify a tree, he can catalog people. So, though he might not know how a snake sheds that dusty old skin to come shining around in a sleek new suit, he's got the guy down the block pegged as a chameleon, because clothes and a car do not fool him.

Country living may be the idyllic existence, but when the country moth comes from the cocoon, it sometimes does not learn that the bright lights are hot until it is too late. As a clam lacquers a protecting film around the grains of sand that irritate it, the city teaches the boy to close his mind to any sights, sounds and smells that are of no concern to him. He becomes impervious to the roar of traffic, never notices the tannery smell, and walks unafraid among the multitudes. From infancy, he builds walls against the invasion of his privacy by anything undesirable. And if he is not callous, he is as smoothly hard as the shining pearl the clam creates in neutralizing the grain of sand. Like the pearl, he wears well and commands a higher price than his country cousin at almost any marketplace.

Miraculous Trees

There are many magical things in this world, but none more magical than the trees that shade our city streets and country lanes. Not necessarily because any is more lovely than a poem, but because without them the world might have remained barren and lifeless. When trees finally evolved into their present form from soft, primeval plants, the continents became sheltered places for living things. The gales that swept the globe were quieted. Moisture that fell was trapped, so rivers were tamed and food assured. The trees also gave oxygen to the atmosphere.

I thought on these things, especially this winter past, as I fed oak, ash, hickory, mulberry, box elder, hard and soft maple, basswood, elm, aspen, white and red cedar, white and red pine, white and black spruce, to the fires of our insatiable fireplaces. The woods were all mixed up, and at any one time I might have had three or four different kinds burning in the fireplace. Then, if the cedar crackled and spit sparks, and the basswood smoke was uncommonly heavy, my chunk of ash, oak or hickory — any of the hardwoods — burned with a steady, quiet, almost fierce heat.

And it was like burning history. Of all organisms, none lives longer than a tree, and within its bark lies a complete record of the warm and beneficent summers, the icy winters, the assaults from wind, lightning and tiny bug. Just imagine, I told my children, there still lives a tree that was already nearly three thousand years old when Christ was born. And indeed, on western mountain slopes, there are bristlecone pines that are older than any other living thing. They watched humans struggle up out of the dank caves, and they watched us fly to the distant moon.

So my children talked about trees, and they wondered if trees could feel "and do they bleed when the sap runs from a cut?" And they wanted to believe that a tree groans, literally, when the wind bends it. But in the end, they found true stories about trees as fascinating as fantasy. I told them, for instance, that the great burr oak, which we could see from a window, lived on a tender, thin network of cells. I pointed out that only a very small part of the great oak was alive — its root tips, the inch coating of cambium just under the bark, and its leaves. All else, I said, except for a sparse and almost haphazard scattering of cells in bark and root and twig, was dead, turned to wood.

But wood! What a miracle is wood itself. Strong. A natural insulator. Durable. Hardwood floors wear well for a century under constant stress. Timbers nearly three thousand years old have been unearthed. Houses of wood nearly four hundred years old still stand. Elastic. Wood bends, and so frame houses weather hurricanes and earthquake shock. And dead wood buried by time is not lost, but is eventually converted to coal.

Then my children said that if all those things were true, it was a shame to burn wood in the fireplace. But I told them it was not, because wood is a renewable resource. Then I added that an acre of growing trees removes, in twelve hours, as much pollution as is spewed into the air by eight cars. Then I saw a new respect in their eyes for magical, miraculous trees. So we got into other interesting aspects of tree life. Some trees, I told them, have both male and female cones or blossoms, but others are strictly male trees or female trees. The seed, I added, is a miniature tree, all ready to go with a tiny root, soft white thread of a trunk, and a leaf or two. Some seeds, like the hard maple's, burst quickly alive with the first freshening rain, but jackpine needs a searing-hot forest fire to break the life free from its iron-hard seed shell.

By then, it didn't matter to my children anymore that trees could not feel, could not sorrow or rejoice, because they understood the important role trees have played on earth, even creating soil by sundering rocks with their roots, and then adding their crumbly dead trunks to the rich humus for other living things. By then, my children knew that it was the tree that helped man out of the caves, because he learned how to make shelters first from brush and finally wood. And then, when the fire in the fireplace burned low, and the cedar had stopped snapping sparks up the chimney, they went to the window and looked out at the burr oak, which was by then but a silhouette in the evening gloom. And they knew how trees had helped make life on earth possible. And knowing this, perhaps, when their time comes, they will have enough respect for trees to use them wisely and well.

⋙ *Opportunity* ⋘

Swallows come from all points as the lawn tractor comes roaring out to cut grass. They know the whirling blades will send insects aloft, out of hiding. It happens especially in July, when the hatch begins to taper off and the birds must fly overtime to fill their own crops and those of youngsters not yet airborne. Grass cut, the swallows leave. But in the wings waiting, grackles, robins, blue jays, blackbirds, even cardinals drop down, as if on some silent signal, to clean up insects killed or wounded.

I marvel at the adaptability of the wild ones, at their talent in using humans. Many is the time, looking up from the snarling chain saw, I have been amused to find myself surrounded by deer waiting in the snow, to get at the browse. Seagulls are especially perceptive, and come in white clouds to the grubs and worms turned by a farmer's plow, to the fishing boat spilling out entrails as the catch is cleaned, and to put a screaming umbrella over garbage barges on their way out to ocean dumping grounds.

Terns, by what means I will never know, learn to hover near fishermen using minnows, so they may get the discarded dead ones, but ignore the boat in which anglers are using artificial lures. Turtles come to fishing bobbers because they know about the bait below and how to steal it. Even on the edge of the Arctic, where people are seldom seen, eagles and ravens appear as if by magic along any rocky shore when the fish filets begin to fry for the noon luncheon.

Cardinals have a regular route that takes them to bird feeders specializing in sunflower seeds, bypassing perhaps dozens offering less succulent fare. The raccoon, on his garbage can route, soon knows which houses have built-in garbage disposal systems. The cowbirds know, before you do, that your neighbor has put all his fields to cash crops and the cows are gone. Even an ant knows about the housewife who leaves the covers off her jam jar and sugar bowls.

≫ *Reeling in the Memories* ≪

To take a kid fishing, it is necessary to go back to that time when the rivers in passing whispered about all the secret things below, when the lakes mirrored the skies with such innocence as masks the mysterious depths of love in a woman's eyes. To take a kid fishing is to believe once more that below the water's surface, in rocky caves and weedy jungles, are creatures as alien as those that walk or fly or crawl on black nights beyond the bedroom windows.

There must be that very beginning when it is indeed a scary thing to lower three-year-old fingers down to where crayfish with crushing, sharp pincers crawl, or down where turtles lurk, turtles whose heads must be severed before they will open their jaws to release their victims, or down where there may be water snakes which, though cut in many pieces, will not die until the tail stops twitching at sunset.

To take a kid fishing, you must remember your first sunfish, as big around perhaps as a dollar, reflecting sunlight like a prism: bright reds and blues and silvers as it dangled at the end of your line, prize of prizes saved for a swim in the kitchen sink to be visited again and again during the night.

To take a kid fishing, you must remember the sleepless nights of waiting, the stinging cold of dawn, the welcome warmth of the rising sun, the fish that, with a thrust of power, shattered the water's calm, broke your line and left you trembling. You must remember the smell of a wood fire, smoke hanging in the low branches of the trees, the sizzling sound of fish frying, the smell of coffee. You must remember that nowhere in the world was there a better place than this rocky shore, that never would any day be as perfect, that truly, heaven could wait.

To take a kid fishing, you must remember the sunset, a time to rest the oars, the holy time when there is gold in the sky and the shore maples seem to be on fire. You must remember that interlude, the moment in between, when daytime creatures are going to their night camps, and the owl and other nighttime creatures wait and watch. You must remember because, even as a child, you may have had a premonition that eternity is wrapped up in this interlude when a day beyond the horizon is beginning as this day ends.

Then, most important, when you take a kid fishing, is to remember that even after all these years, you never can be absolutely sure what will come up on any line you lower. That, no matter your experience, there is no predicting which cast will bring up a boot or a world-record musky. So take a kid fishing. Then, as it is with you, there always will be that part of him that will never grow old.

⇛ *Fire Scar* ⇚

It was one of those breathless hot July days. A Wisconsin warden and I were walking through a forest to set live traps for beavers, whose dams had been backing water into some backwoods farmer's turnip fields. It was an exercise in futility, because, of course, the beavers would be back. The forest was a desolation of scrub oak, stunted jackpine and, in the low places, brush willow and alder thickets. Except for the occasional raven, some chickadees and downy and hairy woodpeckers, it was devoid of life.

"What a waste," the warden said. I agreed, and when we sat on a log to rest, the warden said: "I'm tempted to throw a match into that brush and set the whole damned place afire. Then you'd see things come to life!"

Immediately I remembered what my wife and I had come to call the Bunny Belt, a twenty-mile-wide swath of low, green hard and softwood saplings running like a bright ribbon through a higher forest of stunted jackpine and spruce. It was a ten-year-old fire scar, and every morning and evening for a week, we crossed it on our way to fish a stream especially blessed with trophy rainbow trout. We enjoyed traversing the grassy road through the Bunny Belt even more than we did catching the vigorous trout. Nowhere, except perhaps in the Florida Everglades or some Central American jungles, had we seen such a profusion of life.

There were hundreds upon hundreds of snowshoe hares wearing their summer suntans. Preying on the hares were great horned owls, so unafraid that if one had a carcass in the road, we had to get out and drive it from the kill before we could travel on. There were more moose and deer gorging on the budding browse than I had ever seen in a single area. There were foxes and bobcats, and coyotes, fat as lap dogs, running leisurely ahead of the car, dodging at the last second to escape being run over. There were ravens, eagles and hawks, and thousands of jays and low-nesting songbirds. It was a veritable Eden, bordered on either side by a desolation of trees.

I told the warden about it as we sat there resting on the log. Then, a month later, I read in the papers about a forest fire in the area. I wondered if the warden dropped the match.

≫⟫ *Ghost* ⟪≪

A ghost walks with me these mornings. I feel it nudge my knee as the
chill of night leaves the marsh. I hear it whine softly as the sun rises and
a breeze vibrates through the reeds. I know it is there, this friendly ghost,
because when I walk in the swamp, the cattails, fat and bursting, scatter
golden dust as something moves among them.

Sometimes the ghost is beside me. Sometimes it is at heel. But sometimes it runs out ahead, and then cottontails squirt left and right off the
trail long before I am close enough for them to see or scent me. It is there,
too, when I stretch out in the brown grass on the side of a wintry hill,
because I feel its soft muzzle resting and warming the back of my hand.
Unless, perhaps, I am being deluded and it is only the touch of an errant
ray from a waning sun coming through the branches of a leafless tree.
Even in the night I sometimes am awakened by the same ghost, warning
me that an intruder — coon? skunk? human? — is trespassing. But when
I sit up in bed, the better to hear, there is nothing.

But I do not believe in ghosts. I do not, for example, believe that it is
the ghost of my mother, but only a troubled conscience, that whispers in
my ear: "You know you shouldn't do that."

I do not believe it is the ghost of my father, but only a voice in a
predawn dream that awakens me, always with the same whisper: "It's daylight in the swamp and the fish are jumping."

And I do not believe it is the voice of a dead brother warning: "You
do and I'll tell Ma." I know the words are but remnants of regret, because
a sibling rivalry made us enemies as often as it made us friends.

Ghosts, I have always told myself, are the ephemeral product of
wishful thinking. Most, I keep reminding myself, are childish inventions
of things that never were, or an old-timer's dreams of things irretrievably
lost. But then there is a spurt of dust on the trail ahead, and a squirrel
goes up a tree like a scalded cat. I move forward and search the ground
for the ghost's paw prints. Of course, there are none. So there was no
ghost chasing that squirrel, and I remind myself that squirrels can be
paranoid, too. But then, perhaps, ghosts leave no tracks.

A lifetime ago, during the early weeks of war combat, some beat-up
veterans I flew with spoke of voices in empty rooms. Flak happy, I told
myself. So, when I began hearing the voices, I visited the flight surgeon.
He called it a normal response. Said it was good because during stressful
times, men need voices, since they are afraid of dying alone. I bought
that. I still do.

Because if it really is the ghost of Old Dog walking the trails with me each morning, then where are the ghosts of the others: Rainey, Brig, Bucko, Ace, Captain, Sergeant? It began to bother me to be accompanied by a ghost on my morning walk. So, for exercise, instead of walking, I rode my bike, the stationary one in front of the television set. Four mornings I stayed in, and then on the fifth, while I was sitting in the quiet house writing at the kitchen table, there came a scratching at the kitchen door.

I knew it would happen. I had been waiting for it. But, of course, when I went to the back door, there was nothing there. I had not expected there would be. On the sixth morning, I sat at the kitchen table again and waited. Nothing. So I picked up my pencil, and after warming up by writing a few throwaway pages, I got into what I call "high writing gear."

At once there came a scratching, a scratching at my kitchen door. Perhaps, I thought, I really should talk to a doctor. No, he would probably tell me the same thing the flight surgeon told me a lifetime ago. So I dressed and went walking. And Old Dog was there. Unless, of course, it was only the wind parting the tall, dead grass out ahead of me. Because I don't believe in ghosts.

⇛ *Fables and Flowers* ⇚

During July, midway through the flowering seasons, may be a good time to reflect on how the world of wild plants has played such an important part in so many societies. Yesteryear, quarreling couples did not seek out a marriage counselor, but gathered wood betony and, wearing it as a love balm, lived happily ever after. Menominee Indian men believed sneaking flowers of the Indian paintbrush among a fair maid's clothing would make her enamored of him.

Beads of the rosary were once made from the hard seeds of the common hoary puccoon, and the common stinging nettle, thrown into the fireplace, was insurance against a lightning strike during a storm. Roadside yarrow was a base for tea, to dispel melancholia in the inhabitants of the Orkney islands. It was also used as a beer ingredient in Sweden, as a vinegar ingredient in Switzerland, and as part of an ointment that healed wounded soldiers at the siege of Troy.

Blackberries were recommended to make loose teeth fast again, catnip was used as a soothing syrup for babies, and Solomon's seal, taken internally with ale or wine, was supposed to knit broken bones. Broth from the cleavers, whose stiff bristles have vexed many an American barefoot boy, was supposed to make a fat person thin, and black medic, more commonly known as shamrock or clover, in addition to being regarded as a fine tooth cleanser, was worn as certain protection against witches.

The common white water lily was thought to have grown from a fallen star, and the chicory, found along every roadside, is an Austrian maiden who vowed never to cease grieving for a lover lost in the war until she was turned into a flower. These, and hundreds of others, are the tales which tell how once the world of flowers played an important role in all except today's modern society. So drive slowly some hot July, where the chicory is thick as patches of blue sky, and perhaps you will hear the lovelorn maiden sigh, even though she sounds a little like the wind.

⋙   *The Nature Snob*   ⋘

A visiting lawyer sat with me in a small clearing from which, with the swing of the head, we could see twenty-three tree species. He correctly identified a white birch, a white cedar and a sugar maple. Then, after calling a Douglas fir a spruce and an ash an elm, he gave up. A nationally prominent Minnesota physician, touring Fish Pond with me, wanted to know if the swallow nesting houses staked out over the water were for wood ducks. I had to bite my tongue to keep from saying: "Many a wood duck is bigger than those houses!"

A neighbor who can identify any plane from World War I Jennys to today's supersonic speedsters, and at altitudes beyond my vision, looks bewildered when I mention such common water plants as spatterdock, wapatoo, coontail and knotweed, although he sees them almost every day. A fine editor who formerly handled some of my copy, on looking out the front window of my home, pointed at a nuthatch and asked: "What kind of woodpecker is that?"

Then there was the friend of one of my daughters, who came screaming across the lawn fearful of an attack by a harmless, ten-inch, green garter snake. There was the boy who threw his fishing pole into the pond and retreated when a saucer-sized snapping turtle took his bait. There was the grandmother who had to have her barbecued ribs served in the sunroom, while we picnicked on the lawn, because a spider sat down beside her. And the young daughter of a friend refused to swim in Blue Pool because the water did not smell right (no chlorine) and the bottom was "icky" (no concrete).

"Can you believe it?" I asked Gwen, who had been listening patiently as I related in considerable detail, and with appropriate gestures, all these stories. "Why, we even had renters once ..." Then I told her how the renters had called the police because a bat had come down the chimney and was flying around the house. And I recalled how a young wife, needing some greens to complement a bouquet of flowers, picked poison ivy without raising a rash, only to have her new husband swell up like a poisoned pup.

"It's incredible," I went on. "A lawyer! Imagine a man with eighteen or twenty years of schooling not recognizing the common trees of Wisconsin. Or a doctor!" I threw up my hands. I paused, waited. When she didn't react, I pressed her: "Well?"

She gave me one of her long-suffering looks, and then said quietly: "Oh, I don't know."

"What do you mean, I don't know?"

She shrugged.

"What's with people?" I ran on. "These trees, spiders, plants, birds all around us. Anyone who doesn't know ...!" I threw up my hands again.

After a long pause, she asked quietly: "What's that bathrobe you're wearing made of?"

I frowned. "What's that got to do with it?"

"You've worn it for eight years. What's it made of?"

Somewhat irate, I said: "Cloth. Cotton, I suppose."

"Wrong. It has very little cotton and is mostly polyester."

"So?"

"Now, don't get huffy, but what's the name of that plant by the book-case?"

"How should I know? You've got twenty or forty plants around the house. Anyway, it's an exotic. It's not native."

"Not native? Its kind have been around longer than you have, and you've been looking at that one for six years."

"But that's different."

"Oh? Can you name the fragrance coming from that candle?" She pointed to a candle burning in a cylinder of glass.

"I'm going to bed."

"It isn't time."

"I'm going anyway."

"Well, okay, and don't be angry," she said, soothingly. "But sometimes ... sometimes I think you're just a bit of a snob."

We went to bed and she was soon purring softly. It was a long, long time before I could fall asleep.

≫≫ *A Starving Man Saves no Trees* ≪≪

An energy crisis is not going to mean much to the man who has had his electricity shut off. Nor is water purity of much concern to a mother whose plumbing never works. A child will not think twice about throwing into the gutter the bag in which a hamburger came when that is all he had to eat that day. Nor can you expect a man to become enthused about the million-dollar purchase of a woodland when there is not a tree on his block and his chances of vacationing in the woodland are about as remote as his chances of getting to the moon.

By the same token, how can you blame a farmer for using a pesticide when he has no substitute, and an insect invasion threatens an investment that represents the savings of a lifetime? What profit it a man to save a wetland oasis when periodically the overflow floods out his fields and the potatoes, carrots and onions rot in the ground?

I once heard a man who had just driven down a skid row street filled with blowing newspapers say: "Pigs! Pigs! Pigs!" What he forgot was that those newspapers were the only "blankets" some men had to keep them warm the night before. I got a letter the other day from a woman who lives in a prestigious, immaculate suburb. She complained about the beer cans and wine bottles that littered an access way to a concert hall in the city. "You'd think those people would have enough pride," she wrote, "to at least find a waste receptacle. Drinking in the streets is bad enough, without making the same streets so unsightly." Likely the lady had a garbage compactor. Maybe she even had someone to pick up her sherry bottles as she emptied them. So maybe she did not know that these men had no other place except the street to drink, and whatever precious warmth they got from the wine should not be foolishly dissipated canvassing a windy, cold street in search of a refuse bin.

If all this sounds like I have suddenly reversed directions to dream up excuses for people who have no interest in the good earth, don't believe it. What I am concerned about is the backlash many well-intentioned conservationists evoke among people whose personal problems are so critical that a pure river, a forested mountain, a teeming marshland or clean air are absolutely unimportant. Last night, while watching television, I saw an angry veteran in Chicago shake his fist at the television camera and shout, "We know what we want, and I'm telling you we'll get it, and we don't give a damn how!" What he wanted was what most of us take for granted: a chance to work and to live like a human being.

Of course, anything I would have to say to him about saving the California redwoods or the Everglades or some sand dunes would either bring a blank stare or a howl of derision. We might as well face it: Nobody is going to wage a war to save the polar bear on an empty stomach. He is going to kill that bear himself and cut it up into steaks. So the farmer whose cornfields are being sacked by geese gets out the gun. So the rancher whose lambs are disappearing puts out poisonous "coyote killers." So the hungry inner-city youngster, whose only meal is one hamburger, cannot be convinced he is littering when the hamburger bag whisks away.

And, as with individuals, so it is with nations. How can an emerging country be expected to keep DDT out of its malarial swamps when the mosquito is there waiting to spread death? How can the farmers be prohibited from spreading human body wastes on the land when such fertilizer means the difference between eating and starving? How can an insecticide be prohibited when it is the only way to avert famine? It is easy to be smug about our sacred cows of conservation, to fight for their priority. But if, in our righteousness, we forget that littering is only a word to the hungry boy, if we forget that the man without electricity could not care less about the energy crisis, then we do both the good earth and humanity a disservice.

≫ *Slaves for a Day* ≪

On that day, outside temperatures went over the ninety degree mark at noon. It was a perfect day for staying immersed in one of the spring-fed ponds, or for sitting with a book behind drawn shades while the big basement fan circulated cool basement air, and the hum of its motor, like the hypnotic drone of bees, produced such lethargy as blurs the print and brings sweet dreams.

But no, we were out under the sun, hands slippery with sweat, part of an all-volunteer crew hauling winter's wood to be stacked ceiling-high, row on row, against basement walls. Then, when the snow became deep, it would be handy. But winter was a long way off. So why, on what seemed like the hottest and most humid day of the year, did we wrestle maple and oak in sundry chunks, some heavier than a small boy, into and

out of a truck and through the narrow basement doorway to be piled as
high as there was muscle enough to heave them?

Expediency: Part of the tradition that prompts our five daughters, and
their husbands or boyfriends, to give as birthday or holiday presents a
pledge to be our slaves for a day, instead of ordinary and rather unimag-
inative gifts. And, weather being the unpredictable hussy that she is, and
summer being vacation time when "slave-for-a-day" promises can be
kept, we were hauling wood in the heat.

But it was not all work. These wood chunks, storm victims, were
remains of patriarchs beneath which these girls (women now) grew up.
When the girls were small, they climbed these trees and swung from ropes
tied to their branches. Coming to puberty, they dreamed of womanhood
and princes in the shade of the leaves. They spied on the robins, raccoons, orioles, opossums and squirrels who called the trees home. They
ate of their apples, mulberries and wild and tame cherries, and harvested their hickory and walnuts in the fall.

As they lugged the chunks, they recognized one or another log as being
part of a flicker's cave or a certain squirrel's cache. A wire mark here, bits
of rope imbedded in some other bark, a scar, an axe slash, were reminders
of the days of childhood that sped by on the wings of laughter and tears.
Of course, the lemonade flowed. And when the last chunk had been
hoisted to the highest and last available space, there was an interlude of
cooling, with pond waters soothing sore muscles and dripping delicious-
ly over parched lips and lids.

But now, of course, the winds bank snow around the house and all the
"slaves-for-a-day" gather around the hearth. And they see memories in
the smoke as logs burn, ring on ring, down through the days of their
childhood, back, back to the days when the tree was perhaps a sapling
swing for some Indian infant. Good wood, strengthened by good earth.
Light and airy poplar to kindle obstinate oak. Resin bubbles on pine
bursting into fireworks of sparks. Reluctant, pithy linden requiring a lift
from hickory splints. Cedar snapping. Apple, fragrant as its fruit. Elm,
victim of disease, blue and hot and quiet and almost forever. Cherry,
swift and bright, subsiding to a glowing red core. Maple, reliant and
enduring.

Then, in the ashes, a twisted metal toy, small car or a mechanical
animal, forgotten in a tree crotch and grown solidly into the wood, the
reminder of some tender time, and reminder, too, of that hot July when
they were all "slaves-for-a day."

⇛ *Soul Therapy* ⇚

Once upon a time, the world was mine. As a boy, I could come down off the back steps of our village home, take off in any direction and walk to any horizon, never detouring around "no trespass" signs, getting only a pleasant hello or a friendly wave of the hand from farmers whose fields I crossed.

It was there, beyond the village limits, that problems truly dissolved. Caught up in the bewilderment of being a boy, I could strike out and, in a matter of minutes, shake off the crushing demands of a society with rules for making boys grow up, whatever their age. Those were the times when the good earth really paid off. At creek or pothole, on steep hill or deep swamp, walking prairie or threading forest: ten minutes with a frog, fifteen minutes contemplating a soaring hawk, half an hour watching a muskrat in its watery salad bed, an hour counting a marsh wren's feeding trips to stuff gaping red maws.

It was necessary only to stretch out on the grass. Smell warm earth holding flower fragrance from fleeing on the wind. Catch a butterfly, but only with an eye. Let cool mud soften callused feet. Put a palm in the warm depression of a pheasant's powdery place, its dusting hole. Move out of the shade for a sun sauna and then, slippery with sweat, roll over into an icy creek. No medicine to compare. No therapy so healing. No escape so absolute as during those tender times when the world was truly mine.

August

IN AUGUST, SUMMER, LIKE AN OVERRIPE
BERRY, SHOWS SIGNS OF SHRIVELING ON THE
VINE. It is the month when the Dog Star, Sirius,
brightest of all stars, vainly pursues the sun as if
to absorb yet more brilliance. It is also a lazy, a
bronze, a brazen month. And always, it is later
than you think.

August ages the land, dries the juices from
dead fish and old men, so I drift down off the
browning hill, out of the sun, into the damp and
shady bottomlands. A pair of hummingbirds is
there ahead of me. They are called ruby-throat-
ed, but in the shade the cock's scarlet throat
looks black, except once I catch a glimpse of
crimson as the bird hovers momentarily in a sun
shaft.

I sit on a stump in a sea of billowing greenery
sprinkled with flecks of fiery flowers. Jewelweed:
half an acre beneath a ragged, broken canopy of
spruce, which have found the footing so wet
their roots knee out of the ground as though
they might be trying to keep their feet dry.
While I am fitting myself more comfortably to
the stump, the hummingbirds leave. But before I
can blink my eyes they are back again. Or is it
another pair? No difference. All day, hummingbirds will come and go, and the jewelweed can be
thankful, because of all the winged ones, it is the
only creature capable of ensuring the plant's pollination.

That jewelweed grows where no humming
birds live may be an evolutionary victory of
some sort. Self-fertilizing buds ensure survival,

It is
a lazy,
a bronze,
a brazen
month.
And always,
it is later
than you
think.

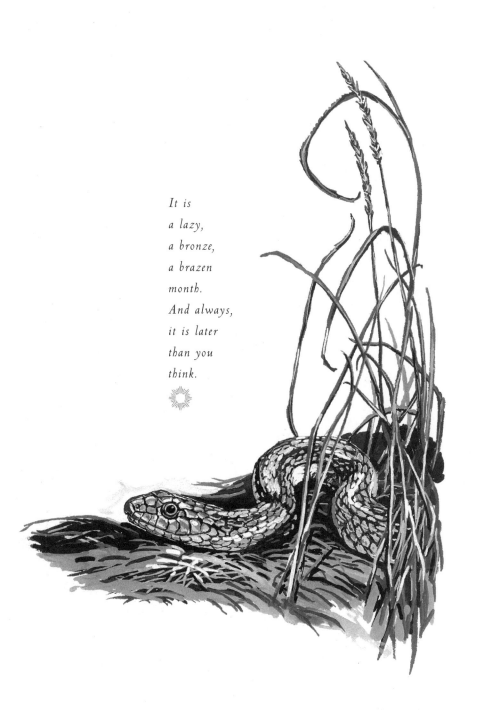

but as the English might tell you, something is missing when there are no birds to sip their nectar. Sometimes, of course, I see no hummingbirds, but that does not mean that they are not there. Fairyland creatures of the bird world, they come and go like bits of sun and shadow, broken and mended by moving leaves.

My August oasis: half-an-acre of such verdant greenery as must be touched to be believed. Half an acre of waist-high plants, all wearing tiny orange-yellow, orchid-like jewels, hanging loosely as gems from a woman's earlobe. Kicking colt and snapweed are two of the many other names for this delicate plant. Children who know come when the seed pods ripen. Touch one or a hundred, they squeal each time a tiny, coiled tendril unfurls like a wiry spring, sending seeds rocketing in every direction.

I have never experimented, but some swear the jewelweed juices prevent infection from poison ivy. The Menominees boiled it to make yellow dye, but let it be only what it is: a cool, glistening gem set into the hot heart of August for my hummingbirds and me.

I can only sit so long before the stump makes too much of an impression. So I take the dim trail back out into the sun and face up to the fact that the martins sitting in a row on the telephone wire are due to go south tomorrow. I know also that some fledgling teal, all feathered now, may follow soon. Whirlwinding redwings make fattening raids on corn and celebrate in fields where combines have missed golden nuggets of grain. They, too, are making ready.

Coming to the barn, I smell summer flowers, dried and pressed now into fragrant bales of hay. In the orchard, some apples are already mellowing on the hot ground. The hawthorn's tortured limbs are red with ripening fruit. The grapes are purpling. If I do not hurry the corn to the house, the milky kernels will have hardened.

So it goes: Herons, done with rookery life, come singly to fish warm back bays pungent with ripening algae. A dead elm is decorated with fawn-feathered

All day, humming-birds will come and go, and the jewelweed can be thankful.

young doves. Tree swallows desert their tree hollows and gravitate to staging areas in larger marshes. There they build forces until, one day in fall, they will lift by the thousands and slant south like colored rain on a north wind.

Of course, summer is not over. Some cottontails are nursing fourth and even fifth litters. Over-sexed wrens and mourning doves, here and there a redbird, and a mallard having lost three clutches, hopefully warm eggs. But mostly, except for such marathon maters as mice, the younger generation is polishing skills that will ensure survival along migratory routes, or on the trails banked by winter's snow.

So I come down the pasture trail and see some signs: Ash, always last to leaf, already ragging. One sumac, embarrassing a whole colony, has turned crimson before its time. Yellow birds, pinned to purple thistles, are finding seeds. Top leaves of a birch have tanned. A maple leaf shows bright veins to forecast its coming crimson glory. Impatient squirrels are whittling husks of walnuts to find the shells beneath still soft. The usually raucous jay is so busy hoarding it permits the cat to nap. The crows, indolent as adult ducks just recovering from the molt, leave the owl in peace. Woodchucks, wallowing in their own fat, prefer the cool depths of their dens, except during the cool of the mornings or evenings. Even the tiny tree frog climbs a fat cattail as if in search of a cooling breeze.

Afternoons belong to the cicadas, their high-frequency song so strident it bores into the brain until, like a perpetual ringing in the ears, it goes unnoticed. Nights there is a haze filtering light from moon and stars. Along a creek, a winding silver ribbon through the tough old meadow grasses of August, the raccoon, eyes bright behind mask, turns a stone and tosses a crayfish ashore for three youngsters. One gets properly pinched by the armored crustacean and leaps squealing, but the dominant male pounces and, crushing life from the crayfish, growls while it peels down to the succulent white flesh.

Some nights, then, if you listen hard, you will hear fox and coyote pups whine their excitement as they follow their first trail, try for their first kill, but are content to eat when a parent makes the kill. In alder patches, buck deer rub ragging velvet from antlered crowns, burnishing them for the November rut. Does kick more often when fawns keep insisting on nursing. An impatient eagle pushes a recalcitrant youngster from the aerie, and after plunging precariously close to earth, the eaglet finally soars.

As in July, there are also arid days. Then the sultry August moon, rising red as though from earth's hot cauldron, must wait to cool to a clear,

Nights there is a haze filtering light from moon and stars.

luminous white in the brittle coldness of space. So August turns sere and brown. Long before Labor Day, sometimes, the valleys have bleached and the hills burned. Waters lie bronze and stagnant, and the floating yellow spatterdock has puckered to a prune. Along the shore, Queen Anne's delicate white lace, ragged for wear, loses its embroidered flowers, and the threads that held them fold forward, a gray-green purse. It is as though the color has bled back into the earth to await the cooling nights, so they may rise again in more somber tones: aster, gentian, joe-pye weed.

But just as in July, on a certain torrid day, the clouds build crag on crag, and when the rain comes, mothers, sensing their opportunity, descend upon stores to fit children's summer-callused feet into school shoes. Then, one night, the owl quavers from its high perch and every living thing listens. They dwell on the owl's prophecy, and old men feel the chill of death as it comes to pimple sweaty arms. August ages the land and sucks dry dead fishes and old men. How could it all have ended before it began?

≫ *Solar Energy* ≪

Solar energy! Wilting sunflower lifting its head for one more look. Morning glory, petals pursed, opening its blue chalice when cloud cover scoots and Old Sol shines. Chipmunk, energy renewed, delays for one more day its retreat to winter's deep darkness. Monarch delays, for one more hour, its flight south. Chilly snake, off on a grasshopper hunt after recharging on a warm rock. Bees, night captives, busy and buzzing as soon as day sops up the dew. Deserted sidewalk, once warmed, becomes a scurry of ants. Old cat soaking life from the sun on a window sill. Old dog, arthritic prisoner, free to check signposts as morning melts his stiffness.

Rain: Sparrows disconsolate beneath eaves. City pigeons, sheltered by each armpit of the statue in the park, fluffed and morose. Blackbirds, bedraggled mourners among the cattails. Wren, two eyes in the doorway hole of its house. Stilted heron, neck folded, head pulled in, eyes blank beneath transparent shields. Redbird, wings drooping, silent beneath dripping pine bough.

The sun! Sparrows chirping, bickering; pigeons billing, bowing, coaxing; blackbirds aloft in a swirl of acrobatic squadron maneuvers; wren's throat throbbing with song; heron stalking, bright eyes searching, stiletto bill on smoothly undulating neck poised for spearing frog or fish. Redbird? Whistling bright, treetop ornament.

Solar Energy! Makes bananas yellow and apples turn rosy. Carrots turn orange, berries redden, plums purple, zucchini fatten, pea pods swell, corn kernels turn buttery. Sun and grass grow rabbits. Rabbits grow hawks. Sun and grass grow milk, bacon and steaks.

Solar Power! Damp, drooping crowd roars with renewed energy as the tarpaulin is rolled back. Ferris wheel, spidery, motionless, grotesque, brightens to a vibrant, scintillating circle after the rains end. And the Midway throbs. The tempo of barkers quickens. Hair dryer? Clothes dryer? House freshener? Sun-warmed breezes through my lady's long hair being fluffed and brushed dry in the backyard. Fragrance for the house through open windows. Freshness in bedsheets billowing on a clothesline.

Lethargic little boy, gloomy behind rain-streaked window, a bursting bundle of energy pausing only to admire the rainbow.

Solar Energy! Dries tears. Warms hands and hearts. Dissolves blues and blahs. Banishes darkness in jungles, even of the mind.

Solar Energy! Eternally streaming with hope between prison bars, in shafts across hospital beds, brightening the worn linoleum of a bare-bulb bedroom, dancing down the dust pillar of a rescue mission cot-crowded loft, scattering broken-bottle diamonds in dirty ghetto alleys. Solar Energy! Everywhere. Even briefly at the North Pole. Sifting through umbrellas of big-city smog.

Solar Energy? Something new? New as an infant's first smile when its eyes finally are able to focus on the sparkling bauble dangling from a string above its crib. Old as the first marine animals and plants transformed during millions of years in Earth's pressure cooker to give us petroleum, gas and coal.

Solar Energy? Life.

⋙ Casting for Sanity ⋘

With apologies to Izaak Walton, I would like to prescribe fishing as one of the best ways of getting close to the good earth. I know some people consider fishing a waste of time. Perhaps they remember the town ne'er-do-well who spent most of his life sleeping on a river bank, cane pole thrust out over the water as an excuse for being there. Well, they may quit worrying. Many of this country's greatest men were enthusiastic anglers.

President Eisenhower enjoyed fishing as much as or more than golf. It was only handier to go golfing. Coolidge and Hoover enjoyed fishing so much that they never failed to take one fishing vacation a year, and usually more. George Washington fished the Delaware and caught smallmouth bass. Commodore Perry trolled Lake Erie and took walleyes. General Lee speared suckers in Bull Run. Abe Lincoln angled in Illinois and once caught a twelve-pound catfish. Bill Cody fished the Shoshone, and records from one day report that he caught eight buffalo fish. Names of famous men who have caught fish from Nile perch to Muddy Creek minnows might, if any had the energy to list them, fill many pages.

And, if that is not enough to convince the doubting Thomases that they are in good company while wading, afloat or even reclining on some watery bank, then witness a report made by the New York police department's narcotics bureau some years back, stating that it had never listed among its dope addicts any individual who, as boy or man, liked to hunt or fish. If even that is not enough, run a check of mental hospitals and see how many fishermen you find. Mix with boys being detained in juvenile hall for delinquency and count the young anglers among them. Try a prison for the list of fishermen. Or even make a random survey of any general hospital and count the number of fishermen in for repairs as against those who do not fish.

No one can estimate what the auto has cost the American people, or the radio, television and the motion picture in active participation. Easy living is steadily reducing stamina to the danger point. Well, we can't all play football or basketball or even golf or tennis. But it is a rare man or woman who cannot go fishing, and one of the most inspiring sights I have ever seen was a group of men in the prime of life, but all paraplegics, who came annually with a young doctor to Wisconsin's Lost Land Lake for a fishing vacation.

During World War II, while flying with a heavy bombardment crew out of a base near Polebrook, England, I saw many men crack under the strain of combat. Near the end of my tour of duty, I noticed that most of those still alive were hollow-eyed and nervous, going to bed with sleeping pills and getting up by taking a stimulant. Except there was one, and he never failed to amaze me, because the strain of combat seemed to run off him like rainwater, and if he was suffering any physical or mental anguish, I could not detect it. It was not until he had but two or three missions left to fly that I discovered he was an inveterate fisherman. Not having any tackle at hand, he was grinding his own flashing spoons out of forks, spoons and knives taken from the squadron mess. He made his own rods out of plane radio antennas, fashioned flies from hair stolen from cats and dogs on the base, and unraveled parachute lines to get a fishline. Then, every time the weather put us down, and in foggy England that occurred quite frequently, he went to the several small rivers in the area. He would spend the day catching pickerel, then give them to the villagers for the privilege of enjoying dinner with them.

Maybe fishing is more than just a chance to be close to and absorb the wonderful healing qualities of nature. Maybe it is a frame of mind. No fisherman can be a pessimist. He has to believe that all good things are going to happen while he is fishing. He has to believe that, or why bring along a creel or a stringer? A fisherman must, of course, be a philosopher, because no matter how hard he concentrates on fishing, he will spend much of his time mentally exploring the wisdom of the natural world that surrounds him. In fact, our schools might meet with more favor, and turn out people who have learned to think for themselves, if students had to spend one hour a day fishing.

During more than forty years of writing about hunters and fishermen, I thought once to make a little survey to see what professional group was foremost among my fishing friends. Would you believe doctors? I once fished regularly with a doctor, and then when my work began to take me farther afield, I lost track of him. So, on one of our rare encounters I asked, "Doc, you still fish?"

"Couldn't live without it."

"You mean literally?"

"I mean literally. Without fishing, I couldn't keep both my practice and my life."

⇶ *Drive-ins* ⇷

A New York Times Service story credited Richard Hollingshead Jr. of Camden, N.J., with opening the world's first drive-in movie theater in 1933. I beg to differ. Ten years earlier, as a sprout of eleven, I was attending weekly movies at a drive-in theater in the all-but-deserted village of Dakota, which overlooks the Mecan River, one of a splendid network of small trout streams that meander through Wisconsin's Waushara County.

Admission was free, but after the movie you were expected to leave your car or horse and buggy, and plunk down fifty cents to get into the dance hall for a night of foot-stomping revelry, sparked by a three-man jazz band and fueled by white lightning from stone jugs, dandelion and elderberry-blossom wine from Mason jars, home brew from catsup bottles and homemade lemonade and root beer in cut-glass pitchers standing on card tables near a door.

There were professional people — doctors, lawyers, businessmen — from the somewhat affluent cottage colony on nearby Crystal Lake. There were carpenters, plumbers, janitors and factory workers from camps and cabins along the shores of one or another of the trout streams and lakes. But mostly there were hard-handed, sun-crisped farmers and their families — men, women and children who squeezed the sand country for all it had to eke out their living.

At the drive-in movie and the dance that followed, they were all just people letting off a little steam and dropping their guard. They were just human beings aided and abetted by music and the fermented fruits of the Earth to forget about the cucumber crop that had failed, business ventures that were going down the drain, a son or daughter seeming hell-bent — trials and tribulations that, in varying degrees, can plague us all.

The drive-in theater was the brainchild of a man who ran the country store, which, in addition to groceries, furnished refills for jugs, jars and bottles, and was also stocked with almost anything to be found in a Sears Roebuck catalog. To clarify further the time in which this drive-in flourished, it would be another four years before Al Jolson would sing "Climb upon my knee, Sonny Boy ..." in the first talking picture "The Jazz Singer," in 1927. And it was eight years after silent-movie audiences gasped in amazement at the first "extravaganza" movie, "Birth of a Nation," in 1915.

The store proprietor painted the side of the tiny pavilion a shining white. The film projector stood on top of a dray wagon so that its beam might clear the crowd, but there was no music unless you counted the sound of the rippling river, the chorus of meadow frogs and crickets, the whisper of poplar leaves, an owl's inquiry or a whip-poor-will's complaint.

That drive-in, of course, was different from the drive-ins of today. For one thing, the cars were parked too closely, so there were no groping couples. Though, if you were watching closely (and some people came to do just that), you would see a couple here and a couple there slip away down the slope to disappear among the tag alders along the riverbank. There was, of course, no wide screen or any color, but the black-and-white picture was clear enough so that it took only a little imagination to see the froth on the flaring nostrils of the galloping horse as the hero, high in the saddle, galloped to "cut them off at the pass."

Then, though the picture sometimes fluttered, a young swain or a still-romantic old buck might swear he could see passion glowing like molten lava in the smoldering eyes of the first queen of the movie vamps, Theda Bara. During intermission, it did not seem incongruous to see a man slip away to fish in the little rapids that rippled below the Mecan River bridge. And often as not, before the movie started again, he would be back with a German brown trout resting on ferns in the creel slung across his shoulder.

So take it from me, Mr. Hollingshead, yours was not the first drive-in theater. And take it from me, drive-in theater proprietors around the world, no matter the popularity of your promotion, none of you ever will match the frog and cricket orchestra of the drive-in I remember, or offer wild trout fishing as a diversion during intermission.

≫≫ *Honing the Senses* ≪≪

Which of the five senses — sight, taste, smell, touch, hearing — do you consider most finely honed, and therefore, most valuable? It was a personal question directed at me, and I immediately blurted out, "Sight, of course!"

That was yesterday. Since then, I have had second thoughts. This morning, for instance, I was sitting at the kitchen table reading. Everyone else in the house was still asleep and, although I never lifted my eyes from the book, my ears told me:

1. A horned owl had come to the big maple near the house, and the crows had found it there.
2. A cat was crossing the front lawn because the crows had quit pestering the owl. Now they were moving along behind the cat.
3. A pair of blue jays had joined the crows to harass the cat.
4. An almost inaudible change in the teakettle tone told me water would be boiling out over the burner if I did not get to it in seconds.
5. The house cat had padded past and was sitting at the back door wanting out.
6. A faint stirring in the bedroom told me it was eight o'clock — my wife was rising. Clock chimes almost immediately confirmed the hour.
7. I also remembered it was Monday because, faintly from the other side of the wood lot, I could hear the garbage truck making the rounds of a subdivision.

Without leaving the book I was reading, I also knew the direction and approximate velocity of the wind by the sound it made in the chimney corner. I was sure it was going to be a hot day because the boards along the east side of the house were already making soft sounds as they expanded in the heat of the rising sun.

I also figured my neighbor across the mill pond had overslept because his chickens cackled an hour late on bursting from their night of confinement in the henhouse. I knew, too, by the alarmed tone of ducks quacking in the north bay of the pond, that a boat was there, probably occupied by fishermen.

I could also tell by the tone of my barking dogs that they were not complaining about a trespasser, but about a cottontail sitting too close to their kennels. I knew also, without looking out, that a daughter of mine, who had slept in the cabin, was approaching the house. A circle of silence in birdsong surrounded her progress through the trees.

I knew, too, that the sun was just over the apple trees and shining through a basement window, because the basement cricket, calling it a night, had quit chirping and retired to its crack in the wall. My ears also told me that since I had not let the cat out, it had caught a fly in the sunroom and was eating it. I knew that the back stoop chipmunk was already gathering basswood nutlets for its cache, that a squirrel had crossed the roof and jumped to a blue spruce, and that it was time I put my book away because there were slippered footfalls on the stairs.

In short, while my eyes had brought me the lives of the characters in Thomas Fleming's "Liberty Tavern," my ears had unerringly cataloged all the events occurring around me. It surprised me, and I never may have realized what a role my hearing played in my life, if the question about senses had not been asked. After breakfast, I took a little time to think about the amazing role my hearing played in my life. I had to conclude it was probably because I had spent much of my life in forests so dense that sight was of little use. I remembered, too, a conversation I once had with the late Ernest Swift, Wisconsin Director of Conservation.

"What you see and hear," he said, "is programmed by what you are looking for."

We were in a forest, and I had seen a deer that he had not seen. "But I'll see a man long before you will," he said, "because during my years as game warden, I hunted men."

I am sure that if we had pursued the subject he would have agreed that he used the sounds of all the animals and birds around to zero in on his quarry, much as I was using the printed word to read my book. Which brings us to the point: Learn to listen. Once your ears are attuned to the sounds of the earth, you will know what is going on up ahead even before your eyes can confirm the activity.

For a greater appreciation of the earth, have all your senses honed, of course. But when the forest is so thick that it acts as a blindfold, let your ears lead you. Sit long on a log and listen. Stop and stand silently before breaking out of the trees into a clearing. Cup your ears and open your mouth wide to better admit sound. ·

And, while you are at it, don't forget you have a nose. The odor of crushed mint may tell of a deer's passing. By smell, you will know how many minutes ago a bear had been grubbing for insects in an old stump. You will learn to smell out weasel and mink, and if you work at it, you will be able to smell out water long before it comes into view.

Our senses have long been dulled, since normally we make such meager use of them. So, hone your senses of smell and hearing and you will be surprised how much more your eyes will see.

⇛ Hoarding Summer ⇚

Yesterday I collected a little bit of August and brought it to the house, so when the snow piles around the door I may reflect on the halcyon days when summer was a softness. No, not flowers to be pressed between pages, nor a knotweed bouquet for drying in a vase. Neither cattails nor stray feathers from a flicker's wing, nor a small turtle jewel for the fishbowl. Not a late songbird egg to shellac so that it may shine where the winter sun lights the window sill.

I do it every summer, and though I make a secret thing of it, no one is fooled. They go along with it, this family of mine, by asking, "How did it happen?" Then, when I leave, I am sure they shake their heads, smile, and maybe say, "He'll never grow up."

When I was young it was not necessary, this penchant of mine. Houses seemed older and crickets found their own way to the hearth. So now I turn a log, and as they scamper, I tenderly palm them, one by one, glistening black singers, and carry a score or more to the house, so there will be survivors enough for a small insect orchestra. Should they eat some small pieces of carpet, or a hole in a Pendleton jacket, I will consider that but small payment for keeping, with syncopated song, the beat of summer.

Since, unlike my Oriental friends, I refuse to cage them, by Christmas they will have names such as Hearth Cricket, Davenport Cricket, Bedroom Cricket, Kitchen Cricket — if all goes well, of course, and they abide in good health.

I would also kidnap a soft russet and white mouse for the basement fireplace wood, so when I am working it may come to stare in starry-eyed innocence. I once had a basement toad, which I sometimes sprinkled with water and then stroked his stomach, so he sang a song as vibrant and thin as the highest note on a violin E string. But crickets are really all I dare. They are enough to sing the summertime song when all the world is white and frozen.

⇛ Teaching Respect ⇚

One of the questions I am most often asked is: "How do you teach your children proper respect and appreciation of the outdoors, of nature?"

My advice is to permit them to learn to love it. Nothing seems to work better. To walk an elementary school child through a forest rattling off the common and scientific names of resident trees, and then expound on how the sunshine recipe (the miracle of photosynthesis), supplies oxygen and food for all living things, is about the quickest way I know of turning that child into a sidewalk adult.

Now, before we go further, I am neither teacher nor professional naturalist. My only credentials are those of a journalist who just never seemed to be happy unless I was knee-deep in a mudhole with some frogs. My children, five girls, followed me into those mudholes, and now, intermittently, I can see one or all of them and their children, home for a weekend, right down the slope in one of those holes in which they first muddied their feet.

Sometimes, I must admit, I wish I might impress my friends by rattling off the scientific names of all the animals and plants. And sometimes I wish my children knew them, too. Except I wonder if the big sugar maple that spans the drive would be as dear a friend if I referred to it as *Acer sacchavan*. And would I be as comfortable walking down a slope covered with shooting stars if I had to think of them as *Dodecathon medias?* And anyway, when I need them, all those scientific names and a wealth of other scientific information are in books no farther than an arm's reach from my chair. To love a thing is to respect it. To respect a thing is to cherish and protect it. Then, sometime, we will be curious enough to inquire into the role of the tree, the frog, the hawk or the wolf, and define their proper ecological niche in a harmonious society.

Some children, being so happy with the flower's perfume, the tree's shade, the cricket's concert, may not find it necessary to wonder about the importance of their inarticulate friends until their own children start asking questions. In others, the questions of how and why may begin tumbling forth almost on the same day they see a spider moving swiftly and effortlessly across the same web that traps and entangles the fly.

I have, in other years, tried with more than considerable profundity to act as a nature guide for groups of elementary school children visiting our country place. Never again! Soon bored, the groups eventually splintered in every direction, and I stood alone, words of wisdom like bones in my throat.

We no longer do it, not on any formal basis. And today, if we did do it, there would be no guided tour and no lectures. Today, if we still hosted groups of youngsters, it would be so they might have fun swimming, fishing, frogging, or only watching ants. Today, if we said anything, it might be to exclaim at the colors of a flower, motion for silence so we could hear a bird better, or pick up an especially attractive stone and say, "Wow! How do you suppose that got to be so beautiful?"

Some educators, I am sure, will disagree, and argue that children can be taught to come by a proper appreciation and respect for the outdoors, for nature. But it is my guess that just as marital love need never dig among the roots of family trees to grow strong, so too a child's reverence for nature requires only a close, exciting and lovable relationship.

⇝ *River Man* ⇜

Once a river man, always a river man, and no ponds or lakes nor any oceans can bring so much mystery — if only you will sit and wait and watch. I would consider any August as a leaf lost from the calendar if I did not find time to buck hazel brush and alder thickets until I have come to a certain sand spit where I can cool bare feet in the shallows, and watch a fishing bobber, hoping a fish will not bother to bob it.

There is much to be said about spring rivers, ribbed and roaring. Autumnal rivers, all decorated with multicolored leaves, are an excitement. But an August river is a ripe woman, experienced in such talents as have seduced country boys to languish in her warm embrace, surfeited by her lush fertility. It is all there in August. On the river. In the river. Along the river. Above the river. Life. All of it.

No chance of seeing, smelling, tasting, feeling or hearing it all. No necessity. Only to come is to be wrapped in the arms of a goddess who, having given life to millions, now wraps them all — fish, duck, crayfish, heron, dragonfly, country boy and life beyond counting — in her voluptuous embrace.

All the mating, the borning, the growing done, she lies back, low in her bed between billowing banks, and with a female smile on her languid face, lets her raccoons, beaver, muskrats and all her creatures, warm to her broad bosom. I feel her slow, contented pulse. I barely hear her sleepy breathing. But I feel her sultry rhythm deep in my loins and know that she is my lover.

⇝ *Web of Death* ⇜

Only rarely does August produce dew. Sometimes, however, when a Canadian weather front drops down unexpectedly to forewarn us of the brisker times ahead, I awaken to an astonishingly sparkling world. Before the sun can get in its licks, I hurry to the bottoms. There, from branch and bush, among grasses and flowers, sparkle hundreds of gossamer webs, the homes and wraps of the ingenious spiders.

Few things are more miraculous. The spider's web is stronger than man-made metals, raw material manufactured at will from the spider's own abdomen, architectural design the envy of the engineers. The spider does not spend years, but spins in one night the web that is its world.

Though I have done it a hundred times, I must stoop at least once to finger strands, to see which are smooth and slick for walking, and which have been coated with the spider's glue. I look for the architect, the builder, and when I cannot find him, I make his web tremble so he comes scurrying from whatever hiding place to see what manner of victim has flown into his trap. He sees or senses my presence and quickly backs off, and from a corner of the web, watches like a tiger in its lair. Even as I crouch there, the dew diamonds evaporate and the web fades into the background, perfectly camouflaged now, as insects rise to the warming air.

I have not breakfasted, but I wait. It is not long, then, before a moth, which should have found its bedroom cranny at the first hint of dawn, pays for its mistake by blundering into the trap. My spider approaches cautiously. Then it pounces. The struggle ends with a few quivering wingbeats. There is no hurry now; the spider, perhaps suspicious of me, retreats to its darkest corner, to come some other time to bundle his prey in spider netting. Stashed away, out of the sun, the tiny moth's juices will not evaporate before the spider has a chance to dine.

⇛ *Trashy but Sweet* ⇚

Like the linden tree, some of us are not worth much in the market-place. Commonly called basswood, the linden contributed but briefly to our world of wood by furnishing piano keys, hardly a mentionable commercial asset, since the by-product, music, is something we can do without. Or is it?

Anyway, it does not really matter, since piano keys are no longer made of basswood. And so the linden, which cannot even warm our wintertime hearths since its wood but smokes and smolders, also becomes something we can do without. Or is it?

There is something sturdy, upright and practical about oak, hard maple, even the vagrant poplar, which is cut to make the paper this whimsy is printed on. But linden? Rather trashy. The linden is satisfied to run rampant in soil even a bull thistle might have second thoughts about. The linden, like many a skid row resident, has little other than a determination to live. Under the circumstances, that seems of small importance. Or is it?

Even when assailed by destructive winds, it does not die in a grand manner. Unlike the oak, which will not break but must be uprooted, the basswood often snaps in the middle, losing only its leafy crown. Come another spring and it sprouts a new crown in an eager, upward thrust of undisciplined branches. But sometimes it seems that there is more dignity in death than in a crippling resurrection. But is there?

No matter that it sometimes grows heart-shaped leaves the size of an old-fashioned hand fan for twirling in the wind, glistening in the rain and shading us from the searing heat of a midday sun. No matter that its tens of thousands of glistening flowers perfume the air and yield so much nectar the trees seem to vibrate with the buzz of honey-making bees before showering down pelts in a rain of gold.

Who cares that the flicker finds such easy access that in an hour it can chisel out an apartment? Who cares if the chipmunk harvests its nutlets in anticipation of winter days in an ice-locked dungeon? What profit that a squirrel survives because once the oak and hickory have long spent their nuts, the bountiful linden still has plenty to spare? Or that an old woman gathers its bracts to make tea and reflect on days in a far country when the roses of youth warmed her cheeks? These are trivial things of hardly any importance and certainly no consequence. Or are they?

Important? Perhaps it is significant that just as people seem to do better in pairs, so side-by-side lindens are more able to withstand adversity and rise to unbelievable heights. Out here at Little Lakes, such a close pair rises above Indian graves, higher than all the trees in our wood lot, which is populated by more substantial leafy citizens. But let's be practical. Beauty for beauty's sake seems an extravagance our technological world can ill afford. Or is it?

⇛ *On Growing Old* ⇚

Once he carried a gun through the forests and was thrilled. Once he rowed a boat and felt strong. Once he cast a lure and shouted when the fish struck. Now the August sun is too much, and he waits until evening to come slowly down the slope. When a ruffed grouse flushes with a roar to go rattling among the limbs of teenage maples, there is no adrenaline to goad his pulse. If he lifts his watery eyes, it is only to make sure he has not strayed from the trail. He sits on a log where a fire lane is a widening glory of silver poplar leaves. His mind is wintry with despair and he never hears the old dog until the gray muzzle nudges his knee.

"So you tracked me?" he says. "Well go track something else. We'll hunt no more."

The dog knows no words, but is tuned to the tone. So he goes, head lifted, nostrils searching, tail methodical as the pendulum of a grandfather clock. Off among the poplars, through the teenage maples, searching. When he returns, he has the grouse.

"Damn fool. Young bird. Broke his neck on a branch."

The feathers are soft. Velvet sheen over Autumn browns. Eyes glistening with the end of day. Arrogant head crest. Regal neck ruff. Fantail marked with bars.

"He'll fry nice. Tender. In ten minutes."

Together, grouse in hand, they trail back to the cabin. Inside, he takes a gun from its pegs, palms the dust from the stock, rubs the barrel with a sleeve.

"Think we could?" The dog answers with his tail. Outside on a stump he plucks feathers, and when the moon lifts over the trees, he lifts his head so the shine of it is in his eyes.

"Next month," he says to the dog. "Next month the season opens."

⋙ *Tenderfeet and Fishermen's Lies* ⋘

I am looking for a musky. Not just any musky, mind you, but a twenty-eight pounder I caught in the first hole of Sawyer County's Chippewa River, just below where the flowage spills over the dam at Winter. I caught it during June of 1949, duly put my mark on it with a toenail clipper, and deposited it in the freezer of the General Store at Ojibwa. As I was sure would happen, I was asked to view the same musky — my musky — six times during the next three days. Each time it was in a different freezer and purportedly had been caught in a different lake.

The publicity seekers did not realize, of course, that the fish they were touting was my fish, and I was not about to tell them. Of course, they got publicity, but though I faithfully took pictures, I did not write about the deception in my *Milwaukee Journal* column. I suppose I should have written an expose, but my integrity in a matter of such minor consequence was not worth the friendship I felt for Conservation Warden Johnny Helsing, who was in on the fraud.

If my failure to expose the hoax made me less a journalist, it did give me, in addition to lots of laughs, a warm feeling of being an insider in a very special world in which Johnny "took care" of those backwoods people who needed him. Though I am sure Johnny got a fine feeling playing the good Samaritan, I also know that he got a big bounce out of fooling the gullible tenderfeet who came out of Chicago loaded with enough fishing tackle to open a store.

Johnny did not dislike tenderfeet. Rather, he wanted to strip them of their pretense and make them into real outdoorsmen, bound to field and stream. Else why, on a deer drive, would he send a man in a pair of new boots through the toughest swamp he could find, and that same night tell him how to harden his feet in a salt solution, and show him how to soften his boots with a skunk and bear fat concoction of his own making?

It was great sport watching Johnny help the small resort operator, sporting goods dealer, even whole villages with his musky and, in turn, his big buck displays. It was not unusual in Johnny's country to see the same whitetail buck hanging as an advertisement in three different villages on the same day. Of course, it wasn't honest. If I had been a young, moralistic, hatchet-minded reporter, I would have stripped hide from Johnny, sentence by sentence. Today I am grateful that by then I already had started to mellow.

It ended, of course, when the really big money began getting into the act. It ended during a time when the world record musky mania was swimming rampant through backwoods lakes. Prizes, including autos and cash from outdoor magazines, boat and tackle manufacturers and big-time resort operators, could run a world record musky into a prize of fifty thousand dollars, or even higher. Things went wild. In quick succession, several fishermen claimed world record fish for Wisconsin, but though I was always in the area, I was invariably refused a view of the corpus delicti until after it was mounted.

One man claimed that Jack O'Connor, a nationally known outdoor writer from Minneapolis, was in the boat with him when he beached his record fish. O'Connor, when contacted, promptly denied being in the vicinity.

Another man's claim to a world record fish became suspect when a warden said he had been on the lake the day the fish supposedly had been caught, and the man had not been there. Yet another fisherman, after having his first "world record" musky topped, claimed a yet larger fish. He said he took it on a certain October day between 5:30 and 6 p.m. on Fleming's Bar in the Chippewa Flowage. He had two witnesses in the boat with him. As soon as that catch was announced, it was challenged by a fisherman who said that he had been on Fleming's Bar from 2 p.m. until dusk that day.

"I didn't see a boat," the man said, "and since the bar is only two blocks long, it isn't likely I'd have missed him."

So it went. A Michigan man trolling on Lake St. Claire with his wife claimed a record. Shortly after, one of Wisconsin's intrepid musky hunters claimed to have a bigger fish. To try to clear the air, Nathan W. Heller of Lie Detector Laboratories of Milwaukee invited all "record holders" to take lie detector tests. None volunteered.

So you see how it was. The big money put Johnny out of the business of giving the little guy a hand up. Johnny is dead. He was fishing precisely where I caught my twenty-eight pounder. Feeling tired, he came ashore, rested his back against a pine, and his heart stopped. I know where Johnny is. But I do not know where my twenty-eight-pound musky is. So if you have one of that size mounted and hanging in your home or office, look for my mark. If you find it, write to me. Just as I kept Johnny's secret until he died, so, too, will I keep yours.

⇛ *Kicking the Work Ethic* ⇚

To savor Little Lakes, I have had to learn to be lazy. It was not easy but, at long last, peace graces these, the twilight years. The work ethic can be as habituating as alcohol. Once hooked, one is forever harassed, and blisters become the calluses of scrupulosity. The trick is to dissemble: If the grass does not get cut, talk about the interesting plants that take over. Forget to prune the climbing rose to see all the places it will travel, and the heights to which it will rise.

Plan it right and there will be no need to weed or hill the potatoes. Plant them in the trough of a gully beneath the leaves of many autumns. Some grow and some do not. Enough do. Barely larger than golf balls, they melt like butter on the tongue. Pumpkins? Press seeds into the dusting saucers of little birds and forget about them. There will be enough for grimacing faces on Halloween, and some pies in the bargain.

Think small and where a shed comes down and weed seeds have not yet invaded, rake in carrots and beets, seeds left over from more ambitious times. Let the vegetables fight it out on their own terms. No sweat. There will be enough for two, even three people to eat. Berries? Maybe there are fifty, even a hundred quarts burdening wild canes arching onto the trails into the sun. Nibble anytime, but pick only enough for one cobbler, three pies, a little sauce and a handful to stir into ice cream. The rest should go to the birds. What they don't eat in summer will dry on the vine for winter treats.

To conquer the work habit, get rid of appurtenances that aid and abet this sin of excess. Pass on fruit jars, freezers and pressure cookers. Turn your cold storage bins into junk bins. One good axiom: Never, never eat anything out of season. Then you will enjoy dreaming of strawberries in winter and sugary snow cones in summer, and what a treat they will be when the time comes to relish them. Harvest wild grapes, but never more than enough for a warming glass of wine or two. Chokecherries? A handful once in a while to mull with sugar in the bottom of a glass. Add icy milk.

Wild ground cherries? For a taste of adventure, peel them from their papery pouches and eat them on the spot while they are warm and mellow from the sun. Mint? Well, yes, for scattering between layers of clothes in a dresser drawer. For a julep? By all means. Puffballs? Once a year. Sliced thin and sauteed in butter. Shelf fungi soup? If it is not too much trouble finding the old recipe. Fish, clams, crayfish for bouillabaisse? Only if there is as much pleasure in the capture of the ingredients as there is in the eating.

A pothole in the driveway? Ride around it. A crack in the sidewalk? Watch the ants who move in to occupy it. A leak in the roof? A pail to catch the water until the roofer can come. Dripping water has a hypnotic rhythm. Let it lull you. Snow? It is as easy to walk down a narrow trail as a wide path. Let the rain wash the windows. Then, when the kids visit, have a gala house-cleaning party with food and drink catered.

Remember: All work and no play really does make Jack a dull boy.

⋙ *Years of Discovery* ⋘

Children come to the fields and forests with me in August. They think I am doing them a favor. How would they know it is I who have been favored? Through their eyes I rediscover the freshly washed colors of a rainbow, which down the years of living has become, if not tawdry, then commonplace. Where children walk, life renews itself, and once again I thrill to the smooth turn of a glacial stone, feel my heart skip a beat at the winged flight of the deer.

They lead me down trails my boots know well, and I am surprised to discover how long it is since I paused to pick a pine cone, reached for a grass stem to chew, put my cheek to the creamy bark of a young poplar to feel the smoothness. As we trudge through thickets and glades, wade creeks and skirt lakes, I am as young as the day I saw my first raven. With them the earth is springy beneath, and the sky a place to climb to, hand-hold to handhold, up the trunk of a sentinel pine.

Once again, with almost adolescent excitement, I hear the eagle scream, spy on the blue heron stilted in a back bay, am breathless at the speed of a hunting kestrel. Through their eyes, the August haze that holds the valleys truly looks again like smoke of Indian encampments. When at last we call a halt to build a careful fire for our hot dogs, and we are seated in a circle, it occurs to me that people whose lives are uncomplicated by children are not really living at all.

Hot dogs gone, fire only embers, sun ablaze in the west, we begin, during the deepening dusk, our eerie march back among the ghost-like trees, coming at last to that place where the car is parked. Exhausted, the children fall asleep at once. Behind the wheel, I am as awake as I will ever be, and alive with the memory of how grand and glorious was every day, during the young, young years of discovery.

September

SEPTEMBER. WOMAN IN WAITING. Still growing toward that final ripening, toward that time when the last seed pod, the last nut husk bursts. Now, from the hot and humid south, up both seacoasts and the Mississippi Valley, on across the grain stubbles of Saskatchewan, and into the apple-crisp heart of Wisconsin, there comes a briskness on the wind. Hot August has had it. Now the moldering. Never quite summer, nor yet autumn. A time between.

Martins gone, but bees still bustling. North Country aquiver as feathered migrants congregate at staging areas. South Country aquiver, too, awaiting the arrival of vacationing robins, geese, orioles, redstarts, fat mallards, swift teal. Now, nature braces, looks to its energy reserves: Thick winter fur. Fat, layer on layer, on bears. Seed caches of chipmunks. Hidden acorn lodes of blue jays. Eggs laid away for the hatch of spring insects.

September, the month that cannot quite make up its mind. Up from the tan grain stubble grows new grass. Between ragged corn rows are surprising paths of green. Even sometimes, a North Country violet, flower of spring, blooms. But no one is fooled, because there against the moon, the first southbound herons are silhouetted. It is the altered angle of the sun. And all things, except humans, obey. Reluctantly, perhaps. But the turning world will not, cannot be denied. The quickening is even in the fawn, which sheds its spots as the flowers die, to take on the tawny shades of the wilting woods.

Now,
nature
braces,
looks to its
energy
reserves.

Change must come. Change does come. Ultimately. Inevitably. And only humans angrily, sullenly, sadly revolt before submitting.

September. It rhymes with remember. And so we must store up, for rigorous days ahead, the memory of green leaves, of plants reflecting the shine of waters in fertile forest ponds. September. A song it truly is. A sonata foretelling death for many, but for others a brisk march played by heralding trumpets of geese, a courageous bugling, signal for all to marshal their forces, measure their strength against the winter to come.

September leads the year into autumn: Red leaf held by shining spider's web. Green garter snake crawling for warmth to the sunny surface of a blacktopped road. Acorn cupped by fallen leaf. Apple red on leafless bough. Weed seeds to the wind, reluctantly. Sugar of wild plum sweetening, bursting like resin through the fruit's skin.

September: Rime of frost on grass blade at dawn. Sun hot by noon. Morning mists over the meadows. Reaches of the sky higher as cold disinfects the atmosphere. Ragging hedgerows. Colors: Tincture of crimson along the sharply blue waters of Lake Superior. Quite suddenly, brilliant thrusts of yellow down the valleys. Reds coming south with forest fire speed. Willows, poplars and birches pallid in the lowlands. Hardwoods leaping the hills with scarlet maple, bronze oak and brown hickory. Roadsides firing up with sumac. Rivers sucked low by summer's sun thread quietly, ready for the ice, anxious, perhaps, to become gorged by winter snows for a torrential springtime spree.

Peaceful some days. Tomatoes are canned. Berries frozen. Potatoes dug. Carrots in sand. Only rutabagas and turnips, and in some fields, bright yellow pumpkins await their turn. Some corn to be husked. Water weeds go down on more northerly lakes, and the water turns crystal clear as microscopic plant and animal life finally comes to the end of an unbelievable fertility cycle of billions and trillions beyond counting. Algae on stones

In an hour, as many butterflies drift by as there are days in a year.

fades and turns from green to stunning white. Creeks show their multi-colored stones again. Deer, staring at his image as he drinks, never knows his summer red has faded to match the more somber gray of winter woods. Ducks floating on the lazy current, once so drab during the August molt, are brilliant again and strong of wing.

So smell September. Taste it. Feel the coolness of her nights. Follow the sun to where it is drying dew from dragonfly wings, where pickerel weed still hides some winding waterways. September. Hawthorn scattering red fruit for grateful grouse. Bracts, tea leaves of the linden, spinning down. Plates of purple elderberry pretty well picked over. Fat cattail, showing signs of wear, bursting a seam.

So I loaf, take a day to sit and watch migrating monarchs, gift of the milkweed, making their slow march. Finding a warm spot of sandy soil on the side of a hill, I begin to count. In an hour, as many butterflies drift by as there are days in a year. How can it be? This fragile filament, orange and black and shades without names, floating south a thousand miles. So if half are eaten by bird or toad or squirrel, or if ninety-nine percent go down on wind-tattered wings, there will be enough come spring to home in on my milkweed. Then the eggs, the striped caterpillar, the bright green chrysalis and, miracle of miracles, bright butterflies to form squadrons for another southern flight.

It is getting late and still they come, but now the phenomenon. The drifters, as if drawn by some magic magnet, turn and begin alighting on a huge yellowing sugar maple. Ten, twenty, a hundred ... I stop counting. Where? Why this tree? A thousand. Ten thousand. Thirty thousand. No. It cannot be. Never that many. The yellow maple flames in their winged embrace. Lower limbs get layer upon layer, like bees swarming to their golden goddess, until a scarf of monarchs cracks a branch and there is an explosion of color, butterflies bursting like fiery shrapnel from an exploding bomb made of quivering wings. They settle back, and when it is dark I do not believe what I have seen. And maybe it was a dream, because when I come at dawn they are gone.

Next day I walk another trail farther from the house, and more monarchs are migrating. I measure their flight, estimate their speed. Four miles per hour. Eight hours of daylight, maybe nine. Thirty-two miles. But maybe they fly at night. If not, thirty-two miles a day. Ten days, three hundred and twenty miles. One month, almost a thousand miles and they are home free. But I have seen them while flying. So perhaps they are loafing when days are warm and waiting on a north wind before climbing to altitude, to be whisked the length of my state between dawn and dusk. Birds do it. So why not butter-flies?

I say good-bye to them, and in my mind, like a child, I say, "See you next spring." A cloud passes over the sun, and suddenly I shiver. If they come back, will I be gone? I hurry toward the house because I want to hear voices. I want to feel the new, brisk tone of September in the heightened feelings of people, surfeited by summer, now brisk once more as the freshening breeze. As I near the house, I know for sure it is September. Wash is on the line. The automatic dryer is getting a day off so the briskness of autumn may come into the house on the fresh smell of clean sheets.

Smell September. Taste it. Feel the coolness of her nights.

I turn onto the road, and from afar, voices that were doleful on the opening day of school are shrill now with the excitement of September. I plod far as the little village. I sense a tightening of community spirit. Vacations over, old routines are again in force. Elks, Eagles, PTA and Bridge Club have resumed activities. People are more friendly, perhaps because they remember how during last winter's storm they needed each other, as much as bees that buzz in unison to keep the hive warm, and so survive during icy times.

Everything is all right, except I am troubled when I see the old men leaning against farm fences or sitting in the village square, turning as the sun turns, hoping in vain to store September's thinning warmth for comfort beneath October overcoats.

⇛ *Learning to See* ⇚

There are worlds most of us never see simply because we do not pause long or often enough for those other worlds to come into focus. Instead of pulling to the side to observe people and events as they flow around us, we abandon ourselves to the current and, like woodchips on a river, join the race to the sea of comfortable complacency.

Impatient even as a youngster, I remember an old man, Bob Nelson, calling out as I frantically paddled past him to take over a fishing hole on the Rock River, "The fish aren't going anywhere." Some weeks later, he coaxed me into spending a quiet evening with him on a hillside. Then, as mammals, insects and birds began to accept us as part of the landscape, they began to show themselves.

A kestrel alighted within a hand's reach, every feather etched into the finest of penciled lines. A grizzled badger threw up showers of gravel in his digging pursuit of a gopher. A walking stick on a hazel branch moved after an hour, so at last we knew it was not part of the bush but an elongated, wingless insect. It was the beginning of my a career as a watcher.

Learning to see is no mean accomplishment. When I take a sharp-eyed bird watcher to an observation stump, he may count more feathered ones than I. But when I ask what he thought of the shelf fungus at the base of the stump, he confesses to not having seen this purple, green, red and yellow jewel, though it is more strikingly beautiful than a whole aviary of hummingbirds.

Of course, sight plays a major role in all those wild ones marked as victims in the life cycle. So a cluster of juncos feeds unperturbed when a passing crow is followed by its shadow on the snow below. But should a shadow of the same size have the symmetrical dimensions of a hunting hawk, the cluster of juncos explodes like a grenade to places of safety among nearby branches.

So it is that a visiting forester sees and measures my wood lot in board feet of lumber, whereas I see the trees as food and shelter for the wild ones, and a soothing sense of fresh, green, aromatic solace for my weary spirit. When I had the legs and the lungs for it, I would reward myself by walking a fox trail at dawn, until I put Reynard out of his day camp. I had no intention of killing or capturing him. I simply wanted the experience of being, for one day, the traveling companion of a fox. Since the animal certainly would not agree to such familiarity, I had to interpret his every move by the script of a night out as he had written it in the snow. Sometimes it would turn out that the two of us, fox and I, got little more than exercise.

But then there would be the night a horned owl stole the rabbit the fox killed. And sometimes on the surface of a river or lake I would read in the snow about the nuptial dance. There was the orchard gone wild where the fox was forced to dig for little sour apples to keep from starving. There once was the skirmish of two male foxes over the affection of a vixen. The more I came to look, so also my ability to see was sharpened. So, if life seems dull, learn to see. You might be surprised at the excitement in some corner where the broom missed the incredibly fantastic snare of the enterprising spider.

⋙ *Misdirected Charity* ⋘

I used to feel godlike when, come September, the bird and squirrel feeders went up, and along with the rest of the wild society, even the backdoor chipmunks went on relief. Now, after having lived awhile, I know that, except in times of extreme emergency, my charity has for the most part been misdirected. Within days after going on the dole, the drive that ensured survival of chipmunks through thousands of perilous years shriveled. Instead of scurrying from dawn to dusk, the two backdoor chipmunks took to waiting. Then, if I entered or left the house without paying a toll, I did so at the risk of being severely reprimanded.

What is more, before the days of my benevolence, the two chipmunks apparently were happy scurrying to gather nut and seed and fruit and any edible thing. Then they lived in comparative peace. Now, they quarrel for favor. In addition to taking away our chipmunks' self-reliance and industry, we robbed them of such dignity as marked their kind as among the hardest working and thriftiest of creatures. Now we cannot give it back to them except by withholding all support. When we do, we get a chirring reminder about the error of our ways. Then, if we extend a hand only in friendship, the chipmunk will bite the fingers that once fed it.

So we relent, but instead of giving nuts for free, we persuade each chipmunk to climb to our lap, perch on a shoulder, hunt through a pocket, go through the motions of earning what heretofore had been free. It is a farce, a circus, a shovel-leaning job of political persuasion. The chipmunks are not to be blamed. Handouts, like drugs, are habit-forming, and charity quickly becomes responsibility.

⫸ *Happiness* ⫷

Happiness is Gwen's smile. It is Buck's tail wag. Mary's laughter. Happiness is a twirling toy prism breaking sunlight into rainbows that chase each other across the carpet, up the wall, across the ceiling. It is the leaves looking in the window. The chair shaped to accommodate old bones. Happiness is a painting that alters its mood with the changing light. It is the iridescent bluebottle fly banging the bay window. It is the lotion that soothes and softens weathered hands and callused feet. It is tea icing a throat. It is the melodious chiming of a very old clock.

Happiness is a peaceful night in which to sleep. It is the coolness of fresh sheets, the faint perfume of a soft pillow, a bird's last song of the day, signal for the frogs to pick up the beat. Happiness is a book, the vehicle for a journey exciting enough to forget bills due to be paid in the morning. Happiness reflects the wood of an old rocking chair glowing warmly in an appreciative eye. Happiness is looking at pine paneling with its knots standing out like surprised eyes. It is a transparent blue vase and the stems of velvety cattails soft as brown satin.

Happiness comes through the screen on a breeze — the aroma of rich soil. And it comes from the kitchen — voices barely audible in their communion. Happiness is tranquility, the mysterious interlude of calm. It is a sudden surge of thankfulness for eyes that can still see, for fingers that feel, for chocolate still sweet on the tongue. Happiness is old shoes that accommodate feet never meant to be imprisoned. It is a shirt or blouse that falls softly open at the neck, trousers and dresses that are comfortably voluminous but appear to fit.

Happiness is forgiveness. It is compassion for the mouse you must kill, tolerance of someone's muddy shoes. It is remembering to balance the admirable qualities against those you find irksome in others. Happiness is the odd stone finally fitting the awkward gap in the Lannon stone walk. It is the right word at the right time, the final brush stroke, the sprout in spring, the potato up from the dark in fall. It is the grass smooth and green as a carpet, the car purring beneath cleaned spark plugs.

Happiness is a window so clean it is invisible. It is sparkling cutlery, glistening dishes, a polished tabletop. It is coffee warming and awakening a sleepy stomach. It is a curl on a damp forehead, a cool hand on a sunburn, peaches in real cream. Happiness is hearing laughter, drying tears, warming hearts in the glow of a smile. It is a card from an old friend, a kiss from a new sweetheart, holding hands on a night ribboned with lightning, crashing with thunder, roaring with wind.

Happiness is the smell of browning ribs, candles sparkling on a white cake, the crunch of a crisp radish. It is a white sink after dirty dishes, a hot sidewalk cooled by the surprise of a sudden shower, a breeze moving curtains after a hot, stagnant day. Happiness is a sentence well written, a ditch well dug, a tomato finally turning red. It is a well-oiled bicycle, swift and silent down a trail. It is a parking place. It is a bright and merry eye, a mischievous smile, jeans that fit. Happiness is sugar in cereal, salt on steak. It is purple berry juice on appreciative lips, a well-told joke breaking barriers of reserve, a baby's hand clutching a surprised finger. Happiness surely is not anticipation of what tomorrow might bring. Happiness just is.

⋙ *Nothing New?* ⋘

Just about the time you think you know it all, along comes a black bass to fan out a September nest. There is no way of discovering what has happened to make the bass nearly a half-year late. The thing is, if someone told you about the bass, if you had not seen it yourself, you would never believe it. But there it is: A big bull bass of fully four pounds, waiting for a female with eggs for him to fertilize. Eight days he waits, but of course, there are no females with eggs, and on the morning of the ninth day he swims out and sinks from sight.

In September, too, while a favorite pond normally has a dozen cedar waxwings tending to its insect hatch, all of a sudden there are more than a hundred perched in the weeping willows. There are never enough insects for that many, not in September. Yet they stay, and when a hatch starts lifting, the air is wild with birds. That same September, while I am fishing one day, a white-billed, slate-colored, head-bobbing coot is lofted into the air when a muskrat surfaces right beneath it. When the coot lands back on the water, a black snapping turtle, rising to the disturbance, bounces the coot again. This time it seeks the refuge of bank willows, protesting such indignities.

Banded nighthawks usually feed at considerable altitude. But during a September migration, just like the monarch butterflies, there are days in succession when they keep drifting lazily south, considerably below the tops of higher trees. In a lifetime of observing the migration, I have never seen one give chase or take time to feed. Then yesterday, one bursts away from a squadron of six and, flying in a straight line inches above the water, puts on a burst of speed to catch a dragonfly.

So you have to concede that perhaps you do not know it all, have not seen everything. Of course you haven't. No matter how ordinary the flight of a duck flock, it is always different. Even the setting sun never sinks into the same surroundings, not at any time since there has been an earthly horizon to receive it.

A Time for Sunfish

September, and children, looking mournful as chickens caught in a downpour, drag in funeral procession back to nine months of forced imprisonment. Even as they do, their elders plot to some day soon do away with this, the child's precious summer hiatus. I will not join in such skulduggery.

Granted that it may be immoral to permit the buildings that house our pupils to stand empty for three months of the year. Granted that the whole system of summer vacations is an antiquated hangover from the days when every hand, large or small, was needed to plant the fields and bring in the harvest. Yet I wonder where I would be today if not for the months when school doors closed and my education continued on river and in fields, on farms and in forests.

Those were three precious months, and if I did not learn Newton's law by falling out of an apple tree, I did discover that this was a great world, one worth loving. No teacher could tell me how a calf was born better than having the cow herself show me. No teacher could explain the intricacies of the spider's web better than the spider herself, by putting on a demonstration where a ray of light came on a long slant down the cavernous haymow. I could smell the clover because I could lie in it, and if dark and desperate days lay ahead, the memory of how the clover once smelled might pull me through.

All living cannot be learned behind school doors, in classrooms. So I rise in futile rage when my children have so much homework that there is no time to learn how to bake a brownie or train a dog. There must be a time for books, but there should also be a time for woodpeckers in a hollow tree, for sunfish beneath a bridge, for daisies nodding to their own reflections in a pond.

≫≫ *Flirting with Death* ≪≪

Kids around town came to call it the hanging tree. I am not sure if it still stands behind a home on North Main Street in Juneau but, more than a half-century ago, people passing the house would point and say, "That's where that Ellis kid almost hung himself."

I will never forget because I carried the rope burns into maturity, before sun and wind finally erased them. It happened on a quiet, peaceful autumn afternoon. As usual, the street was deserted except for an occasional farm wagon rattling by or a car trailing dust along a street that was destined to wait awhile before being buried by concrete. A year-younger brother and I were the only ones at home. He sat on a stone wall cracking hickory nuts. I sat beneath the box elder contemplating a single rope, all that was left of a homemade swing. Sometimes a breeze moved the rope, and my eyes followed its motion hypnotically.

I was contemplating a hanging. Not my own, of course, but one I had seen in an old Wild West thriller on the silent screen. In my mind's eye I could see it again, vivid but perplexing. I could hear Louella's funereal mood music coming from the rattling old piano she played during all films in my home town. For days, and especially nights, I had been seeing the man hanging as the lynch mob spurred their horses away from the hanging tree. Over and over and over.

How? That was what perplexed me. They couldn't kill a man. Not to make a movie. That much I knew. But then, how? There on the screen, plain as day, I had seen him, kicking a little at first, then, like the pendulum of a giant grandfather clock, swinging slowly back and forth. I had spent a sleepless night pondering the question, and when you are ten, spending a sleepless night for any reason verges on the impossible. And the next morning, I sat on the stone wall in the backyard, pondering.

I tried holding my breath. Was that how? Had he been able to hold his breath while the camera filmed the scene? I held my breath again, a little longer this time. That had to be it! A hundred times I had been on the verge of asking someone, anyone, how they thought the scene had been filmed. But I could hear their ridicule: "Why, you dumb kid!"

My mother, of course, would have been charitable. But, I already knew her answer: "Honestly, Melvin. I would have to see it. Why don't you ask your father?"

I knew his answer, too: "Some trick, for sure. Don't bother your head about it."

But what trick? The victim wasn't a dummy. I had seen him kick, then go limp. Getting up, I went over to where the single rope hung. It was just out of reach. I jumped, but couldn't quite touch it. I looked over to where my brother sat. He would be of no help. He couldn't even crack hickory nuts. Instead, he crushed them with a stone, eating what nutmeats fell free, then brushed the rest off the wall. Once more I jumped, and this time my fingertips touched the rope.

Next to a nearby chicken coop stood some crates. I piled one crate on top of another next to the rope. Climbing up, I reached for the rope and fashioned a crude noose. I'll swing off, I told myself, and then swing right back to the top of the crates. I stamped to test the crates. They seemed solid. So I put the noose around my neck and, taking a deep breath, launched myself. The pain filled my head. Like lightning, it flashed down into my toes. Daylight shattered into hundreds of shiny splinters of light. Reaching up, I pulled until I could catch a breath, and almost instantly came crashing down again. I reached for the crates with my feet, and in my frenzy kicked them over.

The rope cut off my air supply with a searing jolt that sent flashes of pain shooting even out my eyes. The only help in sight was my brother and, unfortunately for me, we hated each other's guts. So there I dangled, a human pendulum, about to swing right out into eternity. Fortunately, I was a string bean and tough as a leather bootlace from swimming and running in pursuit of anything that ran the other way, and I managed to pull myself up on the rope again to rasp, "Help!"

But my brother went right on cracking hickory nuts, perhaps not fully aware of my predicament, but more likely pleased that I was at long last getting my comeuppance for the hundreds of times I had made him knuckle under. My kicking and squirming became less frantic. The back-yard began to blur ...

My mind did not begin to take pictures for future reference until I saw my mother's tear-streaked face above me. She was moaning, "My God! My God!" I was still lying on the ground. The rope burn was a bright red welt around my neck. My stomach ached from vomiting. My eyes were still bulging. Of the rescue, I have no recollection. But as my brother told it many times that night and for days thereafter, "I just went over, put my head between his legs and stood up."

I carried the rope burn to full manhood, and sometimes today, when I run my fingers down my throat, I can still feel the circle of death.

⋙ *Inspirations* ⋘

A man, of course, is the sum total of all his experiences. Weaving in and out of his life are winds great and small, all playing their own special tunes on his heart chords. Then, when he has come to maturity, he must look back, and that is what I am doing this day, searching inside for those special people who fostered my love of the land.

I am not sure who taught me to love music. I am not certain who inspired me to write. But when it comes to my concern for the good earth, I have no doubt. Towering above all others are two men whose works are burned into my brain. One was a writer, the other an artist. Both were crusaders who saw clearly, years ago, what most of us are just beginning to understand today: that humankind must live in love and harmony with our surroundings or ultimately perish, victims of our own perfidy.

The first of these men was Jay Norwood (Ding) Darling. Even before I was old enough to read well, I was looking at his hard-hitting nature cartoons. The second man came along later, when I was already working for a newspaper. I knew him a little, but worshipped him a lot. His name was Aldo Leopold. He was a master ecologist. He was a gentle man, a poet, but also very practical.

It was fitting and fortunate for me that Ding Darling was the first of these two men to enter my life. When his cartoons first caught my eye, I was so young that if I had attempted to read Leopold, I would never have understood what he was trying to say. But with Darling there never was any question. You saw his cartoon. You instantly got the message. And days later, if you closed your eyes, the cartoon would flash back into your mind: The filth and pollution in one panel. The grandeur of nature in the other. He drew a lot of "side by side" cartoons. They were before and after cartoons. The land all swimming in sunshine and flowers before man moved in. Then the dead, bloated white fish, the dying ducks, the stinking river.

They were "gut" cartoons, because that was where they hit you, and hit you hard. They made me angry, and I cut them out and pasted them in a school notebook. I decided that one day, I would draw the mantle of Darling over my shoulders, and, like him, show the world in pictures the dirty tracks people were leaving on earth.

Unfortunately, I could not draw a straight line. I eventually settled for a typewriter, and soon after I did, Aldo Leopold came into my life. Unlike Darling, he came gently, almost as quietly as mist, and at first I hardly knew he was there. Reading him in the beginning, I only enjoyed hearing the geese as he heard them, seeing the chickadees as he saw them. I was too word-conscious as a cub reporter to hear anything except the music. Then one day, though I do not remember the exact clause or sentence or paragraph that stopped me, I saw a glimmer. I reread it and saw a gleam. And suddenly the whole flood of his wisdom broke over me and made me giddy. Much later, I met him and talked with him briefly, and my only sadness is that he did not write more often and much, much more.

Both men are dead now. Leopold in 1948 died at age 62 while fighting a forest fire to save the Wisconsin acres he loved. Darling died in 1962 in the fullness of his years, a two-time Pulitzer Prize winner and an otherwise much-honored man. And now, if this has seemed to be an autobiography, it was never so intended. What I have been trying to say is, "Lord, give us another Ding Darling. Lord, give us another Aldo Leopold. Please. Because we, and our children, are sadly in need of men of their ilk."

⇒⇒ *Horse Sense* ⇐⇐

The sun has just risen, but I have already been up awhile, chasing, of all things, horses. We found them — Taffy, a palomino-spot mare, and Rebel, a red gelding — about a mile from home, cavorting across backyards. They had broken their pasture fence and obviously had been out all night, and had left deep hoof marks in the lawns from one end of our village to the other.

"Do you think they're worth it?" my wife asked, looking out across our own lawn, which now resembled a football field after a game played in the rain. Good question, one to which there is no easy answer, because when you count up the trouble and expense of having horses, you have to balance it against the happiness they have brought our girls, and the discipline and self-reliance the girls have acquired while training, caring for and riding the animals.

Many choices involving the good earth are not unlike horses. They are neither all good nor all bad. So the automobile pollutes, but it also has made us creatures of great mobility, with the power to do immeasurable good for ourselves and others. With the motor vehicle, the steer gets to market and the steak to our tables. With the auto, people get swiftly to the hospital, flee disasters, visit the old folks, and on and on.

There is a man in north-central Wisconsin who dug a pond and planted it with fish, and was very happy and proud of his accomplishment. Then, when otters moved in, he was almost ecstatic to have as neighbors such interesting animals. But when the otters ate his fish, he thought perhaps he should trap the otters so that he again might have fish. He waited, and the otters, having no more fish to eat, left on their own. So the man bought more fish and, of course, the otters came back once again to eat them.

The dilemma is not unlike that of the man who wanted a forest and also a great herd of deer. The deer ate and ultimately killed off all his seedling trees. The forest declined and, having eaten everything within reach, the deer left. Without deer, the young trees again flourished until the deer found out about it and came back.

It is a fact that in some areas people cannot have light, heat or even jobs unless the beauty of a swift river is destroyed by erecting a power dam. It is equally true that some rivers should never be dammed because alternate power sources are available. It would be an easy world if everything were either good or bad, black or white. Unfortunately, gray areas are usually the rule, and if the corn in my garden is to mature, I have to shoot the blackbirds because they know all about scarecrows. If I want water for my fishes, I have to trap the muskrats that sieve the dikes with their burrows. If I want tomatoes or melons, I have to fence out the pheasants and shoot or trap the ones that fly over the fence. Mostly, I try to plant enough of everything so there is a little left over for me. But in a hard-nosed world of cutthroat competition, trying to raise enough wheat for both the great flocks of ducks and geese and for the market is apt to bankrupt most farmers.

What I am getting at is that every environmental rule of conduct must be resilient enough to measure up to economic as well as esthetic requirements. And that is where, very often, the Simon-pure environmentalist gets into trouble. He will not yield. If a freeway is scheduled to strike out along a lakeshore, he will insist that it be routed inland. So the freeway is detoured, at perhaps double the cost, and to the consternation of a driving public forced miles off the direct route.

Likewise, limited and supervised strip-mining can provide enough energy so we may have oil for our furnaces and gas for our cars next winter. Clear-cutting forests, though unsightly, could put the price of lumber down sufficiently so a house would be within our price range. Pesticides judiciously used could help increase foodstuffs so the starving of the world might be fed. The salt on the winter highway may kill road-side vegetation and rabbits, but it might also save lives.

If this be heresy, it is also common sense. Rigidity among environmentalists has enraged many good people. Whole communities have turned away from a good earth program because environmentalists would not yield, would not compromise at a time when compromise was called for. Simply put, if I want my children and grandchildren to have horses so they may learn about self-reliance, then I must be willing to get up some mornings and chase horses. And if we want to keep warm next winter, maybe we will have to agree to strip-mining yet another coalfield. It is a hard, hard decision for a Simon-pure environmentalist, but common sense still is the better part of any crusade, including that of the good earth.

Velvet Ghost

September, and the mice move in. Predictably, on the night of first frost, we hear them touring all such dark and mysterious places as are necessarily part of a house built around the heart of an old log cabin. The mice we can cope with. It is another forager which, for twenty years, has had us mystified. We are reasonably sure it is a rodent, and if we lived where pack rats abide, that busybody would be the number one suspect.

More than anything, I suppose, it is a blow to the pride of an old woodsman that he cannot identify, much less trap, a creature who almost nightly moves what seems like mountains of peanuts, valleys of popcorn, hills of jelly beans and other assorted candies. Precautions seem futile, and if jar lids are secure on the peanuts, he manages to start a leak in the sunflower seed sack. If the toasted sunflower seeds go under glass, he has found garden seed packets left over from spring planting. Garden seeds in tins, he has gnawed his way to the heart of ornamental gourds, and their seeds are gone.

We have never even found a dropping that might be a clue to his identity. So each September, as he moves in along with the mice, our paranoia takes fresh root, as we hear double-jointed peanuts scraping as they are dragged between the walls. We laugh about it. Then come the nights when we sit wide-eyed in bed, staring into the dark, listening to the ghostly chomping of goodies, with which he has obviously insulated the entire house.

At first a chipmunk was suspect. Having dealt with many of the striped ones, we ruled that filcher out. Now we have reason to believe it might be one of those bug-eyed, fawn-colored, velvet-soft flyers of the night. Of all creatures, none is more secretive. I once heard an old lumberjack tell how a hollow oak beneath which he often napped, on being felled, spewed forth a whole colony. In all his years in the woods, he had never seen one before. They are long-lived, thirty years or more. They are small enough for the alleyways in our walls. They may live in the trees of a yard, and never once leave a track in the snow. They are elfin creatures, the flying squirrels.

⋙ *The Case for a Kitten* ⋘

Johnny is mentally retarded. He has not smiled in more than a year. So, concerned friends gave Johnny a young goat. Yesterday, Johnny smiled. Rita, an aging single woman, sat out her dreary days behind drawn curtains. A visiting nurse, fearful for her sanity, brought her a canary. The shades have gone up. The sun shines in because the bird will not sing unless it does.

Steve, a paraplegic, lost interest in the books around him. His record player gathered dust. He gave visitors short shrift. Then an uncle gave him an ant colony, and Steve has embarked on an ambitious study of the insects of the world. Mary's only sister died in an automobile accident. The child was inconsolable. Her parents bought her a pup. Mary goes outside to play again.

You do not have to be very young or very old or very sick or very sad to find not only solace but inspiration in animals' contribution to human society. There is something almost mystical in certain animal-human relationships. The dog faithful even after death, the lions protecting their masters from other wild lions, the escaped timber wolves who eventually turned their backs on their wild heritage to return to the place at which they had been held captive — these stories are not all fiction.

But such fidelity is not necessary on the part of either animals or humans. Nor does a person have to possess an animal. It is enough for most only to see a squirrel busy in its own squirrel world to get the feeling that there have to be some things still right on this mixed-up earth. In twenty years, our household has accommodated literally hundreds of mammals, amphibians, reptiles and insects. There have been big and little turtles, fish of many kinds, and hawks, seagulls, muskrats, opossums, foxes, frogs, pigeons, owls, horses, dogs, ducks, geese, chipmunks, blue jays, practically every critter indigenous to our corner of Wisconsin.

I have never doubted that they engendered in our five girls a respect not only for the animal kingdom, but for the very earth itself. Any child who watches an egg hatch or a pup being born, and then is made custodian of the newborn, must ascend to some sort of stewardship requiring the kind of responsibility that can nurture concern for a better world. Conservationists plead often for the endangered species of the world, and their concern deserves everyone's attention. But we should also be concerned for the animals, domestic and wild, who contribute so much to our everyday living.

I will not get maudlin, but yesterday, when I sat in the sunshine on our front lawn and a big woodchuck came out of a culvert beneath the road and began to graze, I could not help but feel I had done something worthwhile by nursing its auto injuries and then setting it free. I get the same kind of feeling when a kingfisher comes all the way up from the ponds and goes rattling loudly back and forth over the housetop, because I can remember the job the girls had feeding the feathered orphan before it was strong enough to be turned free to catch its own fish.

Then there is the wild Canada gander, Duke. He lived here once, and every spring he returns for a short visit. This year, he came out of a blizzard and sat in the marsh only a short time before continuing on to the grass flats on the edge of the subarctic.

It could be we have a natural affinity toward animals. Maybe an 18-year-old woman from North Carolina summed it up when she pleaded her case last summer before a judge in Ocean City, N.J. She had been arrested for carrying a kitten on the Ocean City boardwalk. In court the clerk read the charge: "It is unlawful for any dog or other animal to be on any portion of the boardwalk at any time."

The young woman protested: "But man is an animal, too."

The judge frowned, ran his fingers through his hair, and then, with a smile, declared the girl not guilty, and ordered her twenty-five dollars' bail returned.

⋙ *A Fable of Waste* ⋘

Many, many years ago, a drought settled into the valley of the Ammericuss, home of herders of goats. Hot winds withered the grasses, dried the streams, shriveled the fruits, wilted the greens of their gardens, until often there was barely enough milk and cheese, and the children whimpered in the night because they were hungry. But drought, if not common to the valley of the Ammericuss, had visited before. Grandfathers, and many, many preceding generations of the Ammericuss clan, had developed procedures which, if uncommonly rigorous, saw them through each crisis, until that day when rains once more greened the slopes.

Then the nanny goats grew fat again, and their udders bulged with richness. The falling pink and white blossoms left behind green nubbins, which ripened into rosy, rich fruit. The streams ran so full and clear that even fishes, which had retreated to the bracken bays by the sea, came back to sport in the riffles. So abundant became the riches of the newly watered valley that those who had never lived through such trying times as a drought listened to the telling as they might some fairy tales. And the younger ones, who should have well remembered, preferred to forget, and even scoffed if some old man, with the warning wag of a gnarled finger, prophesied that the drought would return. So in this, another time of crisis, only the old were ready when the scorching winds came.

They trudged, then, to rebuild such rock and boulder barricades as would stay the hot air's thrust on rocky slopes where no trees or bushes grew. And some went where the old wells were marked to see if, digging deep again, they might not find enough to spoon out water for themselves and the thirsty, bleating goats and whimpering children. Others of these old ones began gathering all such straw and hay and fodder of every kind, even thatching from their houses, and thorny sticks and stones from the hillsides, to spread and anchor the precious grass roots of their valley. But the young, having heard from passing persons of other, even greener valleys, did not go with the old ones, but grumbled that there must be some other way. Instead, they sulked in the thin shade, which was no protection from the blistering winds, or wandered, as is the inclination of such as are losing their heritage.

Thus it was that one young man, coming to a far away high place, did look upon a valley as green as any. With great joy, he brought the news.

And so the Ammericuss clan, except for some of the old ones who wished to die where they had been born, began their exodus. Then they thrived for more than a generation in this rich, new valley. It was a gifted place, almost more talented in producing life than the valley of their inheritance. But this time, when the drought came, there were so many more to feed that the devastation was a quick and heartless thrust right to the core of existence. During their bewilderment, an old and feeble man, reminding them that it was he who as a youth had in the first place discovered this valley, said that now it was time they return to the valley where he had been born.

And so they trekked, lifted by the promise of those who remembered, back among the hills. Some began to laugh and cheer even before they reached the summit. Then, when at last they could look down, they stood in such dreadful silence that even the sound of a faraway lizard scurrying across the sand reached up from that barren place to greet them. They stood for a long time, dry-eyed and numb, before filtering down the slope to where the hot winds had burned the unprotected grass roots and filled the creek beds with sand, to where the fruit trees had turned into gnarled skeletons and homes were leveled without a trace, into the valley they had wasted because they had not stayed to watch and care for it.

The goats were first to bleat, and then the children whimpered, and finally the women wailed. The mourning continued until they had no strength for that, either. One young man finally stepped forward to say, "There is nothing left except to find another valley."

"Never!" cried an old but surprisingly strong voice.

It was the old man, who as a boy had found the valley that had provoked the first exodus. Walking out from among the goats and people to where all could see him, he held up a skull he had found in the sand. "There is nothing left except to find the old wells and dig them out. There is nothing left except to rebuild the barriers against the winds, nothing, except to work until we have reclaimed our valley."

"But there must be other valleys," the young man replied.

"And so there may be," the old man answered, "but even if you find one, and another, and another, this," he said, holding the skull high, "is the inevitable end for the Ammericuss, or any clan that thinks it can survive by forever wasting valleys." And, so it was, thirsty, hungry and tired almost unto death, that the Ammericuss clan, with an eye on the sky watching for rain, began again to reclaim the land they had wasted.

⇛ *An Oak for Tomorrow* ⇚

He came one September asking for acorns. I said, "Help yourself." He filled a threadbare gunny sack, tried to lift it but could not. So I said, "Let me help."

He had come two miles, and by the time I dropped him off, I learned that he was eighty-six years old and lived alone. That, no, the acorns were not for the pigs; he was going to plant them. All the way home I wondered about the spirit that moves some men to worry about how the world will look a hundred years from now, because surely, his slow-growing oaks will not be much more than knee-high when he dies. I cannot be sure, but I had to conclude that planting the oaks gave him the same satisfaction that comes to a man who builds a house so well he can envision the countless generations that will be sheltered by its walls.

That afternoon, I planted a bushel of acorns. Later that night, I felt the same contentment I sometimes experience when I have written a verse I feel may bring tears or laughter to some of tomorrow's children. So, what profit a man to plant an oak at eighty-six? Likely the same satisfaction as brings peace to the deathbeds of those who have planted the beauty of truth in the hearts of their children.

OCTOBER. A CERTAIN SADNESS. The beginning of the end. A sharp reminder that no one
lives forever, that no minute of any summer may
be reclaimed.

October. Flight from death. The Arctic cold
begins its relentless march from northern lakes
already iced — down, down our global earth,
icing tail feathers of tardy migrants, sending
reluctant bears into earthy dens among tangled
roots. Ice crackles and falls in bright shards from
fishing nets lifted for the last time. Boats go into
drydock with icicles festooning rails and rigging.
Far northern Canadian planes change to skis.
Farther south, thinner oil and thicker tires for
autos awaiting the onslaught.

Trees leafless in the northern halves of
Canadian provinces, and flaming in one last celebration from there on down into the states. A
painter's dream — undisciplined, quick, brilliant
— the last breath, dying gasp of summer.
Acorns rattle on the roof. Beetles retire beneath
bark. Seeds twirl and sail on the wind. Sharply
blue water gets a flotilla of birch leaves tanned
and curling at bow and stern. Gentians bloom,
fringes closing flowers against the frost.

Then the big freeze. Greens blacken. Reds
rust. Willowy weed stalks become stiff-standing,
brittle skeletons. Yet, before the devastation, one
last time of glory. Like fire creeping south, the
flaming forests are extinguished turn by turn,
and out ahead of the cold fly a thousand, ten
thousand, a million migrants. Nights are vibrant.
Wings across the hunter's moon. Days are hectic.

Nights
are
vibrant.
Days are
hectic.
The
sacrifice
begins.

Shorebirds swoop and settle to scribble quick tracks in the sand before flying again. The canary grass gallops in golden waves when the wind is up, and the marsh ripples in brown and green currents of color. Billowing green willows are threaded with the gold of dying leaves.

The sacrifice begins. Ducks of Canada are first to the white linen altar for ritual feasts which will be repeated and repeated as the year grows older, on down and down across the countryside to the Gulf and beyond. Now, the first hunting horn, perhaps in Virginia. Now, hounds baying a wolf in Manitoba, a coyote in Dakota, a raccoon in Wisconsin, a possum in Florida.

Sharply blue water gets a flotilla of birch leaves tanned and curling at bow and stern.

Time for the fall shuffle. Cottontails move from open fields to brushy edge areas. A fox comes off the hillside den site to better hunting in the marsh. Squirrels dare rivers to cross where there is more mast. Raccoons move down from wooded hills to where meandering creeks hide crayfish in the meadow. Mink dens are deserted as young go forth to forage. Now, for them, any hole is home. And nights, young coyotes quarrel over a first kill. Smoke on the wind and a tear, perhaps, in an oldster's eye, because he remembers when everybody burned leaves during other Octobers, and he ran on young legs to a glade to look up as wild geese came clamoring.

One day a cold rain comes. Spirits sink until a drying wind has them soaring again like new smoke from old, smoldering fires. Slowly, the drying wind boxes the compass, until it holds steady out of the north. Grass gallops, reeds bend, rushes flag and flutter. Colder, colder. Biting. Prophetic wind. Winter's warning. And can we meet it? Will it be an adventure? The day was when we were stirred to unusual activity. We dug potatoes and stored them in deep bins in dark fruit cellars. Kitchens became canning factories, and across the work-worn tables moved an endless variety of vegetables and fruits destined for jars. Wine-making time, too. Grape juice running rich purple. Bottle homemade ketchup. Hang dill. It was butchering time. Hogs were scalded and hams hung. The sausage machine stuffed spice and meat into scrubbed white casings. Like chipmunks, we made last, frantic efforts to see that we were adequately provisioned for winter. With every quart of berries, every side of bacon, came a feeling of solid security.

Life has changed, but perhaps we have not changed with it. Perhaps there still exists the need to box the house foundation around with an insulation of leaves. Perhaps, underneath, there still exists the need to stack wood against winter. And now that we burn oil or gas, we are subconsciously bewildered and fearful that we have not made adequate preparation. Perhaps this is why sleet against the window brings a feeling of uncertainty, a foreboding. To assuage our feelings of concern, we rush outside and rake and cut and curry as if to make things right. The gods must chuckle, knowing full well that the trees store needed moisture beneath the leaves they bank, and seeds sprout from the decaying corpses of the plants that bore them. No need to put the comb and brush, or even fire, to the tangled grass. What better winter protection for the seed? What better blanket for next spring's pale, green sprouts.

But my mind is on soup, mushroom soup, so let the rake rust and the barrow stand idle. I am down the trail, eyes searching the underbrush for one of the most abundant of fall mushrooms, *Armillaria mellea*, though I will welcome any edible fungi, whether from bog or high bank, since the kitchen is a gallery where artistic skills can turn a peasant plant into a royal repast. When I discover a colony of brilliant red, orange and in-between ochers, I will harvest only enough for one batch of soup. As I walk, I try to remember the recipe: dice one onion, two cloves of garlic, two stalks of celery. Cover with water and boil. When the celery is partially soft, add sliced mushrooms. Add water sparingly as needed. Cook until almost done. Salt to taste. Just a smidgen of pepper. Then add one-eighth pound of butter or margarine, make a brown sauce of lard and flour, and thicken the soup. Bring to a boil and get a napkin under the chin and enjoy. That is the way I remember it.

It takes concentration to locate mushrooms, and my attention is diverted by a timberdoodle fluttering from a copse; by a ruffed grouse, young of the year, sitting low like a fool hen, confident that I cannot see it. Quite surprisingly, a vixen appears as if by magic from the underbrush. Never turning to look, but knowing surely that I am there, the fox stays but a slingshot ahead. I have been fooled before, so I stop, and so does the fox. She is in glorious winter pelage: groomed and slick; as red across the back as the oak leaves rustling overhead; unwrinkled black stockings; puff of white, silken as milkweed floss, at tail's end. She never turns her head to look, but if I take a step, so does she. So I sit in the trail and wait, and this, as I knew it would, unnerves her. She turns her head just enough to take a quick look, and then darts left, north off the trail.

I rise and go softly in the other direction, stopping often to listen, and then I hear them, whimpering softly, growling quietly. I part an alder and there they are: Three nearly grown kits arguing over the mottled carcass of a snowshoe hare. Instantly the brush parts. It is the vixen. I have not fooled her. Without pausing, she snatches up what is left of the hare carcass and is gone. The kits stand momentarily bewildered. Then, sensing that something is amiss, they run low to the ground, following in her wake, and disappear like sparks on a wind.

The Arctic cold begins its relentless march from northern lakes already iced

I have forgotten about the mushrooms, and return to the trail, and follow it until I can hear the quiet voice of a tiny creek. I know about all the creatures who live there. So I come slowly, and at last, leaning against a swamp ash, I peek around and he is there as I guessed he might be. We know each other well. Five times I have fooled him into accepting a Muskrat's Regret, and five times, on banking him, I have carefully dislodged the artificial fly from his jaw and slid him back into the water. Today, he would not be interested in a fly. Today, he is waiting for a lover. He has built a nest, dislodging stones as big as my fist. Now as he hovers above the hollow, I see he has been fighting. There are small cuts on one side, and a pectoral fin and his tail are ragged, though moving the rocks may have done that.

Injuries aside, his markings are astonishing. His bridegroom colors are reds and blues and whites as brilliant as a brand new flag. His lower jaw has a thrust to it. There is power in the sweep of his tail, as a mud minnow drifts too close. Fifteen inches of passionate fury, I think he might fight me if I stepped into the water. Stepping from behind the ash, I show myself. Backing off a few inches, he eyes me belligerently. I chuckle at such impertinence, and wish I might remind him how I have bested him. But then, perhaps he would like to remind me of

how he broke a leader and wore my fly three days before he could dislodge it by rubbing among the rocks.

"See you in spring," I say.

Turning away, I wonder, as always, if I really will. Then I remember
that it is *Armillaria mellea* that brought me down the trail. But the sun has
gone, and I can hear the wind rattling the bare branches of the high trees,
and I no longer have an appetite for mushroom soup. I turn back. It is
not cold but I shiver. A half-dozen raindrops strike my face. Tomorrow
it may snow. October. A certain sadness. Beginning of the dark days.

⇛ *Watching Place* ⇚

To fully appreciate nature, we should become attuned to even the
slightest change in the voice of the wind, and know in the dark how it
whispers through the tall grass, laughs among the poplars, sighs in the
long-needled pines, and sings through the tight, vibrant spruce. Unless
we come quietly and just sit, even for hours, we will never get to see the
woodchuck or even the rabbit, and never know a fox uses a mouse
meadow unless we happen to see the tracks.

In addition to some skills, appreciating or even getting acquainted
with nature requires a sort of humility. We can best hear, see, feel and
smell the meadow, the forest and the denizens thereof by coming alone,
like supplicants. Then we must immerse ourselves, blend our presence
into the landscape, so we are no more nor any less than the rock or the
bush we sit beside.

For the urban-oriented, this amounts almost to self-denigration and
requires almost too much discipline. But the country boy never feels any
strain, because he lives alongside the slow-growing, and he has learned to
wait for the world to come to him instead of rushing around every corner
to catch up with it. So I know within minutes if my visitor is from the
city or the country just by the way he walks across the lawn. If he has
come to terms with the outdoors, he will pause at the first pond and
stand for a long time to see what is afloat, submerged or using the banks.
Not so the urban-oriented. He will hurry from pond to pond and pause
only if there is some eruption, as from a school of feeding fish or a black
maelstrom of wildly twirling blackbirds.

The urban-oriented will, of course, miss the flitting warblers among
the leaves, the migrating monarchs (unless they are en masse), the watching frog or toad, the tiny dayflowers, the cocoon cemented to a branch,

the spotted ladybug on a cattail stem, the bittern standing like a statue among the reeds. But the urban-oriented may learn, like his country brother, to identify even the voices of the wind if he will take the time and make the trips. No matter if he fails in the beginning to identify what he sees. That can come later. First, it is only necessary to learn to wait. Maybe this is why duck hunters are such a knowledgeable breed. They sit quietly for endless hours, and all of the marsh becomes as intimate as the yarn in the sleeve of an old hunting sweater.

Of course, there are some tricks that help. One is to use a boat as a vantage point. Most things along a shoreline will not object to anything out on the water, and will go on about their business as if they were not being watched. It is wise also to come early and late, because it is then that the night creatures are still to be seen. Always stay home on windy days, because then the wild ones are wary.

If there is a breeze, come to your Watching Place so it is blowing into your face. Then your scent will not be carried to animals in the arena you are watching. Wear neither solids nor bright colors, but such clothing as provides camouflage. Leave off perfumes, hair tonics and other such things as can be smelled at a distance. Wear low boots with soft soles that grip. Always dress more warmly than you might think necessary, for being still any length of time slows the pulse — unless a deer should come daintily stepping or an osprey dive.

If you sit and see nothing the first time, come back anyway, and always to the same Watching Place. Finally, every tree, bush and blade of grass will become so familiar that nothing can invade the premises without your knowing it. Eventually then, the Watching Place will become like an old home in which every floorboard creaks in its very special key, and you can tell about the wind by the way it talks down the chimney, and whether the day is hazy or bright by the coloring of the carpet, or whether the temperature is rising or falling by sounds in the walls. Then, when the Watching Place is as familiar as your own home, you will be outdoor-oriented and not even a spider will be able to leave a new web without your knowing it.

⋙ *Halloween Spirits* ⋘

When I was a boy, Halloween was the time when the good citizens of my hometown battened down the hatches and left the yard and porch lights on from dark to dawn. They were following in a tradition that goes back at least two thousand years before the time of Christ, a tradition that calls for caution on a night when spirits, usually evil, are believed to emerge from the shadows.

During ancient times, the Druids, who were nature worshippers, decorated their homes with fruits of the earth and lighted fires to frighten away evil spirits. The electric lights in my hometown served the same purpose. Still, the evil spirits were not much discouraged, although many of them were sent to church the next day — All Saints' Day — to seek forgiveness for their sins.

What sins? Moving every outhouse that wasn't bolted to a concrete base to a more prominent place, usually a downtown street corner. Running a hay rake up the flagpole in the courthouse square. The pranks were a ritual and if they were vandalism of a sort, it happened but once a year. People came to expect it, and the smart ones nailed down everything of value, leaving just enough property of little consequence lying around to keep the boys busy. Always then, on November 1, the day after Halloween, Main Street looked like a junkyard struck by a cyclone.

Except one year. That memorable year, Main Street, except for a few soaped windows, some junky lawn furniture strewn about and a dilapidated old sofa obviously put out by someone hoping it would be taken, was clean and clear. Townspeople could not believe it, not until school opened and the mouth-to-mouth telegraph system began to clickety-clack. Then they marched off to school to see for themselves. And, sure enough, there on the main stage of the high school assembly hall, which was on the second floor, was a sight to behold: A litter of eight piglets and their huge sow, all in a big crate in the back of a huge lumber wagon with iron-rimmed wheels and a heavy wooden tongue so long it draped stiffly out over the stage into an aisle. Magnifique! Especially since the doors of the school had been double barred and padlocked. Magic? That was what it looked like.

Of course, it was not magic but a feat of engineering that still stands as one of the finest freelance efforts ever successfully handled by the young Halloween spirits. Word spread fast about how the spirits had taken the wagon apart. How then, piece by piece, they had hauled it up the fire escape with block and tackle to the platform outside the second-story window. How the crated pigs followed the wagon parts. How the wagon was reassembled and the crated hogs bedded down in the wagon box. Quite a crowd had gathered in the assembly room when the school superintendent finally took the stage. Almost shouting to be heard above the sow's grunts and the squealing of the piglets, he read a list of names.

"You boys," he said, "will take the wagon apart and remove it down the stairs, through the front door and reassemble it in the street. As for the rest of you, you will meet with your teachers at the courthouse square. You will then clean up the streets. Furthermore, this routine will be followed every November first from now on. The School Board has so ordered."

It was then the Halloween spirits knew they had been set up. They knew the farmer's horse had gone conveniently "lame" and had to be unharnessed alongside the fire escape. They knew the hawser, the block and tackle and all the tools needed to do the job had been planted in the toolbox beneath the wagon seat. And they realized that one of their elders had surely planted the idea by mentioning that "by morning the kids will have found some way to get that wagon inside the school."

The Halloween spirits had been conned. They had blindly taken the bait. And from that time forward, Halloween began its abysmal descent from the one night of the year when evil spirits made a shambles of my hometown to a night of trick-or-treat — when all you had to worry about was alum in the apples, laxatives in the bubblegum or a dose of evil-tasting salts in the soda pop.

⋙ *Death of Dream* ⋘

I come through the autumn woods and break out precipitously into a clearing to look out on the debris of a man's dream. I approach with sadness and in awe. There, with axe and adze, are logs, gift of the forest, notched to rise tier on tier. A touch of class, shingles, each hand-shaven. A man's castle. I hesitate because it is no small thing to leaf through the diary of another's dreams, especially when that dream has moldered and is turning to dust.

The naked windows and the vacant door tell the story even before I feel the stones of a forgotten path beneath my boots. Still, I must go in, and it is with an almost sacrilegious feeling that I poke about in the old bedroom, wondering what words of love may still be hovering like lost echoes. From a crack in the floor, I retrieve a button black with age. Rubbing the button on my sleeve, I am startled to find a quick shine. With my red handkerchief I clean and polish until the mother-of-pearl catches a slant of sun through a crack in the roof and shines as brilliantly as the day it was some woman's prized possession.

In the kitchen, below a leaning sink of decaying cedar, I kneel where an animal has left a smooth trail through the dust, and I wonder if the dark marks are water stains or tears. Most of the morning I piece together clues to the laughter and sorrows, solitude and sweat, success and the ultimate failure that changed the place from a living home into a crumbling cabin.

Poke and pry. Pick and pluck. Scatter, sort and search. A child's shoe, sole worn through. A picture so faded I cannot make out the faces. A rag which, when I shake it, becomes a tattered shawl. A torn calendar page with the date, April 1, 18 ... I cannot read the rest. At last I can no longer bear the forsaken feeling. Deeply depressed, I walk across the crumbling boards, through the door and out into the light. Dejected, I thrust my hands deep into my pockets and feel the button. I bring it out and hold it up, and the sun finds pink as well as shining ivory. Between my fingers it becomes a shining talisman, epitome of perseverance. I walk away, and the hope grows that the man and his family found some other forest, and that this time their dream came true.

⋙ *The Magic of Books* ⋘

It still offends me to see the name of one of my favorite authors on the cover of a mutilated paperback awaiting oblivion in a trash can. When I was young, no book ever was thrown away, and few childhood sins were as serious as dog-earing a page to mark the place at which to resume reading. I am not sure what engendered my respect for books. Necessity may have been the reason, because I can remember a year when textbooks were in such short supply that two and three children shared the same geography or arithmetic books. Needless to say, a thumbprint was enough to invoke a reprimand, and a torn page reason enough to bring on corporal punishment.

Still, I think it was something more, because necessity, though it may ensure compliance, rarely ensures respect. My guess is that it was attitude, the attitude of some of my early teachers and the attitude of my mother, an omnivorous reader until, at a relatively early age, she went blind. Though memory is untrustworthy, since romantic thinking has a way of wanting to take over, I still can see my mother, long after she no longer could read, sitting with a book in her lap. So it likely was a combination of attitudinal forces, none more powerful than that invoked by the school principal, Oscar Bauer.

Our principal's office was on the second floor among the high school classrooms, and he rarely ventured down to the first floor, where grades one through eight held forth, unless his mission was to reinforce discipline. One time, however, he came carrying a book instead of his scepter, a sturdy yardstick. It must have been a very special book, though I cannot even remember its title or who wrote it. What I remember vividly, however, is the smell of the leather binding. So, even to this day, fine leather has the odor of wisdom for me.

He held the book up for all to see, and the gist of his lecture was that pearls of wisdom should come in a proper package, just as a rare and beautiful diamond should rest on plush, purple velvet. Then the book was passed from pupil to pupil. We were cautioned not to open it but to look, feel and smell. It was an elegant book of embossed leather, cool to touch. It felt soft yet strong as the rippling hide of a moving horse. It smelled old, yet it smelled new, not musty as old things often do.

While the book passed from desk to desk, Bauer talked about how the words of those from centuries ago were ours to ponder because of the magic that is a book. "More than any other thing," he emphasized, "it is the book that has brought humankind from the dark ages to these days of enlightenment."

But what I remember most about that day is how the fine leather felt beneath my fingers, and how it smelled. Perhaps that is why I decided to have a library of my own, and though I never obtained any leather-bound volumes, I accumulated a few good books. During the Depression, I had my books shipped via freight train after I arrived in Los Angeles. Unfortunately, my first little library of books became forfeit when I could not scratch up two dollars to pay the weekly rent on my room.

Since then, books have poured in on me. Reference books and fiction. Biography and poetry. Astronomy and archeology. Mystery and romance. Philosophy and fantasy. A few are excellent. Many are good. Too many should not have been published. And in some, the typographical errors offend me on almost every page. A bibliophile would call my library trash. Still, I keep them all, and only sometimes do I wish they were all great books bound in fine leather.

As for the discarded paperback in the trash can, I tell myself how wonderful it is that modern printing and distribution have made books available to all, even the most deprived, because they are often cheaper than food. Surely, out of that, something good must surface.

⇒⇒ *Ghosts of the Past* ⇐⇐

Life treads on life, and heart on heart;
We press too close ...
To keep a dream or grave apart.
ELIZABETH BARRETT BROWNING

The marriage, sixteen years ago, was a joining not just of two people, but of two families. The five children, ages four to twenty, gathered wildflowers for the fireplace mantel in front of which we would exchange vows. They wore their most beautiful dresses. Their faces were scrubbed and their hair brushed until it glistened. The house was cool and fragrant. Bird songs came through the open windows on a soft breeze. Waukesha County Judge William G. Callow was gracious. His words, though official, were comforting with their promise of happiness ahead. The ceremony went beautifully until it was time for the oldest daughter to sing, "Oh, Promise Me." Instead, tears welled up in her eyes, the words would not come, and for a breathless moment, it seemed as if even the birds stopped singing.

The ghosts had arrived. But, of course! How could they have stayed away? They were a beautiful part of the past. They belonged. What we were, each of us, was in large part a result of their sacrifices and their love. We had all agreed we would not, could not, forget them, love them less. But now, without warning, as our families were to be joined, it seemed for one terribly upsetting moment that we were shutting them forever out of our lives. Judge Callow, sensing the sudden sadness, said quietly: "This is a new beginning. Now if you have the ring ... " Later, when we piled into two cars to drive to the restaurant for the family wedding dinner, the mood remained somber.

At the long table, the conversation was cordial, but not convivial. Not until the wedding cake came and the orchestra began to play: "Happy birthday to you. Happy birthday to you ... " did the emotional logjam break, the tension melt. We laughed until tears came. Happy birthday? Well, judging by the ages of the bride and groom and the passel of kids surrounding them, I suppose it was a natural mistake. Now, everyone talked at once. Regrets for things gone, and fears of things to come, were swept away on a wave of merriment. The yearning for two people who had died moved close to its proper place among memories.

Not that there would be no more tense times. And, even as we parted, the children in one car and Gwen and I in another, the mood, if not somber, was subdued. Our honeymoon was to be a one-night event. It was Saturday, and I was scheduled to go on a magazine assignment more than a thousand miles north to Saskatchewan. We would stay in Milwaukee for the night. But, on arrival, there was no room at the inn. It was Saturday night, the Packers were in town, and I had not made reservations. Finally, on Wisconsin Avenue, a desk clerk said, "Well, we've got one room, but I don't think you'll like it."

I looked at my new wife. "Any port in a storm?" She nodded. The bellhop left us at the door without waiting for a tip. We opened the door and stepped in. We found the light switch, and batteries of lights glared down on more than an acre of shiny, bare floor. The only visible furniture was a single, folding bed standing tiny and inconsequential in the center of a mammoth convention hall.

We stood bedazzled and bewildered. Then Gwen asked, "Shall we dance?" We roared with laughter until our sides ached. After a tour of the place, we prepared for bed, each in a snack bar at opposite ends of the hall, while conversing on house phones, since it was easier than shouting across a room that was longer than a football field. In night clothes, we met in the middle of the room and sat together on the bed. Windows went all the way from the floor to a high ceiling, and there were no drapes. The lights and the roar of Saturday night traffic on the avenue gave us the feeling of being in bed on the median strip between two flowing freeways of cars.

Perhaps not, but I thought I heard two ghosts snicker. Except for the comic relief, you might say it was something less than an encouraging beginning. And, when we got home the next afternoon, the children were already quarreling. So they, at least, were settling down, working out the pecking order, so the days might mold themselves more comfortably into weeks, months and years.

It was not easy. It took awhile for me to remember to leave my shoes on the sun porch before tracking across the carpeting. Gwen learned, too, how much I hated spinach but relished oysters. I straightened out her checkbook and did all the accounting, and she learned to use a chain saw. I hung my muddy clothes in the basement. She stopped drying her lingerie in the bathroom. I wrote. She researched. And the ghosts of the past faded until they were no longer ghosts, but old friends about whom we often talked. That wedding was a long time ago. All the children are adults. There are teenage grandchildren. And at the wedding anniversary now being planned, perhaps we will ask our oldest daughter to sing the song, "Oh, Promise Me." This time there will be no tears. Because, you see, the promises made so many years ago have been kept.

⇛ *A Chilling Verdict* ⇚

Interlude: An owl holds court. Herons answer to jury duty. Ducks gather to give witness. The verdict is written in fine lines of frost. The owl came on my first call to perch above me in my favorite oak. Black-capped night-herons, looking for a night camp, accepted my invitation to rest, not with but near the owl. And a duck flock, little more than a swift shadow on sizzling wings, veered down, when asked, and splashed out of the night sky on pond waters beneath my knoll.

Together we wait on the moon, which is a glow along Horizon East. Sometimes one of the ducks splashes, and a gabby hen invites down a passing shadow. Sometimes the herons mutter in throaty gutturals. Only the owl remains silent, motionless except for its head, which swivels slowly like a feathery vane in a lazy wind. The moon rises blushing, then regains its composure to turn white enough for reading frost's forecast in fine lines on bending grass.

It is time. The night is bright. The herons fluff, sleek back their feathers and, complaining, lift to continue south in single file. The ducks, on some secret signal, vault aloft, circle to check for stragglers, then in a bundle follow the herons. I look up. The owl is gone. But I know where: to another oak that guards a glade where he can glide down through moonbeams to catch mice.

I walk off my knoll, through a shadowy cedar aisle, across a narrow causeway between ponds, to a marsh. On a footbridge above the creek I sit in a leafy amphitheater of billowing willows. At first nothing, nothing except shine and shadow changing places with movements of the trees against the moon. Downstream, rushes and reeds finally shiver, then part, and here comes my first visitor. It is a raccoon, and with talented paws it begins fingering the creek bottom for crayfish. I squeak through pursed lips. The coon, half grown, lifts its head. I squeak again. Eyes bright as white stones, the raccoon forgets crayfish and comes humping toward me. An air current betrays me. The raccoon retreats. I squeak. It stops, looks back as if puzzled. It shrugs. I swear it shrugs. Then it concentrates on feeling for crayfish and moves slowly through the shallows out of sight around a bend.

Hearing a splash, I turn. A muskrat's shiny mahogany head emerges as a silvery vee. Fur glistening, the muskrat comes ashore, digs at the base of a reed, and then begins nibbling with teeth as white as the root it devours. One root, two roots, then a shadow from above. The muskrat dives. Ripples run in rings and are lost. The pond and the creek are calm. I turn, but the raccoon has not come back.

Between my legs a moth flutters in a web stretched between bridge boards. I rescue it, but too late. I pinch it dead and toss it on the creek current. Like a lance, a fish darts from beneath a bed of cress. It positions itself downstream from the floating moth. It waits, then lifts. The water dimples. Moth and trout are gone.

The moon no longer looks soft but brittle, metallic. And now I leave tracks. Frost has whitened the grass. Ahead, a cottontail is a darting shadow on the trail. It spurts off into a bramble patch, leaving behind only pawprints. On a milkweed pod bursting with silk a bug-eyed grasshopper moves, perhaps for the last time. The cold will congeal its juices. By morning it will be dead.

Where the trail turns up onto the road, a shadow crosses. It is a skunk on what is perhaps its last foray before going below. I see it beneath the pines. It sees me and waits to see how brave, or how foolish, I am. "Keep going skunk," I say, "because it's later than you think."

As I approach the house, the Old Dog likely smells me in his sleep. He comes from the kennel, tail somewhat less than enthusiastic. "Cold, old boy?" His tail droops in agreement. The frost is pinching my vulnerable lungs. I go inside, grateful to come to my bed and my partner's warmth. For a time I watch the moonlight move across the wall from picture to picture. I hear geese, and they are high and far, far away. I hear a mouse. It, too, has read the frost's forecast and is glad to be between walls. Even the house, though only boards — bones, if you will, of once-living trees — shrinks from the cold. As the wood contracts, it creaks to close cracks. Old, old, in settling it groans.

The sound awakens Gwen. "Your feet are cold," she says.

"I know. By morning there'll be ice in the inlets."

As if on cue, the furnace kicks in.

⋙ *A Mucky Duel* ⋘

A cold night. An open fire. Friends. A warm drink. Time to remember. Time for a hunting story. The hunt took place in autumn 1938 at

Horicon Marsh. It was only a few years after the dam was finished and closed to back up water and create the great, lush oasis that eventually became a home and halfway house for hundreds of thousands of water-fowl. An early, wet spring that year produced a bumper duck crop on the nesting grounds to the west. Then a drought settled in. By fall the great duck factories of the Dakotas and Canadian provinces became pockmarked with crusty craters into which the ponds and lakes seemed to have seeped away, right through cracks in the mud. Great hordes of ducks, fleeing the dusty barrens, moved east, many into Wisconsin.

For Wisconsin hunters, and the ducks, it was a homecoming at Horicon. Central Wisconsin had escaped the drought and, that fall, water behind the dam backed up out of the Horicon Marsh ditches and river channels into the poplar stands and beyond, into the pastures. So the ducks came by the tens of thousands, and I knew whereof my great-grandfather spoke when he talked of flocks hiding the sun. It was enough to bring my brother, Bun, home from college, and me back for a short vacation from newspapering.

In hip boots, we waded the poplar stands, and it was no challenge to kill a limit of ten birds. As usual, when we were together, the old sibling rivalry surfaced. We had to make the next hunt a contest, not only between the ducks and us, but between each other. Under our rules, we each took ten shotgun shells into the marsh. We agreed to kill only drakes. If by accident we killed a hen, it would be subtracted from the score. So a bag of five males and one hen would count as four points. Ten, of course, was the perfect score.

I collected six drakes and one hen with my ten shells, for a score of five. Bun was still among the poplars when I came out, so I went to the sheltered nook next to a rock pile where we had agreed to meet. The sun felt good, and I fell asleep. When I awakened, it was dark. I sat a moment, listening. Then I called out. All I got was frenzied quacking from the mal-lards in the marsh. I stayed by the rock pile for an hour. Having no shells to sound a signal, I called out at regular intervals. Finally, I walked up the slope and down the lane to the farm where we had parked the car. The car was still there. The farmer had not seen Bun. The two of us went back to the marsh, built a fire, and waited. After a couple of hours, the farmer suggested we call the sheriff.

"He may have fallen into a peat burn," the farmer said, voicing a fear I had felt right from the beginning. Some of the peat burns were more than ten feet deep and thirty feet across. Cattle had perished in them. In the dark, it might be difficult to avoid them. Soon the sheriff and three deputies arrived. We began shooting and blowing the sirens as signals. An hour went by, and nothing. I thought echoes might distort sound direction and suggested we tie oil-soaked rags to a windmill at the farm and light them to put out a beacon. We were about to start back for volunteers to begin a search when the farmer said, "Listen!"

It was a voice, heard above the clamor of the ducks. We shouted and shot our guns. Then Bun emerged from the trees, and in the beams of the flashlights he looked like a snapping turtle just up out of the mud after a winter of hibernation. He had lost his hat. His boots bulged with water. His face was plastered with mud. We helped him to the rock pile, where we gave him a drink from a bottle provided by the sheriff. I lit a cigarette and gave it to him. Another drink and he was talking.

He had lost his way and then had gotten stuck on the edge of a water-filled peat burn. We waited for the rest of the story but instead of continuing, he turned to me and asked: "How many drakes? What's your score?"

I told him I had scored five.

He grinned, then nudged his bulging hunting coat. I pulled the flap and shook it. Nine drakes rolled out.

All I could manage to say was, "Well, it isn't a ten!"

He smiled through the mud, reached into a pocket and pulled out a shell. Holding it up, he said, "I've got one shot coming. Tomorrow ... ."

⇛ *Moose Country* ⇚

Hudson Bay,
Saskatchewan

This is moose country. Here in the shallow bays among the timbered slopes, the largest of all North American land animals thrusts its long muzzle down for water weeds, and we have come to kill it. Why? He has not harmed us, nor has he any desire to. We do not need his flesh to eat, nor his hide to keep us warm. Nor do we need spreading antlers to hang above the fireplace to bolster our egos when winter has driven us inside, because there are many other ways and many other things which can make us feel more like a man than killing a moose.

Our most immediate excuse is that we come for the same reason other men go to the office every morning. It is our way of making a living —

by catching and killing things so we may write about it. Silly? I suppose so. But probably no more foolish than selling cigarettes, building war planes or washing fast cars.

We have many excuses for killing if there is need for lubrication to salve our consciences. We can point out that if we do not kill and harvest the moose, disease or old age or the wolf will. We can point out that there is as much justice in harvesting a moose for meat as in killing a cow. We might add that if the moose herd were not controlled, it could conceivably destroy its own home, the forest. But when all arguments, valid or invalid, have been examined, we must in final honesty conclude that we kill the moose because still lurking somewhere deep inside is a strong instinct to search out game and, like our naked ancestors, best it.

We are still hunters. We have not come far enough to deny our heritage. At least today we have come far enough so it matters how we hunt. It is becoming proper to hunt by the rules. So it is with moose hunting. There are right and wrong ways to go about it. Some men do it the wrong way, just as some men obtain money the wrong way. Some men search with airplanes and then land and get out and shoot the moose as if it were a cow in a corral. Others meet the moose on more equal terms. They hunt it on foot or in a canoe along rivers and lakes. Then when they finally find it and kill it, they know they have taken only a little advantage.

Hunting the moose brings an ancient satisfaction. During primeval days, killing an animal as large as a moose made a man a hero, and his tribe celebrated for days because there was so much meat. For hundreds of thousands of years, man was concerned almost exclusively with finding meat to keep life in his body. For all but a very short time during his existence, hunting and killing were the most necessary things in life, and the big fires and the feasting that followed were indelibly marked on his brain.

So that is perhaps also why I am up here to kill a moose. Maybe, deep down, I want to crouch in the marsh grass and bellow like a bull moose to see if my challenge will be answered. I know for sure that when a bull answers my challenge, all the little hairs on my body stand on end. I know that adrenaline sharpens my senses. I know my heart beats faster. I know, when that great bull comes crashing through the forest looking for his adversary, that I will hold my breath. Then, when the bull comes charging into the open where I can level the gun and put the sights on his side above where the heart beats, I know there is elation, whether I want to admit it or not. Then I am the hunter, as were tens of thousands of hunters before me, and I am satisfying that primeval desire to be a hero at the campfire around which there will be great feasting.

Once the bull is down and there is blood on the grass, the feeling quickly leaves. My brush with civilization comes to the fore, and I feel sorry for the moose and even for myself. Now I no longer feel like the great hunter. And some day, a hundred thousand years hence, descendants of mine will wonder how, in the first place, I could shoot the moose.

⫸ *The Lesson of Eekim* ⫷

On a cold, clear morning a few days ago, Eekim, the tawny Chesapeake with the head of a lion, was unable to rise from his bed when fresh water was carried to the kennels. Now he has gone to join the buried in the long rectangular cemetery shaded by tall spruce, fragrant lindens, ancient apple and mulberry trees, and ground cover, which in season includes wild asparagus, rhubarb, hollyhocks, wild roses, violets, goldenrod and many more wildflowers.

As a hunter, Eekim would probably rank last on the achievement chart listing the scores of dogs who, during a lifetime, have accompanied me to the marshes, fields and forests of this continent. Eekim never got to know about the sharptails, ruffed grouse, fat mallards, Hungarian partridge, pheasants, quail, cottontails, or raccoons, and it was obvious that he could not have cared less. If he had any talents, one was as a fisherman. Bluegills, green sunfish and the large goldfish that swim in the crystal waters of Blue Pool drove him into a frenzy when they surfaced to slurp floating pellets, a commercial fish food. Then, he would cock his huge frame much like a gigantic cat getting ready to spring on a victim, and execute a power dive that catapulted him down, down among the schooling fish.

It did not matter that he probably averaged but one fish in one hundred tries. His zeal never diminished, and even when he could barely walk he could forget the misery in his old bones each time the fish came from all directions to gang up at feeding time. He would even go off the diving board, except we rarely sprinkled pellets there, since his entry into the water from that height was flesh-pounding punishment.

Still, his principal role in life was not fishing, but loving. He was not a lover of other dogs, but of his children, the Little Lakes Rebels, whom he adored. They returned that love with succulent tidbits, and a daily grooming that triggered eye-rolling ecstasy when the stiff brush went through his curls to scratch his belly.

And, lest we forget, there were the muskrats. He hated them with a snarling passion ever since a trapped animal slashed his nose while he was still a bumbling, big-footed pup. So, in his lifetime he accounted for a fair share of 'rats, and for this we were grateful, since the animals have cost us thousands of dollars in damaged dikes. He dug them out of their bank burrows with such ferocity as left him with a mouthful of stubby teeth, broken on roots and rocks as, with almost insane savagery, he persisted until there was a dead 'rat on the bank to be carried to the house by one of the other dogs.

For those who came this way often, he was a regal front lawn adornment, looking like a stone lion. And for those who did not know him for the cream puff that he was, his presence put mischievous interlopers scurrying, since his jaws looked massive enough to sever a leg with one bite.

In the beginning I tried, of course, to show him what was expected of a retriever. Then, though in an astounding record ten days I trained his black kennel mate, a Labrador named Buck, to sit, heel, take a line and obey hand signals, Eekim would have none of it. Only Rebel tears kept me from sending him off to become someone's house dog.

Illness had me confined to the house on the day he died and was buried. Mary, the youngest Rebel, had cut classes at Madison to come home, and I watched from a window as she and Gwen dug his grave, wrapped him in a shroud, and put him to rest. Now Buck, a great-great-grandson of our yellow Lab who had been called Bucko, is alone in the kennels built to house a dozen. For days after Eekim's demise, Buck would not eat. So there was another who, despite the Chesapeake's shortcomings as a field dog, held him to be something of a fine fellow.

It seems I cannot weep anymore, but I am sure Gwen and the girls shed enough tears to make up for that. Not that I didn't feel sad, but more important, I was reminded once again that each of us, no matter how seemingly common and ordinary, has talents which, upon reflection, are very special. The tragedy is that it takes death to trigger such reflections as recognize and appreciate a person's or dog's contributions to the little world in which she or he orbits.

So, I know already that on a warm, summery evening, as I sit under starlight on the banks of Blue Pool listening to a hooty owl whimpering in the big burr oak, it will be my memory of Eekim that comforts me in these, my waning years. Love, it seems, is a gift more precious than talent, because love has a way of living even after death.

⇛ Some Questions ⇚

I wonder: Would I still be content to look for hours at the natural world beyond my window if television had come into my life fifty years earlier? If my mother had not been such a precious person, would I have such reverence for womanhood? Would I continue to be fascinated by the flight of a duck had I not seen one limp and lifeless on a boat seat after I had shot it? Would I still think the spider's web wondrous if we had left Earth for the moon fifty years earlier?

Could I weep, if no one had ever wept for me? If I had never held a baby, raised a child, guided a graduate, would I still hope for the world? If I had never stood in a bread line, would I still savor each meal, value each morsel? If I had never lost a partner, would I so treasure my wife? If I had never been compelled to kill a man, would I be so outraged by murder? Could I understand another's despair if I had never despaired?

If I had never stood in awe as the sun set, would I anticipate the sunrise? If I had never frozen my face, would the fire on my hearth still fascinate me each time the flames put bright tongues up the chimney? Would I welcome rain if I had not known the Dust Bowl? Or watch for clear skies if I had never been caught in a flood? Would I be a thief if my grandmother had not punished me for stealing a penny? Could I forgive if I had never been forgiven?

If I had never been locked inside looking out, would I know about freedom? If I had never been parched by thirst, would I know how cool and precious water really is? If I had never been a loser, would I want to be a winner? If I had never relied on the horse, would the automobile still seem magical, the airplane miraculous? Could I love, if I had never been loved?

If I knew beforehand what would happen, would I look forward to tomorrow? Would I be so incensed by the crimes of the spoilers if I had never known the green-and-blue beauty of my river before they began to pollute it? Would I continue to be comforted by my bed if I had never slept on hard ground? If I had never seen the other side of the mountain, would I be satisfied with my corner of the world?

Could I know joy, never having been sad? If I had not wished upon a star before learning how forbidding and lifeless they are, would they still shine for me? If I could conceive of space beyond space, would this world of mine still be the center of my universe? Would I know the majesty of a virgin forest if I had never seen one burn? If my letters had never been censored, would I understand the privilege of freedom of speech? Could I be brave if my father had been a coward? Would I be writing this if a certain professor had not said: "You can do it if you're willing to pay the price."?

I wonder.

≫ *Eager for Winter* ≪

Beautiful as summer can sometimes be, in October I walk woodland trails eager to feel the cold sting of a winter's wind. No season stimulates like winter. Hearing the first frost crunch beneath my boots, I sense the adrenaline beginning to sing vigorous songs in the heightened awareness of storms to come. Perhaps it all hearkens back to prehistoric times when a man had better be at his best in winter or perish. Now, having little need to battle the elements, we turn this survival strength into other channels of endeavor.

Or go back but half-a-century. It took some spirit to get a Model T started on a cold morning, or to get the stiff harness over Old Dobbin's back. The snow had to be shoveled, and there were many wood- and coal-burning stoves, and furnaces with reluctant drafts, and such an accumulation of ash to be disposed of. Physical fitness programs were never necessary.

Perhaps this need to meet and overcome obstacles when winter comes is still present in humans, even though our streamlined existence has all but eliminated worry about the weather. In summer, we are energetic, no doubt about that, but there is less discipline. Somewhere, deep within our subconscious, there is perhaps the sure knowledge that during the warm days we do not have to struggle to survive.

Coming to the crest of an October hill, I search the sky for low, black clouds carrying snow. It is strange, but I am almost eager for winter. It is sharp and real. Biting and bitter. Reviving memories of how now is the time to fight!

November

DISCONSOLATE ON A BARE BRANCH SITS THE
KINGFISHER. Shining ice covers his fishing hole,
and he must wait on the sun. Then, when the ice
melts, he dives again. One day, of course, the ice
will not melt. Then the fishing bird will be a
blue arrow lancing south. Sometimes his journey
is delayed, as when a high pressure front from
Canada is stalled by a warm front up from the
south.

Grandmother called this "Old Woman's
Summer." Today it is called Indian Summer, a
day, or days and days, of lazy, hazy mornings and
tissue-paper afternoons, tinted blue and glistening with the tinsel of spiders ballooning along on
silvery strands. It is as if the world has gone
under glass. Temperatures lift to summer levels.
Plants revive. Birds en route south pause, and
sometimes even return to old nests where eggs
hatched, and from which fledglings took wing.
Indian summer. Sun warm on bright maple leaves
caught in conifer skirts, shiny as ornaments on a
Christmas tree. Blue blink of aster, gentians in a
wintry brown bog, walnut tree wearing fat, furry
squirrels flattened on branches to absorb the heat.

Indian summer, if a reprieve, it is also a trap.
The flaming wood duck returns to puddle for
acorns where the oak puts branches out over his
favorite pond. People venture afield in short
sleeves. Geese return from more southerly watering places to Wisconsin's winter wheat fields. We
put out decoys to await dawn and ducks. The
sun lifts red, turns silvery in the haze. Robins
sing in the willows. Killdeers call from stubble

It is called
Indian Summer,
days of lazy, hazy
mornings and
tissue-paper
afternoons.

fields. Sandpipers bob and run, bob and run, along the foam fringe of shoreline. A stranded night crawler looks for home. A gold-crested warbler, hardly as large as a walnut, investigates the reeds of a duck blind for any edible thing. On the edges of a narrow sand pit, golden dandelions look like dropped coins.

Beyond gun range, far out on the lake, great rafts of ducks delay their journey south. All across Midwest marshes, hunters doze in their hunting blinds. There is nothing to indicate that before this day ends, the lake and the land will be in the grip of an ice vise.

First warning is a sudden breathlessness. Air is sucked aloft and into the vacuum; winds from all sides clash and create a vortex. Rafting ducks are blown like leaves from the water. Forced north at feather-bending speeds, they are turned back with astounding vigor. Churning air currents send them spinning upward, only to explode their flocks in all directions, like ash from the hot column of a forest fire.

A coyote howls and a fox barks, and the wind catches up their voices and tears them to tatters.

In the time it takes to button a coat, the temperature has dropped thirty degrees. In the time it takes to put on gloves, it drops another ten. But some have no coats and no gloves. Then the snow. Needle-sharp crystals sting cheeks. Everyman's world becomes a tight circle with white, swirling walls. Waves break high over skiffs. Hunters are quickly armored with ice. Geese are slammed to earth. Birds are slammed against buildings and trees. All day the elements battle. Nighttime ends the conflict and the moon looks down on a world of ice.

Indian summer has ended. Surviving mice move from fields to barns and houses. Boats overturned on barren beaches get a covering of rushes as dispossessed muskrats quickly improvise to build another winter home. Suspicious squirrels wait until noon to come down and sort through husks for missed nuts. Pheasants look forlorn as for the umpteenth time they glean an ice-locked field. One last acorn on a roof. Rolling, rattling.

Slowly, the cold retreats. Ice melts in noon suns and freezes again under stars. Slowly, the earth recovers.

Autumn is back on course. Days are cool and nights are cold. Signals rise from fireplace chimneys. Stems rigid as sailing masts, poplar leaves continue creek journeys. Leaves windrace, whispering their excitement. Grapes along fence rows continue to ferment, wine for raccoons. Forked sumac lifts branches bare and bronze as antlers. A single apple bobs from a bare branch.

Ponds wear shawls of mist against the morning chill. Clouds filter sunbeams through their lace. Jealous prickly ash catches thistledown for adornment. Bare roads, as if embarrassed, borrow leaves. Brown ferns prepare fodder for spring's fiddleheads. Reeds stand broken, rushes bent, green mist of asparagus yellows and drips with red berries. In an oak, auburn leaves, never unseated, are ready to rustle all winter.

In a sheltered nook stands one circle of late phlox, lavender diadem. Ivy still clings, a red runner up a green cedar. Acorns are bald, fuzzy topknots gone. A fir cone bristles. Spruce cones wait for the ultimate cold before lifting skirted panels hiding secret seeds. Hawthorn fruit lies scattered like blood drops on brown grass. Spun silver drips from an exploded milkweed pod. Frog and turtle have gone to live burial on pond bottom.

Brown creeper, starting at the base, works up a tree until it reaches the crown and, flying down to the base of another tree, repeats the maneuver. The nuthatch, wedge of blue flint, chooses to start at the top of a tree and come down headfirst. A sapsucker prefers to circle the trunk, and a black-and-white warbler scrambles helter-skelter. Now crow families, having united, come in raucous gangs to communal roosts. Owls are more voluble. A coyote howls and a fox barks, and the wind catches up their voices and tears them to tatters.

Slowly, cautiously, hunters venture forth again. Virginia, Florida, Wisconsin, Montana, hound music, thin from a distance, growing louder and louder to pass beneath a bedroom window in a fury of pursuit. Then, diminishing, growing distant. But hunters remember, and they are wary, though mostly November bluffs with scudding black clouds, angry waters and fits of snowy temper. Mostly, the wind only whines beneath the eaves, nibbles at the shingles.

Even while the bears den, cardinals flutter like red kerchiefs at bird feeders. Late-hatching turtle egg congeals, freezes solid, and who will believe that miraculously, come spring, it will not only thaw but hatch? Blue jays come closer to the house and a cocoon reminds a man that the butterflies will be back.

⋙ *Zzzzzzzp!* ⋘

November, and the saws begin to sing. Wild, snarling, thoughtless saws cutting from this day back through the decades. Soft, whispering saws: hypnotic *zzzzzzzp, zzzzzzzp, zzzzzzzp*. Two men, poetry of muscle in motion as they pull, but never push, pull but never push: *zzzzzzzp, zzzzzzzp, zzzzzzzp*. Far back among the trees. Alone except for chickadees looking for lunch. Alone except for a raven in gargling protest, finding a pinnacle pine from which to watch.

The saw teeth cut quickly through last year. They send sawdust of a decade to sprinkle with white the broken brown bracken in a scandalously short time. Oh, how the years are wiped out. Generation after generation, war after war, storm after storm, peace and plenty of rain. *Zzzzzzzp, zzzzzzzp*, the saw eats history.

In minutes, the saw is among the rings that mark the years of my youth, when people of the Roaring Twenties swore civilization would flounder on the immorality of its young. Another minute and it is sawing through Flanders fields where "poppies blow between the crosses row on row." Swiftly to the turn of the century with its sawdust wars, miners' strikes and troops shooting down labor's efforts to unite and break the monopolistic grasp of a hardcore of wealth and power and greed.

Back to the Chicago Exposition of 1893, where George W.G. Ferris stands and surveys with pride the first Ferris wheel in operation. Back, back, past the backyard where Henry Ford tinkers with his flivver. Down the bloody roads of a South promised reconstruction and given destruction. Down to a rail-splitter who changed his fur cap for a high hat. Finally to the core when the tree was a sapling, though Wisconsin was not yet a state.

Now the saw slows. It is nearing the notch. *Zzzzzzzp, zzzzzzzp, zzzz . . .* the tree groans. It leans, tries to hang on, to straighten itself. There is a sigh and then a swish and crashing death. Nearly two centuries. *Zzzzzzzp.*

⋙ *Bracing for Winter* ⋘

Only the young can brush aside November as an interlude between the full summer of life and the fresh, crisp challenge of winter. The Old Man knows better. In November, he stays abed a little longer each morning, and goes to his easy chair a little earlier as the day wanes. He has seen the winter cripple and kill. He knows none are exempt. Then, if this is not the winter of departure, the time is not distant.

So he recounts forced marches of twenty miles through thirty-below-zero weather, to shoot a buck in the last light. He tells of trapped muskrats chopped from fields of solid ice, sledded home to thaw, and of a pike up from an ice hole, its fins brittle with frost on the first and final flop. He remembers aloud binding himself to an island tree to sleep while water rose above his waist. He speaks of the grizzly that crushed his rifle stock in a single bite, while he watched from his pine tree retreat. He talks of slides, shale and snow, near an eagle's aerie. There was the winter of the year when frost buckled the basement floor. There was the winter of the year deer stood in the yard with the cattle, while he wheeled steaming manure from the barn.

The young grow weary of his tales. They nod when trapped into listening. They find other places in the house. Grandpa sits alone, winter crowding at the window. Little do they know that Grandpa is not boasting, nor does he care whether they listen. He is talking to impress no one, but only parading ghosts of winters past, to revive what courage he once had, and to strengthen his faltering spirit so it may come to one more springtime.

⋙ *You are Invincible* ⋘

To my daughter Mary:

I could not sleep last night because I was thinking of all the things I wanted to say before you left home this morning to be swept back into a whirlwind of university activities. I even tried rehearsing my lines but then, while the rest of the house slept, and we were sitting in the quiet kitchen breakfasting, all I could think to say was, "Did you brush your teeth?" Now you are upstairs finishing the packing, and there is only the ticking of clocks to break the stillness. And I find I lack either the courage or the talent to marshal in logical sequence my reasons for believing that you, because you are a woman, may some day become a part of that female army that will save this good earth.

We men — boys, really — will never do it. If anything should have convinced you of that, it was the recent posturing of politicians. Did you ever see so many role players, such a political Punch and Judy show? But it isn't the boys I want to talk about.

I do not believe it was an accident that the French gave the Statue of Liberty a female form. I do not believe it was an accident that a blindfolded woman holds the scales of justice. I am sure sailors refer to their ship as "she" because safe passage is synonymous with womanhood. And have not the peoples of almost every culture referred to our world as Mother Earth? So why, you ask, have women waited so long to assert themselves? To me, the answer is simple. In a hunting society on a thinly populated, pioneering planet, the male had to dominate lest the female be forced to give up her role of incubating and rearing the generations necessary to inhabit the earth.

Well, that day has passed. The world is overpopulated. Hunters are as unnecessary as guns. Strong minds are preferable to strong backs. Hairy chests are necessary only on apes. But do not tell us, the hunters, who since the beginning of time have dominated through brute strength, that our manly skills are no longer necessary for survival. Do not tell us there is no longer any need to kill, because, not having tigers or bison, we will kill one another and collect the flags of nations instead of the skins of animals.

Unless you stop us. Unless, having been custodian of the home fires and little children, you now bring the tender sanity our world needs to survive. Ruthless though you have sometimes had to be, mostly you fought not for your life or the life of the world, but for the life you clutched to your bosom. But be wary of us. For centuries we have preached equality, and yet it is not so many years since a French woman was unable to have a personal bank account, or sell her own belongings, or seek employment, unless she had her husband's consent. Be wary of us, because it was not so many years ago that Chinese men were first prohibited from beating their wives. Be wary of us, since your grandmother, my mother, was not permitted to vote, and if she had showed an ankle, bobbed her hair, smoked a cigarette or entered a tavern, chances were good she might have been run out of town.

But Mary, your day is dawning. How you and your girlfriends around the world conduct yourselves will determine how quickly you will come to that place in society where the fate of the good earth is in your hands. Perhaps, since for centuries your sex has had to play second fiddle, you are frightened that you may not have the courage for it. Well, take heart, and think on what Aristophanes, writing before the time of Christ, thought of women: "There is no animal more invincible than a woman, nor fire either, nor any wildcat so ruthless."

Or consider the opinion of Matthew Arnold, the 19th century English poet: "If ever the world sees a time when women shall come together purely and simply for the benefit and good of mankind, it will be a power such as the world has never known."

Love and good luck,

Dad

⫸ *End of the Trail* ⫷

The Wisconsin deer hunt will not become history until Old Leather Stocking corrals relatives and friends at Christmas to relate how, with his trusty rifle, he brought the antlered King of Bucking Back Ridge crashing to the forest floor. Well, I have a deer story, too. If it is no match for Leather Stocking's dramatic rendition, it is at least unique. Because, you see, I did not get the deer. The deer, you might say, got me.

So you may know that I am not exactly a novice, let me say that I have left boot tracks in wild places both below and above our nation's borders, and in at least half the states in between. I have forgotten about many of the deer I have shot, and there are some I wish I could forget. But there was one I remember clearly, and when the moment of truth came, he was not afraid because we both knew I would not, could not, shoot him.

Perhaps it was the strain of the hunt. I had been tracking him for two days. Perhaps it was the mood of the forest: silent, somber, not another hunter for six, maybe eight miles in any direction. Perhaps, as one of my daughters suggests, those stars involved in my destiny had entered into some inexplicably mystic alignment. I do not know, except what I write is true.

TIME:
November 1959

PLACE:
Roadless tract northeast of Summit Lake in Langlade and Forest Counties.

WEATHER:
Windless. Low, gray ceiling. Temperature, twenty degrees. Snow predicted.

FOREST:
Cutover. Grown back to mixed hardwoods, mostly deciduous except for small balsam clumps.

TERRAIN:
Fairly level with a few swamp pockets and some low ridges.

UNDERGROWTH:
Meager to medium.

HUNTING CONDITIONS:
Excellent. Two-day-old snowfall of six inches on the ground.

I saw the buck jump a fire lane shortly after dawn on the second day of the hunt. He was a ten-pointer in good flesh, and I decided at once that he was the animal I was going to hunt. Since the country was too big for organized drives, my hunting partners had no objections when I said I was going to track the buck — to the end of the trail, I hoped. I had been told that northeast of where I had first seen the deer, a roadless wilderness stretched for thirty miles — no large lakes or rivers of any consequence. I hoped, of course, that the buck would not head that way.

Tracking was fairly easy. My buck (I was already calling him *my* buck) left a good trail, and even though it often intermingled with tracks of other deer, and once was joined by those of two fellow travelers, I had no trouble following it. At noon on the first day of tracking, I got a glimpse of my buck. He had not struck out for the Big Country, but had been content to repeatedly circle out and circle back. I was seated on a log eating a sandwich when, from about a hundred fifty yards away, he peered out from behind a small balsam to see what manner of creature was trailing him. My arm stopped, sandwich poised midway to my mouth. Then he was gone, and I finished my lunch.

At dusk, I saw him again. We had come nearly to that place where I had first picked up the trail. He was too far out for a shot with open iron sights, so I satisfied myself with a long look. Even in the fading light, his antlers glowed faintly. It was enough. I marked the spot. My friends had the car motor running and the lights on when I got back. Next morning at dawn I resumed the hunt. Indications were that my buck had browsed but briefly during the night and then bedded down. With me on his trail, he had not slept the previous day.

I had been on the trail for about an hour when I heard him leave his camp in an alder clump. I began to push for an early confrontation, since the prediction was for more snow, and that would have ended the hunt. My buck dawdled, and I saw him a half-dozen times, well out of rifle range. Then, at about ten o'clock, perhaps annoyed, perhaps tiring, he struck out at a killing pace to put some distance between us, and headed straight for the Big Country through which men rarely have any reason to go.

Not once through the day did I stop to eat. Night does not lower into the forest. It creeps upward until only the branches of treetops brighten briefly, even on overcast days. I knew I had come as far as I dared. It was time to turn back. Then, as deer hunters will tell you is not uncommon, quite magically, there was my buck, not more than a hundred feet away, standing open and clear, statuesque as if bronzed. I could have shot him from the hip, without raising my rifle. It was then I saw my image in his eyes.

Had my life depended on it, I could not have shot. I am sure my buck knew. So, with day fading, I started back. Four times I turned to look. He never moved. At the time I considered my decision a weakness, and I excused it by telling myself that it would have been impossible to drag the carcass out without help. And since snow seemed certain, it was unlikely that I could blaze a trail in the dark to direct me back to the tree from which I would have hung my buck.

At midnight, as was our custom when a hunter was late coming out of the forest, shots guided me back to the car.

"Get him?" they asked.

"Hell, no," I said. "Last time I saw him he was heading for Michigan, and judging by the way he was cutting it, he's probably in Canada by now."

So if you come to shoot something, man or beast, avoid his eyes, because you may see your reflection, and then you will forever wonder what part of yourself it was that you killed.

⋙ *Old Shack* ⋘

Dear Mel:

The Old Shack still stands. The food tastes better and old lies are more believable there. The pump still has the sweetest and coldest water in the county, and the beer tap is still in use. Tales are still told of a deer-hunting journalist who waded through the tangle of a tag-alder swamp while friends, who were supposed to be making the drive with him, sat out of sight on a nearby ridge shouting about how tough they were having it. So, you see, you are still part of our history. And now, if you will drop me a reminder, I'll send you a quart of our latest batch of maple syrup."

Barb Helsing and son Jim
Barron, Wis.

Everyone should have an Old Shack. Preferably, it should be a place in the woods. Simmering on the range for the community supper should be a stew of turnips, spices and meat chunks — rabbit, partridge, deer and, if pickings are slim, even porcupine. Though the Old Shack might be anything from a dormitory to a lodge hall, I am thankful mine is the Helsing fishing and hunting shack. Now, when life seems to be cutting me right down to the bone, I give my mind permission to go back to where I sat among the unshaven occupants of the shack to take sustenance for my sagging spirits.

There were no written rules at the Old Shack. But if you went to the beer tap too often in an evening, then the next day, hung over or not, likely you rowed the boat and someone else fished. Or, if it was deer season, you were given that place in the line of drive that would take you through such God-awful country as would make a goat back off. Make the mistake of taking another person's turn on the clothes-drying line above the stove and you might slip into a bootful of water next morning. Shirk kitchen duties and, on coming to the bottom of your bowl of stew, you might find a mouse.

If you were a tenderfoot, you got the worst of everything, whether you deserved it or not. But then, if you did come back and abided by the unwritten rules, you never had to worry that someone might rig the seat and in the dark you would fall through the hole on a visit to the outhouse. We use the word "love" so carelessly these days that I hesitate to label Old Shack camaraderie as such. But for all, male or female, who became regulars on the roster, there was a closeness that only soldiers who fought shoulder to shoulder for each other's lives can understand.

If you are alert, you can see the Old Shack from the road when you go north out of the Sawyer County village of Radisson, with your car pointing toward the Chippewa Flowage. If there is a woman framed in the doorway of the Old Shack, likely it will be Barb. Or, if there is a younger man cutting wood, it may be Jim, her son. Because, as Barb writes, "The Helsings are alive and well in the Northwoods."

Charter members on the Old Shack's roster — the brothers Bob and John Helsing — do not come anymore. But if, as some insist, there is life after death, they have probably made ready a replica of this, their earthly shack. And perhaps, just perhaps, they're wondering what's keeping me.

⇛ Backdoor Bums ⇚

Most gray squirrels at Little Lakes are fat, sassy and even impudent. Instead of getting out among the trees to harvest the fruits, nuts and seeds that ripen in abundance, they sit at the kitchen door waiting for handouts. Gwen, being a sucker for panhandlers, does not disappoint them. Every time the backdoor opens, they sit up and, with front paws folded over furry chests, watch bright-eyed to see what goodies will come flying out onto the turf, a turf they defend against chipmunks and any bird hoping to share the largess. Even when Gwen forgets, they do not forage, but come crawling up the window screens and peek in to remind her that they are hungry.

But down from the house a piece, where the waters of the last pond, Clear Pool, cascade over a dam into Watercress Creek, things are different. Here is a land of reeds and rushes, some spruce groves and many billowing willows. Except for a single butternut tree, there is little to recommend it to a squirrel. This, however, is the land where Skinny Gray Squirrel lives, alone. I come here often on the Gray Ghost, my electric tractor, because it is a fascinating place. I sometimes see bitterns standing motionless, unless a wind sways the rushes. Then the bittern sways with them, hoping I will not notice that it is feathery, that I will think it is just another clump of grass. And there is usually one blue heron measuring at least three feet, standing in the creek, hoping a fish will swim its way.

Ducks come up from the mill pond into the creek — gaudy wood ducks, mallards, sometimes teal — so I keep the creek bottom salted with corn to keep them coming. That corn is a cruelty for Skinny Gray Squirrel. I am sure he can see it beneath six to twelve inches of crystalline water, and all he can do is look. But Skinny is not wasting time wishing for something he cannot get. He keeps hustling butternuts to three caches, and sometimes buries them where a low winter sun softens southern slopes enough to make digging possible, even in zero weather. The butternut is fine fare, unless, of course, you must gnaw through the sharply corrugated shell for each smidgen of nut meat.

But, if there is one thing Skinny does well, it is work. While other squirrels spend much of each day sunning on high limbs or lining up for Kitchen Door Relief, he keeps moving from the time dawn lights up the eastern sky until evening douses the lights in the west. All summer and fall I have watched until I know all his routes through the treetops above the marshlands, open water and brushy jungles where a fox might hide. Here, where Skinny lives, there are no hollow trees. There is no place for a home unless you count a metal wood duck house, which this year had no renters. Skinny has tried every which way to get into that house but, of course, it is so designed that even a coon cannot get a paw through the doorway.

Often, I have been tempted not only to put corn on shore for Skinny, but also to hang a branch by the duck house doorway, so he might be able to get in. It would be easy to do, and charitable, I suppose. But I don't do it. So, of course, he has had to build his own house of leaves fastened to branches on the southern side of a weeping willow. He has had to build well, not only for warmth, but also so he and his home will not be whisked away on the biting breath of a blizzard.

So, why doesn't Skinny leave for more fertile acres? Well, squirrels have territories, and there is the pecking order, and even the bums at the backdoor must defer to the head honcho, usually a big female. And this place is Skinny's Place. So I respect his rights and stay just outside the invisible boundaries of such space as he requires and watch for hours as he performs breathtaking aerial antics. Of course, by now, I know all of his maneuvers. All, that is, except one. And that continues to be a mystery.

In the middle of Watercress Creek, downstream from the dam, is a thicket of brush willow growing out of an old muskrat house. It is surrounded by water, though a willow billows high over it. I have seen Skinny drop five feet from the tree's branches to the brushy island. Yet, after a summer and autumn of watching, I still do not know how he gets ashore again. If I am present while Skinny is on the island, he stays there. No matter how long I wait, he will not move. Sometimes I become so irked I throw a stick. Then I am ashamed. So I retreat for a few minutes, and when I come back, Skinny is high in the big willow.

Though gray squirrels are good swimmers (they have been seen swimming the Mississippi River en masse during years of acorn failure), Skinny is always bone dry. I know he cannot fly or jump far enough to land in the tree. So how? How does he do it? Perhaps I will never find out. It is not important. The important thing is that I know Skinny is ten times as much squirrel as any of the Backdoor Bums who wait for life to hand them a living. I can take heart from that.

⋙ Becoming a Writer ⋘

A lot of young people ask me, "How do I become a writer?" The process is tied up with searching out the truth, particularly about yourself.

It is a worthwhile but difficult experience for anyone. Of course, there is a lot of standard advice for prospective writers. It usually goes like this:

"Words are your tools, so while in school, learn to use them. Set aside an hour every day to sit at your typewriter, even if nothing comes of it. Write about things you know best. Study the masters. Take a course in creative writing. In the beginning, write for your own amusement and amazement, and the day may come when you will be amazed at how you can write to amuse and amaze others.

"If you want to become an author of consequence, be prepared to forget money, friends and even marriage. That is because you will need eight hours a day for writing and another eight hours for a job that will bring in money for food and typewriter ribbons. Forget about traveling to strange places seeking exotic experiences to write about. Enough happens during the ordinary day of every ordinary person for at least a paragraph or even a chapter in a best seller. The trick is to learn to recognize how truly meaningful is every moment of even the dullest day.

"Get a big barrel to hold your rejection slips, unless you have a room to wallpaper. A small envelope will suffice as a file to hold letters of acceptance."

There is more, much more, and it is all good advice for beginning writers. Until recently, I used to run through the list of "dos and don'ts" for youngsters required to write a paper titled, "How to Become a Writer." Lately, however, especially if I see a special spark, I take the tack about seeking out the truth. I am surely not going to live long enough to see whether my new advice is going to produce any writers of merit, or even a few hacks. But since it is an excellent therapeutic exercise, especially for anyone who may need to see an analyst anyway, here goes.

(But first, a word of warning: If you are over age thirty, it likely will not work, since you have already been lying to yourself for so many years you will not know how to be completely honest.)

First, buy a strongbox with a foolproof lock. You cannot let anyone — teacher, parent, spouse, friend — see what you are writing. If someone has access to your thoughts, you will start lying, every time!

Second, write at the end of every day and begin each effort with the salutation: "Dear Diary." Diary, you see, will not tell a soul. But, remember, this will be no ordinary diary but sentences about such deep-down feelings as you would never even whisper to another. It will not be easy. Nothing is more difficult than being completely honest with yourself. So if you hate a schoolmate, your mother, your husband or one of the kids, tell it to Diary. Do not hold back a thing. Try to analyze your hatred. Dig into it until you feel thoroughly ashamed, or you understand it and it dissolves.

At first it will be impossible. Even as young as sixteen, you have probably learned to lie so well to yourself that you will be searching not for truth but for alibis. At first you will do a whitewash job, trying to prove to yourself that you really are not a thoroughly despicable person at times. But, as the months pass and you become satisfied that Diary will keep your thoughts securely locked in the iron box, the truth may begin to shine through.

If already you have decided to forego such agonizing experiences as can come from being truthful, know that hatred is rare and there will be beautiful visions of a bright future, boundless enthusiasm, tenderness, sympathy, kindness, gratefulness, concern, understanding, moments of almost blissful awe. In the beginning, it will be like learning to walk. Time and time again you will fall into cliches, and lie and lie and lie. But then will come the day when you unlock the box to talk to Diary, and the inhibitions will be gone. You will write the truth — good, bad, kind or evil.

Then perhaps, after five or ten years, you not only will be a more splendid person, but also waiting to spill out will be the thousands upon thousands of words you have told Diary. And, who knows, you may have written the book to make you a candidate for the Nobel Prize. Try it. What can you lose?

⋙ *A Tribute* ⋘

Dear Gwen:

How do you put up with it? Whence came this patience? From what depths do you dredge enough courage and strength to daily live with a writer who cannot even find his pencils? Yours must be an uncommon talent, else how could you sweat over a lavish dinner, only to find that your writer-husband has forgotten what he has eaten even before the dishes are done?

You, the tidy one, following a trail of pipe tobacco from bedroom to bathroom, sweeping pipe ashes from the floor wherever your husband leans to tie a shoe, pick up a paper clip, peer at a spider. And then the nights! Up for a glass of milk. Up for a smoke. Up to make some notes.

Up to check a reluctant paragraph. And your beautiful house! Drawings, proofs, carbons, folders, all spread across your best davenport. Newspaper and magazine clippings sorted into piles on the fireplace hearth and mantle. Your coffee table hidden beneath pamphlets, magazines and more clippings. Books spread out all across the floor of the living room, each open to a pertinent page. Boxes of used material by the big chair waiting to be filed. Stacks of magazines in the TV room waiting to be scanned. Letters, letters everywhere. I wonder why don't you just blow your cool and announce, "Well, Mel, I've had it!"

Even your own closet is piled high with carbon copies of book manuscripts — two carbons for every book spilling out into every room of the house, and a filing system in the basement office is crowding the chair, desk and typewriter out into the furnace room. And those pencils everywhere. Thrusting up out of flower vases. Under couch cushions. Even in the bed. And dictionaries, atlases, Bartlett's Quotations, Roget's Thesaurus, Guinness Book of Records, twenty or thirty reference books stacked around the big writing chair. Books, books, books, spilling out of the shelves onto the floor and beneath the TV, stacks and stacks from basement to attic.

And the attic! Bulging with published works in newspapers, magazines and books until you have to squeeze to put your summer coat away for winter. It must drive you up a wall, you who cannot stand to see a spoon placed on the wrong side of a fork, who hates flies because they leave behind specks. How did you ever get trapped? And being trapped, how do you ever tolerate a man who grouses around the house all day in bathrobe and slippers while you tour office supply stores looking for his special silk typewriter ribbon?

Secretary. Sister. Housekeeper. Maid. Wife. Accountant. Lover. Handyman. Mother to a headache, pulled muscle, sore toe. Chauffeur. Yardman. Seamstress. Confidant. Critic. File clerk. Research assistant. Cook. Nurse. Editor. Proofreader. Frontman on the telephone, at the front door and at a cocktail party. Keeper of the kids and the dogs. Sage. Priestly guardian of inspiration. Confessor. What roles you must play in our home, which is a word factory; in a house where even your jewelry box and the flower vase on the kitchen table get notes about the things you must do tomorrow, next week, next year.

How can you tolerate a life that hangs by a paragraph, goes to bed with a question mark, comes barefooted to the cold floor with an exclamation mark? Don't you wish your husband drove a truck? Taught school? Went

to an office? Practiced law? Dug ditches? Certainly I should at least share
my byline with you. Though if I could, I would have you canonized,
except you would be sure to say, "Now what's all this foolishness? Here,
I've cleaned you a pipe. You need an aspirin? Come to bed. Sleep on it.
Maybe by morning it will write itself. Hold me. There. Isn't that better?"

Yes, my love. Oh yes!

⇛ *The Mice Know* ⇚

Mostly, this is a story about mice. And birds. It is also a story about
the day I was born, which happened to be during the coldest winter on
record. What got me skidding off on this tangent were reports of
various TV weathermen trying to explain why the winter this nation just
staggered through was so cold. One weatherman blamed it on sunspots.
Another claimed it was a mysterious misdirection of ocean currents
thousands of miles from American shores. Still another was sure it was
the result of polar electrical disturbances causing a massive shift in upper
air currents.

I am not saying any of them is wrong, or any of them is right. My
quarrel with them is that to a man, they claimed that there was no way of
predicting the winter's severity. They were wrong. I knew it was coming.
The mice told me.

We have lived in this house almost a quarter-century. Each November,
a few mice migrate from the fields to the basement. We trap them, usually
three or four, but never more than half a dozen. Last fall, they kept
coming and coming and coming until we had tossed twenty-eight out the
basement door for the owls and foxes.

Thanksgiving Day, with some of the children home for a visit, I said,
"Things are gonna happen; watch out for this winter."

They said, "Yeah, Dad, we know," and went on attacking the turkey.

Then, in December, the evening grosbeaks, which spend their winter
vacation here, did not come down from their more northerly habitat. Nor
did the crossbills, or the snow buntings, or the redpolls — not a northern bird. At Christmas, with all the kids visiting, I repeated: "Watch out.
Things are gonna happen this winter. The birds know it."

And, of course, the kids said, "Yeah, Dad, we know," and went back
to opening presents.

Then, winter lowered the boom, and I could not wait for my February
birthday, when the kids would be home again, so I could say, "I told you

so!" Well, they all came, and it was a long time before I could get a word in edgewise as, one after another, each talked about frozen water pipes, snow-buried cars, days without milk, being marooned at work.

Finally, during a lull, I said, "It was colder the year I was born."

"Yeah, Dad, we know."

And I suppose they did, because weather summaries made a point of listing the coldest winters on record. Except I felt that it might interest them to know that the doctor could not make it to the old farmhouse for the birthing. But the children were busy castigating engineers who failed to place water intakes deep enough to keep from being clogged by Lake Michigan slush and ice, causing water pressure to drop so low they had to take sponge baths instead of showers.

"Reminds me of '36," I cut in quickly. "Lake Michigan about froze over. As a cub reporter, on a vessel sent to rescue fishing tugs, our boat froze in. We didn't have food … "

"Yeah, Dad, we know. You showed us the clipping."

Gradually, I straggled back from the past to hear them comparing temperatures. "Thirty below one night. Never got up to zero for three days."

Not one to be shut up for long, I pooh-poohed with some vehemence. "When we bombed from 35,000 feet, it was often fifty and even sixty below."

"Sure, yeah Dad, we know."

I wanted to tell them it was during the days before B-17 bombers were heated and had Plexiglas windows, and before fliers wore electrically heated suits. Then I noticed the grandchildren were as bored as I. So I took them to a bedroom, closed the door, and began an embellished story about the mouse invasion. They were enthralled because it will be some years before they begin telling their own fathers, "Yeah, Dad, we know."

⫸ *Eleventh Commandment* ⫷

Church attendance always shows a decided increase during November, according to a survey. It may be that people, done with summer's fun, have more time for worship, or that, seeing the decay all around them, they ponder on their own demise. Regardless, since we have all gathered this Sabbath, my sermon for November.

Religion is, of course, more concerned with the hereafter than the here and now. But its basic premise is that there will be no happy hereafter if we do not have a healthy concern for the here and now. One of the first things we learn in Sunday school is that murder of man is a sin. So should not our children also be taught that the murder of mankind through environmental neglect is the more mortal sin? Yet what denomination has come out with encyclicals flying to pronounce global strangulation a crime, not only against man, but against God?

Many are shocked at the way young people have been turning away from formal religion. The youngsters claim their churches no longer relate to the world of today, but are preaching a gospel that went down with the last virgin pine. But, religion's responsibility to youth aside, how about religion's duty to a world many are certain is hell-bent on destroying itself? If indeed our churches do exert as great an influence on our lives as do our homes, are not religions derelict in their duty if they do not officially and energetically and loudly proclaim and explain the eleventh commandment:

"Thou shalt honor the earth!"

December

DECEMBER. MONTH OF RETREAT. In the frozen half of the world now visited by snows, some members of the two-legged tribe head south to be greeted by the birds which preceded them. Not accomplishing that, they opt for merriment. And in their frantic efforts to be joyous, Christmas comes to them with the hollow resonance of a pretty gourd left dry by the constant beat and bleat of seasonal entreaty. Hoping to take the sting out of winter, they wallow in a spending orgy to create a tinseled euphoria, and even their charity becomes "as something brass, or a tinkling cymbal."

But there are other ways, meaningful country ways — watching soft snows wrap around the spruce and a redbird come to perch on the white bough. There are warming country ways with a fire bright each night on the hearth, and the yard light on so the wind can be watched as it whips horsetails of snow across the frosted windows. Big city or country lane, there are old-fashioned ways with popcorn and homemade presents among the store-bought gifts hidden where everyone knows — under the bed. There is giving, even if it is only to the birds: one pigeon on a city window sill, or a country bird feeder oasis, axis of a feathery orbit.

December is the first month of winter, but none who sit watching pre-Christmas television programs are likely to see it come. Winter is out there where the snow comes, first sharp as sand to snicker through cattails, then growing to a smother of white, so only the creek is blue-

Now,
seeing is
really
forever
through
crystalline air,
across field
after field
of iced grasses.

black and restless in the silent serenity that follows the storms.

We bar the doors of our mind, anesthetize our instincts, and never venture into the blue-white wonder through a glittering forest of trees fringed with white lace. But winter was long before we were. With or without us, it suddenly is on the hill, along the valley, laying a white sheet for all the wild society to scribble their daily and nightly diaries. Now, seeing is really forever through crystalline air, across field after field of iced grasses dazzling as diamonds. Sunsets are volcanic, brighter than fire.

With snow cover, no night is really dark, and moon-favored nights turn snowbanks into sculpted statuary. Its beams, through forest branches, sketch the white canvas with works of shadowy, fluid art, picture after picture, a million sketches as the planet marks the arc from dusk to dawn. Sad that for the uninitiated, the winter woods seem forsaken, creeks silent and corrugated with ice, snow hummocked high on deadfalls. Trees are reaching skeletons; fire lanes barren white raceways. And where marshes intrude, there is only the rattle of cattails, like bones in the wind. To the stranger the forest must seem desolate, eerie. Where now the riotous birdsongs of spring, the throbbing insect orchestra of summer, and the whistling wing-beat of big birds in fall? Could this place ever have been the birthplace of thousands, tens of thousands?

But the seeming emptiness is an illusion. The forest dwellers are still extant, eating, sleeping, living, dying. The signs are there, but reading them is a lost art. So most of us do not know that when day is done, the fox courses, the owl flies and beneath the creek ice a muskrat or beaver blows jewel bubbles like thousands of muskrats and beavers before him.

The printing is in the snow. Wing fingers tracing where a pheasant fled. Stain on an ice fringe, the muskrat's wet belly. Indecipherable scribble where a junco bent a weed to get the seeds. Quotation marks followed by an exclamation mark, a mouse dragging its tail.

Sunsets are volcanic, brighter than fire.

Ghostly snowshoe hare, its arrow tracks pointing not the direction of its flight, but the place from which it came. Faint tracings of an old-fashioned fan: owl wings lightly on the snow as talons reach for the mouse. Sharp wedge: deer. Furrow bordered by finger marks: bumbling possum, prehensile tail trailing. Baby's handprint: raccoon. Pigeon-toed chicken tracks: raven. And the owl hops and the otter slides — it is all out there for any who are bored by "Jingle Bells."

December, for winter a trial run. Time to test, to toughen, to acclimatize all for the rigors to come. In the city, snow turns gray with grit and grinds to slush beneath the wheels of cars, forming interminable traffic lines. The glare of colored lights and the blare of brassy loudspeakers are all that keep some city folk from despairing. Would they could come to the country, there to cut a spruce or balsam, not too large, not too small, and bring it into the apartment or the house.

For the Christmas holidays, just once open the summer cottage, or rent one, if you can. Saw wood for your Christmas fire. Cut a hole in the ice for water. Break an icicle from an eave to chill your before-dinner drink. Be silent often. Speak softly if you must. Put crumbs out for the mice. Cut a cedar for the deer. On snowshoes or skis, permit your muscles to rejoice. Let your mind soar to the highest blue above the mundane years that have imprisoned you. Make angels in the snow. Carve your initials on a drift. Melting, they will not offend any who follow, yet for years and years they will still be there, in your mind.

Catch a fish through the ice. Clean it and see the scales like sequins brighten a log, your cutting board. From a dead birch make a cone of bark. Fill lightly with snow. Light it and watch it sputter and spark. Collect pine cones for remembering. Sleep with someone you love, child or lover, so you may awaken to sit close while a coyote howls. Sit in dim corners, whether in forest or cabin, so the ballet of shadow and light may have full play. Eat one steak and hang one for the chickadees and the shadowy, gray camp robbers. Talk to a raven long enough in his language and at last he may answer you.

Tunnel beneath a snow-covered deadfall. Sit for a while and feel like a bear. Try for the spire of a sentinel pine to look far and away if you want to feel a little like God. Run and slide where wind has bared the ice. Lie down by your fishing hole, draw a blanket over your head, and see what is happening in the water world. Discover there still is peace where the earth is home for the quiet ones at the end of the road, and Christmas is a holy day instead of a holiday.

⋙ *Doorway to the Woods* ⋘

"Bring your snowmobile on my place," I tell my friend, Clarence Fickau, "and I'll shoot the tracks right out from under it." Of course, I would not and he knows that. It is a standing joke, repeated like a greeting. Nevertheless, as one of my rights, he respects my freedom from such mental and physical intrusion.

In years past, I have been a vociferous and, I suppose, a sometimes prejudiced opponent of the snowmobile. Though I still prefer a world having no off-trail vehicles, my opposition has been tempered by the success of manufacturers in bringing the machines' noise to tolerable levels, and by the snowmobilers' efforts to police their own ranks. The snowmobile, when it exploded upon an unsuspecting and sometimes horrified public, was really nothing new. Not to me, anyway. More than fifty years ago, right after World War I, my father and his partner in a struggling auto agency built a ski-footed monster that could navigate unplowed winter roads that stopped even horses pulling bobsleds. To them, it was a matter of expediency. To supplement their often meager income from the garage, they had contracted to run the mail twice a day from Juneau, Wis., three miles north to a hamlet, Minnesota Junction, where rail lines intersected.

During those days, the U.S. Postal Service really held to its pledge, so when a car could not get through the snowy roads, my father shouldered the mail sacks and bucked the drifts on foot. Trouble was, he could, of course, carry no passengers while walking, and since salesmen usually traveled by rail, riders at fifty cents a head were a vital part of the partnership's economy. So he and his partner, Baldy Kuntz, built a monstrosity and, oddly enough, called it a snowmobile. As I remember, it was a V-8 Oldsmobile with skis instead of front wheels, and enormous tires to the rear. It leaned forward like a falling-over drunk, but when it went past our house twice a day to deliver the mail, we children were at the window to cheer our hero.

My next experience with snowmobiles came right after World War II while hunting coyotes on Wisconsin's Stockbridge Indian Reservation. As I recall, these were factory models, and we used them to haul ourselves and the hounds along fire trails far into the forest. Then, of course, the more sophisticated snowmobiles of today burst upon the market in the 1960s with a horrendous snarl and a proclivity for killing riders, ruining habitat, panicking wild creatures and driving people from one nightmare to another. Threatened by all sorts of retributions, including laws banning their operation, manufacturers and customers banded together to make snowmobiling, if not a thing of joy for the average Joe and Jane, at least something the public might tolerate.

Quickly then, the snowmobile's merits as an emergency vehicle were utilized. It went to scientific outposts in the Arctic and the Antarctic. It made lives of Indians and Eskimos more tolerable along endless traplines and on grocery trips to town. Clubs began to police their own activities, and as snowmobilers stayed on marked trails, damage to habitat was substantially reduced. But most important, so far as I am concerned, the snowmobile took the winterbound housewife to a frosted forest paradise she otherwise would never have discovered. It took the aging man who could no longer negotiate the trails back to the winter woodlands he loved. It introduced sprouts with legs not long or strong enough to handle skis or snowshoes to a fairyland not even Disney could duplicate. And now countless handicapped people have access to the winter woods.

So come slowly, softly as you can. Pause often to read stories the wild ones have written in the snow. Pick a pine cone to remember how it was. Build a small fire and whisper. Then, if the wind is right, there may be furred and feathered friends on the welcoming committee.

⋙ *Where Are the Trees?* ⋘

When not restrained, land grabbers level hills, pave creek bottoms, uproot trees and even sell topsoil before moving on, leaving only markers along lot lines so builders may erect homes. Travel any country road within a twenty-five-mile radius of any major city and these new subdivisions, like desert settlements, blister in the summer sun.

Magnificent oaks, fragrant basswoods and sweet sugar maples are cut to remove every impediment to construction and save a few dollars. Then families water spindly spruce or stripling ash, and ultimately spend hundreds of dollars and an entire lifetime trying to get the trees back. But forget the money. Forget the role that trees play as atmospheric filters, as sponges for groundwater reservoirs and as insurance policies against erosion. Forget trees' energy-saving role as shady air conditioners in summer and as a shelter belt to insulate against below-zero winds. Forget that without tree communities, life as we know it probably would disappear.

We take trees for granted, like grass or gravel. Yet, despite our negligence, we seem compelled to crowd into the forests when vacations permit an exodus from city streets. Is there something mystical about trees? Do they, in some mysterious way, heal the spirit, calm the nerves, bring peace to tortured minds? Is there an affirmation of eternity in their springtime rebirth? A friend of mine who is still raising children decided to move from Milwaukee to the country when a stroke of good fortune provided the money. He purchased several acres in a rural subdivision and ultimately built what he and his wife decided was their dream house. Dream home notwithstanding, he and his wife, and especially the children, were devastated by the bleakness of their woodless surroundings. In the end, they sold the country home and were lucky enough to buy back the house they had left. Down the block from the old house is a large, shady park. The children were relieved to be back from the sterile countryside into a habitat where dreaming came easy.

I will not forget a morning many years ago at the Benson Kennels in the Kettle Moraine forest near Eagle. Orin and his wife, Lucille, were in an oak grove across the drive from their little white house, laying out what looked like a giant jigsaw puzzle of boards. They were planning a new home. For days, visualizing the outlines of the building, they studied it, then at last called the architect and said, "There she goes!" So the house was built, and not a tree sacrificed.

Last summer, in taking a bird survey, I visited an instant subdivision built twenty-five years ago. Among the teenage trees, I counted seventeen starlings, twenty-two house sparrows, three robin families, a mourning dove couple and a grackle pair. Two birds per acre, and not a really good singer in the lot.

Trees, whether in a backyard colony, a farm wood lot, city park or national forest, are like buildings in a city. The tall trees are the concrete and steel skyscrapers. The lower story of trees and bushes are the smaller buildings — homes and shops — and on the ground are the gardens growing food. In the high-rise apartments live raccoons, opossums, orioles and tree frogs. In the smaller homes live warblers, butterflies, walking sticks and beetles. In the ground garden live cottontails, mice, crickets and snails. In the earthy basement are worms, grubs, mites and bacteria. And decorating all are climbing vines, ferns, flowers, fungi and mosses. It is a fascinating place, busy and bustling by day, quiet and mysterious by night.

An environmental impact assessment that zeroes in on sewage and water but disregards such a fruitful community is archaic. There are any number of ways to solve sewage and water problems, but only one way to get a tree: Grow it! Still, the land grabbers come and the land grabbers go. And the families come and most have no alternative except to stay. And the kids, at first excited to be moving to the country, take one look at the sterile community and say, "To hell with it." They begin hanging around the corner tavern down the road, waiting for the day they will be old enough to go in.

⇛   *December Dilemma*   ⇚

An unusually heavy fall of early December snow on yet soft earth is pretty good assurance that spring will provide an especially luxurious season of pastels, prelude to a summer of brilliant blooms. Such deep and early snows protect against killing frosts, which take their toll of all growing things. Furthermore, early snows provide moisture banks for rivers and lakes, and create reservoirs to keep springs bubbling through August's heat.

But just as one man's food is another's poison, so these snows exact their toll, and the cottontail must at once go on mid-January rations of tree bark, and the deer are imprisoned in barren, traditional yarding valleys, weeks before their time. Songbird seeds all but disappear as the long-stemmed weeds are bent beneath the drifts; the squirrels must go on a diet of leathery bud beginnings, because their nut caches are buried.

The hunting range of the raccoon and opossum dwindles, and the foxes' mouse pasture is sealed shut. Deadfalls, the chickadees' pantries, being shrouded in white, send the birds looking for dead branches not yet separated from trees. The downy and hairy woodpeckers, finding neither milkweed, cattail, burr reed, knotweed nor any standing stalk, search frantically those trees which larger woodpeckers have already raided.

But then, if the snow has pruned the trees, it might have been accomplished in time, with a little wind pressing the rotting wood. Now the wet, heavy snow takes living as well as dead branches, and lays over young conifers until they crack, and when life returns in spring, it oozes from the wound. The heavy, wet snow puts slush on ponds that turns to opaque ice, and if the winter is long, water plants, having little light, offer no gifts of oxygen, and so fish die. Frogs, salamanders and turtles succumb, too. And when the census is taken, little matter how lush the spring or beautiful the summer. The applause will be subdued because of the vacancies in the seats of the earth's auditorium.

⇛ Vicious Circle ⇚

Gwen says life is a vicious circle. My raised eyebrows prompt her to explain, so she does.

You've got to admit it is a rare individual who would not elect to do things differently, given the chance to live life over, she says.

I cannot argue with that, and my nod prompts her to continue.

It being ordained that we shall live but once, the time comes when we realize we have missed the boat, that life is giving us a ride we hadn't opted for. So what do we do?

She waits, so I spread my palms as if to ask, Well, what do we do?

I'll tell you, she says. Knowing that we've lucked out, we're not about to let it happen to our kids, so we plan their lives as if we were planning for ourselves.

I shrug as though to say, so what?

Don't you see? she asks. Instead of letting our kids live their lives the way they'd like to, we steer them into lives we would have liked to live ourselves. And so there it is.

I wait, then lift my eyebrows again.

Don't you see? she repeats. The vicious circle! We're all living lives someone else planned for us, lives parents wanted for themselves. Over and over. Generation after generation. The vicious circle.

My shrug tells her I think her logic may lack a premise or two.

She rises to the occasion. OK, she says, now let's take you.

My eyes widen.

Yes, I mean you. You're a writer. Well, aren't you?

My shrug intimates she might get an argument on that. But it doesn't stop her.

You make your living writing things. But you never wanted to be a writer. Even to this day, after some ten or fifteen million words, you still aren't happy about it. Right?

She waits. I nod, reluctantly.

You've told me a hundred times you wish you'd never left the farm.

She waits. And waits. So again, reluctantly, I nod.

See? she says almost triumphantly. You are what your parents wanted you to be. You have the career they couldn't have. So what happens?

A long wait, because by now I am afraid to encourage her. But she does not back off. So I tilt my head as if to ask: Well, all right, what happens?

She jumps at the chance: You moved back to the country the very first chance you got. You got a place with plums and muskrats and fish and ducks and ...

I raise a hand to try to halt the recitation.

But she is still running. Well, you did. You got back as close to the land as you could, and you dragged your kids with you.

She's got her adrenaline going now. After a timeout for a deep breath, she hurtles on.

So your kids are captive. You've got the only car to anywhere. They'll learn to love butterflies whether they want to or not. They'll prune trees until they've got biceps like gourds. They'll clean fish until the smell can't ever be scrubbed away. They'll haul rocks until they've got no fingernails to polish, even if you gave them the polish to do it with. They'll saw wood. They'll pick berries, apples, cherries. They'll shovel ...

I raise a hand to protest.

Oh, put your hand down, she almost shouts.

I look for an escape route.

I'm not through, she says.

I put on my hangdog look.

And don't pull that hangdog look on me, she says. While you were out on the road looking for stories to write, you were happy because that part of you which you loved most was back here farming.

With an eyebrow I start to protest again.

Don't con me, she says. You can farm trees or fish or ducks just as surely as you can farm corn or cows. And you were doing it. You were putting muscles on those five sweet girls in places where girls shouldn't even have muscles. Your dream life, the one you wanted, was yours, even if you had to live it vicariously by enslaving poor, innocent children.

I looked shocked!

Look shocked? You should! she exclaims. Because you know what your kids say when someone remarks that it must have been great growing up on a place like Little Lakes? This time she doesn't even wait for an eyebrow of inquiry, but rants on: They say they didn't have a childhood but were draftees in Mel's School for Survival. That's what they say!

I hang my head.

You should hang your head. You didn't get your farm, but you made darn sure your kids were going to get it whether they wanted it or not. And if you're looking for sympathy, you'll find it under S in the dictionary.

Well, I can't handle it anymore and start backing toward the bedroom as she levels her parting shot: Now do you see what I mean when I say that life is just a vicious circle?

To end the tirade, I slowly close the bedroom door. Then later, much later, as Gwen kisses me good night, all I can think of is, Gee, although I didn't say a word, that's one vicious circle that wound up around my neck.

⤜ *Big Business* ⤛

We cannot go back, ever. For most of us, dreams of porkchops from our own pigs, tomatoes from our own vines and wine from our own grapes have precious little chance of coming true. Like it or not, we are stuck with the wheelers and dealers, with the men who neither sow nor spin but, for a price, save us a trip to the potato patch. Try as we might, most of us are in no position to eliminate the middleman. Even the farmer might discover that making his own sausage could be vastly more expensive than anticipated, and the end result could be an inferior product.

So, backyard gardens notwithstanding, individually we will never be able to raise enough wheat to grind into enough flour to bake our own bread. Not that it isn't sometimes fun. And maybe a guy could save a buck by raising rabbits for his own hasenpfeffer, but the self-sustaining man of the land is a purely imaginary figure. Because, the moment we pick up a shovel, we have paid our dues to the miner, manufacturer, lumberman, trucker, storekeeper, stenographer, salesman, executive, you name it. Then, if we agonize that a dollar's worth of material costs us ten dollars by the time we get to use it, only think of the problems we would have to surmount in making our own shovels.

The point, of course, is that we wail too often that many of today's woes are the direct result of man's reluctance to get down on his knees and grub in the good earth. Well, it surely would not hurt any of us to rekindle our appreciation and affection for the earth with some weekend gardening. But at the same time we must recognize that nothing short of today's business methods can feed today's millions. Consider that in 1820, the average farm employee produced enough food to sustain four people. That, by 1950, the same worker could produce enough food for fifteen, and then, as we came roaring into the 1970s, the average farm employee was producing enough to feed nearly fifty.

So farming, too, is big business. If we deplore the disappearance of the small farmer, and if we mourn the passing of man's direct involvement with the earth, we must, nevertheless, worship at the altar of a system that has freed us from bondage, that has provided the opportunity to write songs and sing them and obtain some of the benefits of the good life, no matter how meager our incomes. It is easy today to become nostalgic about the idyllic life on the farms of fifty and more years ago. I have done it myself, but then, if I am honest, I must also remember that it was a time of blistered palms and red, chapped wrists, that it was a time of putting warm feet on cold floors long before dawn, and then putting a bone-weary body to bed as soon as the barn lantern was out and the chores were done.

Maybe it was a more honest time, but who wants twelve to fourteen hours of muscle-aching drudgery, often spent slopping around in ankle-deep manure, with milking to be done (by hand) seven days a week, and haying in the hot sun on the Fourth of July? We are often rapturous of home-grown radishes and homemade goat cheese, when the real miracle is that big business can put dewy fresh vegetables on the shelves of supermarkets hundreds of miles from the fields in which they were harvested.

I can weep for the horse that no longer pulls the plow, and I can yearn to see the rain turn pastures green, and I can wish to turn up a rutabaga with my bare toe and eat it on the spot. But the world would be infinitely poorer if big business, despite all its sins, had not lifted people from yesterday's drudgery, so we might find time to read a book or go see the Grand Canyon.

⇛ *Questions to Ponder* ⇚

Long thoughts on a long December's night: Who gave the woodpecker a chisel bill while the crossbill came equipped with a pair of tweezers? What is with the bittersweet that it needs two parents to reproduce, while other growing things hold this miracle of life in a single plant?

So, if the firefly flashes a sexy welcome to other fireflies, why doesn't the moth do likewise, instead of laying scent trails on the evening breeze? Now, if the male penguin is agreeable to hatching the egg, why does the mallard drake join a bachelor colony and leave all the work to the hen?

Then, why does one snake lay eggs and another afford live birth for its offspring? And how come the killdeer fledgling pops ready and running from the egg, while the robin is blind and helpless? Isn't it strange that a willow will grow from a branch thrust into the earth, though an oak needs an acorn?

How did the sea otter learn about rocks to crack mollusks on its chest, while the seagull flew high to drop the same clams and oysters on the rocks? And why must the robin puzzle with a peanut, which a jay can crack with one well-placed peck? What about the tortoise content to live a hundred miles from water? The catfish that walks from pond to pond? And why won't pike eat grass when the amur (grass carp) thrives on it?

Isn't it strange that the female mosquito needs your blood to complete the life cycle, while the male is content with plant juices? And isn't it a miracle, and somehow beautiful, that a pine can bleed a clot of resin to heal a sore, even as you and I? What's with the mockingbird, which can change its tune eighty-seven times in seven minutes, while a house sparrow only chirps, and a nuthatch is content to mostly buzz?

If the honeybee must die after stinging once, why not the hornet? How come the ostrich never followed the vulture into the sky? What is this about the turtle breathing through the skin around its anus, when its head is at the other end? Why can a seed lie dormant for centuries and then grow, but an egg rots? And if the worm, on losing its tail, can grow a new one, why can't I grow a finger?

⋙ *Kitchen Table Diplomacy* ⋘

Lately I have had the urge to return to the home of my childhood. I would go not to indulge in a nostalgic binge, but to search for a table, a kitchen table of oak and ample proportions across which many decisions were hammered out, and the fruits of the earth were processed before descending to the fruit cellar in the basement. Likely, I would not find it, though if I did, I would crate if for shipment, along with any others of its kind I might uncover, to such prestigious places as Camp David, Washington, D.C., the United Nations headquarters in New York, and such capitals of the world where I might, without argument, be welcomed.

There, in conference rooms where domestic and international controversies are resolved, I would surround it with straight-backed, sturdy oaken chairs and defy any who sat around it to negotiate with kingly disdain instead of humane humility. Perhaps in all the world there is no more common denominator. And I defy people of power to misuse that power while leaning elbows where once a baby had been diapered, fruit jars filled, crocks larded with pork, rummy and old maid played with a deck of worn cards, sorrows and triumphs recounted and family plans formulated.

Twenty-one-gun salutes, the blare of welcoming trumpets, the roar of adulation from the crowds, the cock-of-the-walk inspection of the honor guard, the royal ride with Secret Service men running alongside the bulletproof limousine, would become a mockery when seated at this table where a baby splattered oatmeal, a cat got help delivering a litter, a cut thumb was mended, tears of happiness and sorrow wet the wood, and fists rarely were thumped in anger but to emphasize victory, or as a gesture of defiance against impending defeat. Pope or peasant, president or pauper, prince or peon become equals at this table across which all of Earth's meager or abundant harvest ultimately come to be divided.

Talking across the kitchen table — life's plateau of equality — crowns, scepters or royal robes would be as out of place as neckties or lies. How to sell out mankind across the scarred boards around which all life once revolved? If prodded to emotional oratory in the great halls of assembly, then here at the kitchen table there is the necessity, the requirement of questions quietly asked, and of answers thoughtful and subdued.

Sadly today, many homes have replaced this monument to family tranquility with snack bars or room dividers, and we are the poorer for it. No problem can be resolved at a snack bar, or in any other room, with such frankness as during an eyeball-to-eyeball confrontation across the kitchen table. Here, Grandpa can make a point by merely snapping his suspenders. Mother, serving breakfast in her nightgown, could hardly present a more protective role. And Johnny might kick off his shoes while father guided the kitchen table diplomacy so the best interests of all were served.

All the better if the table is one where root beer was made, horseradish ground, sausages stuffed, apples quartered and strung for drying in the attic, bread dough kneaded, cookies cut, wine bottled — reminders not only of the essentials but of the small luxuries that gave life flavor. Saber rattling would be as incongruous at the kitchen table as a military parade in a backyard garden. Whether seeking more land or oil or wheat, what better place than the kitchen table to remind rulers that it is not power, but the equitable distribution of the fruits of this earth which must be the goal of governments?

⋙ *Riding Out Old Age* ⋘

Is it possible to abandon an old friend who has seen you through a hundred hassles and a few hells? Even when they tell you it is all over, that it can never be the same again? How can I forget, just like that, how season after season we met the weather, and everything else, together: the head-high snowdrifts of winter, the belly-deep mudholes of spring, summer heat that left everyone limp. How can I just turn my back and walk away when I remember the many times we skirted the thin edge of living?

There was the day the venerable elm fell the wrong way and came within inches of crushing us. There was the time the shale of a precipice shifted and we went catapulting together into a rocky ravine. What about the blizzard that surely would have turned us both into icy statues if we had not worked as a team to find a way out of the whirling white? Remember how I warmed you, and you, in turn, warmed me?

And how can I forget the good times? The times when we were younger and traveled to trout streams where the air was sweet with the fragrance of spring flowers? How together we negotiated the "impossible" ascent to the top of a hill, just to watch evening shoot down the day with a flaming sun? How to forget the way we raced through northern forests aflame with fall, forgetting about the grouse we had come to hunt, the deer to stalk, the steelhead trout to catch?

We celebrated life, you and I, even though we were as different as any pair possibly could be. Different, yet the same, as the man who flies the airplane and the airplane itself, which, in reality, is flying the man. Though we grew old, it was good, even if people sometimes laughed to themselves to see us come wheezing and grunting up the road on the way to town. I suppose we never really knew how old and decrepit we had become, even though kids sometimes snickered and dogs sometimes barked as we went by.

Sure, I could find another truck. But now? When only to look at you invokes memories of how together we took all the kids to the Rock River fishing? When I remember all the water we hauled to fight grass fires? And how we dug out many a stump to make a fertile place for flowers we had brought from the land where freeways were coming?

You were always there for the big jobs: hauling fifty, maybe a hundred cords of wood, extracting cars from ditches drifted over with snow or slippery with mud, hauling tons of hay and corn and oats to feed hundreds of ducks, thousands of birds and an assortment of pets. How can I just walk away from such a partnership now that they say it would cost more to make you well than you are worth?

I would never do it to Gwen, and I am sure she would never do it to me. So, Bumpy, I am not going to let it happen to you. You are going in, and no matter what it takes, the mechanics are going to make you well again. Don't worry. It is no new push-button truck for me, with a cab that smells like fresh paint instead of grease, sweat and tobacco. After all, Bumpy, you are only seventeen years old, and I am only seventy. So as long as the doctors can keep me going, the least I can do for you, old friend, is see to it that you keep rolling, too.

⇛ *Christmas Tree* ⇚

Having been raised on the traditional tinseled spruce or pine with its winged angels and all manner of gaudy, store-bought ornaments, it was not until about a decade ago that we switched to what I suppose might be referred to as a biodegradable Christmas tree. Ecology, however, had nothing to do with it. A great aunt, Martha Dedolph of Mayville, Wis., provided the inspiration. House-bound with infirmities, she wondered, during a visit, if we might not have a little spruce tree to spare. Of course! We had hundreds!

"But the only decorations I want," she insisted, "are conifer cones, nightshade berries, a colored leaf or two, perhaps a cluster of mountain ash berries, or if the birds have gotten them, a sprig of multiflora rose berries." And that is what she got: a three-foot white spruce with, among other things, a red sprinkling of highbush cranberries, a monarch and a white cabbage butterfly, both of which had perished uncrumpled, and, to top it off, a cross of red dogwood. (According to legend, that is the wood of which Christ's cross was made, and the tree was doomed thereafter to bush size so no more crosses might be made of it.)

Compared to the flashy trees to which we had become accustomed, this tree was, at first glance, woefully drab, almost ugly. Then a ray of sun through a window put a sparkle on the monarch butterfly wings, and a lighted lamp made the nightshade berries sparkle as though freshly anointed with dew. I moved the lamp, and the cabbage butterfly looked wonderfully alive. Summer had come to the little corner, though just outside the window the thermometer recorded ten degrees below zero.

Next year, we tried it on our children. The older ones agreed: "Great!" The younger ones protested: "That's a Christmas tree?" and went walking in the subdivision beyond the woods to revive their Christmas spirit in the razzle-dazzle of lighted reindeer prancing on rooftops, picture windows ablaze with colored lights, and a loudspeaker with a tin throat trying to imitate Bing Crosby's "White Christmas."

So, next year, down from the attic came all the boxed ornaments, some graceful, some grotesque, and the beautiful tree once again resembled a campaigning hooker all decked out in sequins, rhinestones, trailing boas and, the gods preserve us, a white-winged angel flying next to a multi-colored jet airplane. Well, anything for a happy home, except that toward the end of the following summer the youngest, Mary, came to the house with a little yellow bucket overflowing with milkweed silk. She stood for awhile saying nothing, but then, as though talking to no one in particular, said: "Might look prettier than tinsel ... softer, somehow." So, we were off and running.

That year we stayed with spruce, and though we did not abandon lights, we elected to part with a little cash for the smallest twinkling bulbs the marketplace afforded. The big change came the following year. We abandoned spruce and went to juniper (red cedar) which rivals the tamarack's spring delicacy of texture. We stayed with the lights, but otherwise all ornaments, including three dry, feather-light bumblebees, joined the likes of dried joe-pye weed, and feathers from jay, flicker, cardinal, goldfinch and wood duck. At once it became something of a contest. Abandoned bird eggs (well blown) had to have nests. Dragonflies, iridescent as the day they died, joined even a crayfish's armor, great claws as blue as the water it had once scuttled about in.

The first few years, there was little planning. Gradually, as the children matured, patterns developed. Autumn might have its corner, while spring put its props on the other side of the tree. There was even one "pond tree," highlighted by hundreds of clamshells tiny as fingernails, taking their color from any light willing to shine on them.

Fortunately, our land is well endowed with junipers of all sizes and shapes. After the tree has been selected and marked, it is down to the marsh, the bush pantry, the oak hill, the creek and ponds, the pasture, any nook gracious enough to provide a spider web carefully sprayed and carefully carried on paper, a mushroom varnished to preserve it, or perhaps a shelf fungus plucked in infancy, already a curious convulsion of incredible colors.

⋙ *New Year?* ⋘

The last leaf falls from the calendar at a most inappropriate time. December thirty-first can hardly be labeled year's end, nor the first day of January a beginning of the seasons of humans and the wild society. So, whether we drown reality with a rousing New Year's Eve celebration, or retreat for reassurance to Biblical stories, the winter of life makes no concessions, and neither the deity nor champagne can halt the demise of time.

The rabbit has none of our problems. His god is a maple shoot, and if that is not enough to fuel his furnace for one more day, he begs no one for the blessings of another sunrise, but becomes a complacent corpse. It matters not then that a fox finds and eats the carcass, or if snow keeps it for spring maggots. But if a tree, feeding on what is left, becomes his monument, the rabbit at last has something in common with man.

Immortality being a vision peculiar to minds geared to surviving every tomorrow, man implores Allah, Christ or the golden calf for life ever after, while country cemeteries are plowed and King Tut comes to Paris. Better March, marked by first flowers, swelling buds and owlets already hatched, be designated as the year's beginning. It is the only resurrection none can dispute. There is cause then for celebration, because only survivors are washed clean by spring rains.

Properly then, instead of being walled in by any churchly structure, a man might walk in a wild place where it is all happening. He certainly would return refreshed, and maybe even find immortality in the succession of all growing things, including the children who will find and come down the same trail among the trees.

January

JANUARY. MONTH OF THE INVISIBLE KILLER. Now the time of testing. Now the reckoning. Short days, brittle and bright or biting and leaden, sandwiched between dawn and dusk, sun fires tinting the purple smoke of horizon clouds. Now, one feather awry, a single day of short rations, and during the night a victim falls frozen.

Mostly, January is a cruel month. Once it tested our mettle to determine the purity of our courage, and to measure how much was merely alloy. Wrapped now in our technological cocoon, rarely are we forced to make a stand. When it happens, we find we are unable to get our car from a ditch, much less survive a night in the woods.

Few things in nature are as insidious, as relentless as cold. Ice on ponds and lakes creaks, groans, and then booms as hairline cracks streak from shore to shore. A tortured tree protests with a cannon burst, which reverberates down the frozen aisles of an otherwise silent forest. Snow squeaks underfoot. Bridge boards and cabin roofs crack as though breaking. Iron wheels scream. The ring of an axe carries miles, and a falling icicle breaks into the musical briskness of shattering glass. Finally, when the far-below-zero cold tightens its grip, the ice stops expanding and begins to contract, and an ominous, pervasive, barely audible moan tells of the earth's agony.

Vapor from a spring-fed creek rises to overhanging grass and trees to freeze in a white

Now the
time of
testing.
Now the
reckoning.

fringe. Even rocks are rent where moisture in a fissure becomes an expanding wedge of ice. The moon turns the snow pale blue, but the mouse knows better than to surface from its labyrinthian shelter to see the shadow and shine.

Then, just about the time the hardiest of humans balks at facing the cutting wind, it swings to the south, and the redbird rises to the topmost branch of the highest tree on its range to cheer this unbelievable hiatus, the January Thaw. There, the bird's piercing whistle tells about how, when the time comes, his hen will use this place for a nest in which to lay her eggs.

Encouraged, English sparrows rise toward the sun in excited, feathery flurries. Waxwings flutter beneath icicles on the maples to sip droplets of sweet sap. The red fox comes down off the ridge to patrol mouse meadows now that the ice, roofing the tunneled cities, has softened. The following night, the wind goes back into the north, and everyone knows about the lie January almost always tells. Then, even the crows drift south, and snowbirds, down from the bleak Arctic, swirl in ghostly white flocks where a plow has scraped deep enough for a pinch of sand for an empty gizzard, a weed seed for an empty crop.

The frost probes deeper and, far below, the faint and infrequent heartbeat of a woodchuck or chipmunk flutters, then fails. White bone marrow of yarded white-tailed deer becomes pink and watery. Hides, trying to accommodate the shrinking flesh, stand the hollow hairs on end, and the bristling buck becomes a hollow-eyed, stumbling caricature of the once-noble stag. To descend into the valley of death, where deer stand spraddle-legged among trees stripped as ivory-white as tombstones, is to remember a televised visit to Dachau. The "living dead" is no cliche, but a precise, gut-grinding truth. They stand mute among the fallen — fawns, does and bucks, antlers long gone. In the trees, glutted ravens watch, and around the shadowy perimeter, four-legged meat eaters have too much stomach to move farther than necessity demands.

Across the firelands are wind-whipped raceways, track of coyote and fox.

Macabre herd, prisoners of a tradition, a habit, some instinct that brings them to this barren though buttressed valley, to add their bones to the countless generations who have fed the carnivores down through the years. For most, the hay and pellets come too late. Shrunken stomachs, overwhelmed by such largesse, send shock waves along nervous systems, which snap like brittle wire, breaking heart-to-brain communication. They knee over, chin to ground for a brace, and then roll over and die without a quiver.

Always, however, some few feel the slow, fresh flow of blood, which puts a light back in blank-wall eyes, and these will live. During some other autumn, perhaps, men will come, with and without guns, to scatter and whittle, and shoot or live-trap the herd down to numbers the range will support. Then, where the denuded trees once stood, fresh new greenery will rise, though in some other place, during some other January, there will be another deer Dachau.

That is January, too often, and even the ubiquitous coyote, toughest tendon of life on four legs, comes sometimes to the day when he claws down to find the discarded belt of a hunter and eats all except the buckle. Treacherous month. Sun softens snow in a glade and the ruffed grouse dives at dusk to sleep beneath the warm, white blanket. He never rises. During the night, a crust forms, and next day clouds obscure the sun, and the crust does not soften. So there is one less partridge in the poplar swallowing leathery buds for the green pinprick of life meant to be a leaf.

Not much farther south, gray partridge (sometimes called Hungarian) and quail come head-to-head for a sleeping circle of warmth, and sometimes only the hub of the feathery wheel, the bird in the middle, lives to see the dawn. Ice freezing down to the beaver's feed pile sends lodge members looking for more watery accommodations, and lucky is the one strong enough to make the march, if he does not encounter coyote, remnant wolf or sagacious bobcat. Muskrats, too, trapped by ice that freezes to marsh bottoms, eats his own home, and then wanders aimlessly. Some few find flowing creeks and grass roots sufficient to support a flickering flame, a faltering heartbeat. Many warm a hawk's innards. Some, finding a culvert, plug it to amass water, and die, prisoners of their own folly. Foolish opossum, never meant to cross the Mason-Dixon line, drops an ear, one or more finger-like toes, or a length of tail to the cold, and is a rattle of bones strung together by tendons thin as string.

Being wary of the cold is far different, however, from being frightened by it. Knowing cold for what it can do to the animals, and being prepared to resist its lethal, knife-sharp thrust, we can afford exhilarating hours on shining blades cutting fanciful figures, downhill flights on skis carrying us like wings, snowshoes matting trails back to beaver ponds where now only the otter comes to fish. Beneath the ice of creeks, fish still swim. Among reaching skeletons of trees, a gray jay casts a bright eye. Across the firelands are windwhipped, barren white raceways, track of coyote and fox.

Not all have perished. Some signs are still there, even though reading them is as foreign to most of this generation as Chaldea. A mink makes it, and his twin prints mark where he humped along a route mink have been following since there was a creek. In a forest clearing, white hares have dug down in an ancient orchard to get some of the sour little apples overlooked by the deer. Tracks assure the visitor that many, and especially the cantankerous porcupine, not only have met but survived the assault.

So dress warm and come. Perhaps you will be rewarded by the sight of a flit of juncos, a squadron of crossbills hanging upside down to steal seeds from the spruce cones, or even a huge pileated woodpecker drumming on a dead tree, while in the distance, ravens talk in tongues. Bring matches, and then about noon, kick the resinous heart out of a crumbling pine stump, and put a can of snow above the leaping flames for a long drink of stomach- and heart-warming tea. Rested, move again, quietly. Savor the grandeur of the winter woods. Know that here, beyond the reach of compassionate humans with our affinity for coddling the weak, evolution continues its agonizing process to ensure survival of the fittest.

Few things in nature are as insidious, as relentless as cold.

❧ *Summer Birds* ❧

It is a gloomy day, the kind of day that dampens spirits. Just outside my window to this, my little world, a white birch stands starkly naked, sharp reminder that it will be a long time before summer returns. So why, then, do I hear birds singing? Is it some kind of magic that even though pond waters are freezing, I see tree swallows maneuvering on gifted wings to collect insects just up from their watery womb? Didn't the swallows leave even before August was very old? Didn't I see them but once thereafter out on Waukesha County's Vernon Marsh, which is one of their staging areas?

I remember driving to where the road overlooks the brown reeds and rushes and the sparkling ponds. While I sat there, as if responding to some pre-arranged signal, they lifted in unison. There must have been five thousand, maybe more. They climbed toward a thinly veiled sun through a light sprinkle, and the air seemed suddenly filled with diamond raindrops and emerald birds. When I came back a few days later, they were gone. So why is it that now, when they should be in Cuba, Guatemala or Mexico, I hear their sweet, liquid twittering?

And how about you, little summer bandit with the rapier bill and long green legs that turn orange when you go courting? How come, green heron, I see you poised to spear one of my goldfish? Don't you know how much I had to pay for those goldfish? So why don't you spear some of the stunted bluegills? There are thousands, and they taste as good. While we are on the subject: How come you nested right over a colony of Turk's cap and whitewashed them to death when there were a thousand other more likely nesting places in the same spruce grove? Did you consider the goldfish as forfeit? Are they payment for amusing me by startling strangers with your clicks, clucks and muted grunts? You are handsome in an ungainly, gawky way, but you really are a clown, and perhaps you think it amusing the way you lumber along looking as if, after every measured wing beat, you are going to stall and fall. You know green herons are supposed to be in places like Texas or Louisiana by now. So how come I see you when the only remains of summer are windrows of dead leaves?

You, too, bold flicker! How come I hear you hammering on the metal eave troughs of my house? It is months before you should be sounding that territorial warning! I know you have a chisel-hard beak, but you will not get deep enough to get your favorite morsels which, of all things, are ants. I also know you are a glutton, because I just read where one of your cousins, on being autopsied, was found to have five thousand ants in its crop. So they call you woodpecker, and if that is the family of birds you belong to, why don't you hammer on trees instead of the eaves? Or do my ears deceive me, and is the hammering I hear nothing more than a leftover echo?

Uncanny! But there they are: a roving gypsy band of cedar waxwings darting out from among the hanging branches of the billowing willows that encircle and tower over Clear Pool. There are no insects now, and you should be dining on berries dead on the vine. Then, when you have picked my acres clean, you should be winging on to some other bush pantry. So why these aerial acrobatics to sip insects out of the air when fall's frosty nights have already eliminated them?

I even see a hummingbird, tiny avian helicopter with wings beating as swiftly as seventy-five times in a single second, flitting among a profusion of tiny orange jewelweed blossoms, sipping pinpoints of nectar. You should be in Panama or Mexico or Cuba. Your metabolism is such that to slow down enough to sleep you must lapse into a comatose state resembling hibernation. I wonder if you visit my neighbor. Last summer he counted twenty of your cousins, all dining at the same time from the long, slender blossoms of the trumpet vine that climbs all the way to the eaves of his house.

And how come gold still glitters among the flocks of goldfinches? By now, glittering cocks should be as drab as their hens. And robins! I saw them leave in little gangs, so now why can I count so many on the long lawn that slopes all the way to the ponds?

Of course, the birds are gone. But on such a gloomy day as this, the most ebullient of spirits seems to sink. So, presto! Time for magic. And then the images of the birds of summer fly across the mirror of my mind. Imagination. It is a talent we all have, but one with which the very young and very old are especially gifted.

⋙ Old Age and Trickery ⋘

Being something of an authority on the subject, I would like to pass along a few suggestions on how to have a good time while growing old. For starters, learn to limp. If you can rise from your chair favoring a knee, chances are you won't have to go to the kitchen to get a cup of coffee. Someone will bring it to you. Or wince a little when you walk, especially if there is snow to shovel, leaves to rake, flowers to weed or a sink full of dishes to be washed. If you are convincing enough, someone is sure to say: "Now you just sit still, Grandpa, because we can take care of those things."

Do not, of course, make the mistake of showing too much appreciation. Instead, put on a hangdog look and mutter something about feeling useless. It will get you a generous dollop of sympathy in addition to a nap while someone else does the work. If the wince isn't working, add a wheeze. Then, if you are practiced enough, every head will turn your way and you will get a second helping of cake, or whatever, without even asking for it.

Always, of course, keep a shawl where you can reach it from your TV chair. Then, if you do not want to go outside or to the basement for a smoke, pull on the shawl, shiver a little and finger your pipe lovingly. It is a sure bet someone will say, "Just go ahead, Grandpa. We don't mind."

By all means contrive to get a bottle of medicine from your doctor, whether you need it or not. Keep it handy. Then, when the grandchildren are tearing down the house, or the dog is barking to get out, or someone has turned the stereo to an ear-shattering crescendo, take a long pull from the medicine bottle. Then, close your eyes, lean back and sigh. Things should quiet down promptly. (Always keep the medicine bottle half-full by adding water colored with vegetable dye.)

Whether you need it or not, get a hearing aid. Leave it off when you want to eavesdrop on how your "growing old campaign" is progressing. What is more, using a hearing aid, you can pop in and out of the action at will. Never, of course, hear questions you can't or don't want to answer. Eyeglasses are also a useful tool, even if they are cut from a windowpane. Lose them whenever necessary and you can get out of anything from balancing a checkbook to washing windows. If you decide to spend a day pruning the yews, don't overdo it. Stop to rest often. Someone is sure to notice. Chances are, then, that any chore scheduled for you will be prefaced by an escape clause: "Now, Grandpa, only if you feel up to it."

In extreme emergencies, such as during housecleaning, sit forward with your eyes closed and your hands to your head. Then, if someone asks if you have a headache, be sure to say: "No. Oh, no. Just thinking." After that, one will get you ten that someone will say, "Let Grandpa rest. I don't think he feels good."

Improvise as you go along. There are hundreds of variations to be played upon the same theme. If you are having trouble coming across in a convincing manner, take a lesson from the way a small child manipulates a doting grandmother. Kids always have been masters at the art of manipulation.

If all this sounds simple, it is not. To employ this stratagem, you will have to hone your acting skills until they are worthy of an Academy Award. Now that I have blown my cover to present these words of wisdom, I hope that when I leave this vale of crocodile tears, I will be rewarded with a place, if not on the right hand, then at the feet of that great god of writers, Mark Twain.

⇛ *Little Killer* ⇚

Amazing is the efficiency with which a tiny screech owl kills a rabbit three times its size. But January calls for stern measures, and often macabre and daring exploits are all that stand between death and survival. Walking a trail where deep snow keeps a diary of all nighttime activities, I come upon the obituary of the rabbit, and his carcass, too. It is instantly obvious that death came during the night and from the air. A feather tells me the executioner was a screech owl.

If you have never held a screech owl, know that it is a mere handful of fluffy feathers covering stringy tendons. Though it weighs less than half a pound, it is armed with a sharp, slightly curving beak and strong, needle-sharp talons. Nevertheless, a two- or three-pound cottontail has enough kick to decapitate the owl with a single, well-aimed wallop. I do not perform an autopsy. It is obvious the owl struck the rabbit silently and swiftly directly behind the ears with its talons, and either broke the neck or hit nerves, which paralyzed the victim.

It is obvious also that the owl immediately pecked out the cottontail's eyes. Except for such convulsions as precede death, it is apparent the rabbit put up no struggle. Once the rabbit died, the tiny owl relaxed its grip and, going to the rear of the carcass, dined sparingly on a haunch. He was not strong enough to fly his booty to a cache. So I drape the carcass as high as I can reach in the crotch of a box elder. With help from starlings and chickadees, the owl dines four nights before being compelled to hunt again.

⇛ *Mystery Man* ⇚

He sits there no longer, but when my work took me more frequently to the airport, I would see him on the same bench, newspaper folded on his lap, shoulders hunched into a black overcoat. I must have walked past him twenty times or more, at midnight or noon, morning or evening, before it occurred to me that he was not an inanimate airport fixture but a man, a living being, placidly watching people surge to and fro in eternal haste. Once, when my plane was late, I managed to sit on the same bench. It was then I saw that the newspaper in his lap was yellow with age and likely had never been unfolded. I craned my neck and made out the date: April 1, 1945.

One afternoon, coming home from a Canadian trip, I noticed he was not there. I stopped as if at the edge of an unexpected precipice, teetering in surprise. Then my family swarmed around and swept me toward the baggage room. Hastening out toward the car, I took one look back and saw him shuffle from a rest room, the old paper in one hand, a candy bar in the other.

That evening I mentioned it to my wife. "Likely alone in the world," she said. "Probably poor and senile on top of it."

"I suppose so," I agreed.

Being home was so great, and being loved was so wonderful, that I put the haunting picture of the old man out of my mind and wallowed in the warmth of being wanted. Two days later I was off again, and the old man was there. Just before departure time, a snow squall closed the airport and everybody wandered from the boarding alcoves downstairs into the main terminal toward the bars, the restaurants and the game rooms. But I went to sit by the old man. As usual, his eyes seemed to see everything, yet nothing. He only occasionally shifted weight from port to starboard and then back again. I slid closer, trying to catch his eye, ready, if it happened, with what I hoped would be a warm, inviting smile. But though his eyes crossed my face half a dozen times, there was no flicker of response. Finally, I had to speak.

"Just a squall," I said. "Traffic will resume momentarily." If he heard me, he ignored me. Still I tried: "People get nervous when flights are delayed."

He turned, and in a clear, well-modulated voice, asked, "Am I to presume you are addressing me?" I was so shocked I could only gulp and nod. "Well, in answer to your question," he went on in what I swear was an Oxford accent, "people are always nervous, only more so when an obstacle is present."

I found my voice. "True, true. You're right, of course."

Flight announcements ended what I had hoped might evolve into a conversation. It was more than a month before I got the chance to sit next to him again.

"Good morning," I offered. I had to repeat the greeting three times before he acknowledged it.

"Oh, it's you again," he said, as though it was only yesterday that I had first sat by his side. I assume I must have blushed.

"Yeah ... yes," I said, correcting myself. "My family must have gotten caught up in traffic, since they're not here to pick me up."

There was a long silence before he said: "Everybody's always caught up in traffic."

I didn't quite know what he meant or how to take him, so I agreed. "Yes, I suppose so." Then, getting bolder, "Except you, sir, never seem to have such trouble."

For the first time, I saw a flicker of a change in the expression on his face. Slowly he turned the old paper over and over in his hands. Then he said, "No, I don't get caught up in traffic. Not any more."

I waited, hoping he would elucidate. When he didn't, I asked, "But there was a time ... ?" I hesitated and then went on, " ... that you were, should I say, caught up in traffic?" I don't know why I thought myself impertinent. Surprisingly, it seemed he did not, and I saw just the shadow of a smile soften the grim line of his wrinkled lips.

"I traveled continually for thirty years. Eighteen times around the world." Before my amazement could bring some inane observation to my lips, my tardy family swarmed over me and swept me away. That was the last time I saw him at the airport. After a couple of months of looking at where he had always sat, I could stand it no longer and began making inquiries. It was relatively easy. Every airport employee had been, if not as intrigued, then as aware as I was of his presence. They told me the exact date and time of day he was taken away in an ambulance, victim of what they concluded was a heart attack or a stroke. It was some time before I made inquiry at the hospital, and again I almost immediately found people who remembered his arrival and departure.

"His name is Mr. Torrance B. Rochri," a charge nurse said. Flipping pages, she added, "He suffered a stroke. He was transferred to Olivet Arms, one of the finest nursing homes in the city." I would have gone straight to Olivet Arms, but I had a trip scheduled, so I hurried for the airport. It was almost two weeks before I got to Olivet Arms. I was ushered into a two-room suite where Mr. Rochri, partially paralyzed, sat in a wheelchair, the yellowed newspaper in his lap.

Seeing me, he nodded, and then with some difficulty said, "I assumed you'd look for me. There was something about you."

I felt like a small boy. He motioned me to a chair. An attendant brought coffee. I tried pleasantries, but got little more than nods. Then I blurted out, "But don't you miss the airport?"

"Not at all," he said, pointing to an enormous and brilliantly lighted ant farm back of glass, thousands of insects going nowhere in maddening haste. "Not at all."

⋙ *Sun Seekers* ⋘

Amazing is the ingenuity displayed by the sun seekers. With the mercury in the thermometer threatening to bottom out, we assume that there are no cozy corners outside our artificially heated homes. Be not deceived, because cottontail and squirrel, horse and dog, sparrow and fox, all know about places of warmth. On a southern slope where the sun has cut a tunnel through the hazel brush, a fox may be basking, tail curled to cover his nose, in a dry grass bed that gathers in the heat reflected by the snow.

Venture no farther than the stable. Carry a thermometer, and hang it in the sun where the horses are sleeping in a corner out of the wind, so close to the building that no reflected warmth escapes. Hang the thermometer where the horses stand, and watch the mercury rise. See how the squirrel stretches, head down, on the trunk of a tree, legs so far akimbo that every square inch of his body is absorbing heat from the wood and the sun at the same time.

Come to where the sun shines beneath a spruce skirt, and see sparrows perched in such a scientific circle that they take heat not only from the sun, but from one another. Around the house, notice how birds learn to use chimney corners, window reflections and dry spots close to the foundations where sometimes even the earth does not freeze. Catch a cottontail in his form. Note how the dry, dead grass curls up over his back as a buffer over which every wind just slides. See how the sun shines brightly into quarters that precisely fit a body so compactly arranged, even an ear tip does not show.

And do not feel sorry for the duck because he is squatting on ice. His insulation is the best in the world, and his webs, the only vulnerable portion of his whole body, are tucked tight and safely into the soft down of his warm bottom.

⋙ Souls Laid Bare ⋘

When a favorite tree drops her leaves just before winter, I think of lines from John Keats' famous poem "The Eve of St. Agnes:"

Unclasps her warmed jewels one by one;
Loosens her fragrant bodice; by degrees
Her rich attire creeps rustling to her knees.

So then it is winter and the trees stand naked. Now, should you take the time, there for remembering are the scars of the storms that brought you startled from your bed or sent you hustling from street or field for the shelter of a house. There are the broken limbs, badly healed and growing at grotesque angles. There, too, broken branches that failed to put out new tendrils, and decaying stumps, refuges of insects, pantries for birds. Here at Little Lakes, a huge sugar maple now shows its jagged lightning wound. And, back in the pasture, a smaller burr oak reveals a lightning strike that circled its way down the tree's trunk to leave a snake-like tattoo. But more interesting than wounds of wind and fire are the character and characteristics of winter trees, now that they have been stripped of their finery.

I see the winter hawthorn as a hopelessly arthritic cripple. Standing there naked, the tree seems to writhe in pain. But Gwen sees the tree as an artistic masterpiece of branches curling in a caring embrace. So she brings some branches into the house to give warmth and character to an otherwise uninteresting corner. As for the paper birch, even though it is naked, there are no words I can find to compare to James Russell Lowell's contention that it is the "most shy and ladylike of trees."

Cousins of the birch, the perpetually sighing poplars of warmer days are pale in the icy moonlight and so uncommonly quiet I can believe they are visiting ghosts and will be gone by morning. Then there is the widow maker, the weeping willow. It probably has maimed or killed more wood-cutters than any other, since there is no predicting what it will do, short of exploding, when tortured by the saw. If there be a tree more lovely in summer than a billowing weeping willow, I do not know of it. Out here, we have a row of oldtimers with waists bigger around than barrels. They drape their finery out over Blue Pool. In summer, they dance gracefully on a breeze and gallop in green splendor on a wind. On quiet days, they come down in emerald tiers like trees in a fairyland. But now, in winter, their tresses have been blown and they are a grotesque tangle of dead and living branches, more snarled than a head of long, uncombed hair.

In this winter tree community, the tamarack is the only needle tree to bare itself. Almost ugly now, it is a scab on the landscape. Poking out of marshes, stands of tamarack look as though they have been blackened by fire. The list of trees is long: Mulberry with bark which, like the cheeks of a child, takes on color in the cold. The hickory, shaggy as an unkempt sheep dog. The American elm, naked limbs spreading like the ribs of an umbrella stripped of its canopy. The black cherry, scabby as though from an infection. The ironwood, gray as death.

As always, there is an eccentric, even among trees. It is the red oak. If some snowy day you hear the rustling of leaves, know that a red oak is near, because of all Wisconsin's deciduous trees, it is the most reluctant to appear naked in public. Often it holds its leaves right on through the blizzards of winter, until the buds of spring force them to fall to make way for the green leaves of summer.

Should winter be long, take a lesson from the patiently waiting trees and know that, except for these barren months, spring hardly would be worth waiting for, or cause for celebration when, at last, it arrives.

⇛ *Frosty Morning* ⇚

5:00 a.m. The stars are bright pinpricks in a black canopy of sky as my electric tractor, the Gray Ghost, hums along the south trail through the old pasture, now a tree plantation. I do not need lights because, even in the dark, I know the terrain as I know the wrinkles on my face. Head-high cedars and spruce flank the trail and march in orderly rows on down to Fish Pond. The trees are white with new snow, sheeted ghosts. Their roots are intertwined among bones, because this is an Indian burial ground, and I wonder if the spirits of the dead seep up through the cellular structure of the trees to make them shine so uncommonly bright.

5:30 a.m. I am parked on the dike that flanks the west side of Fish Pond. An aerator, some twenty feet from shore, makes gurgling sounds as bubbles race away from a boil of water swollen by compressed air. On the ice around the large circle of open water are dark patches that I know to be wild ducks. They are hunkered down over their vulnerable webs, conserving heat. I resist the temptation to throw a little corn, since the feeding ritual is the last act, performed just before night returns. I tease them instead by reaching out to rattle the pail that holds the corn. I get a few guttural complaints, but I have fooled them too often, and they know me for what I am. To the west, which is on my left, is the mill pond, a ten-acre white sheet of snow-covered ice stretching across to the highway where drivers follow the path of headlights on their way to work. Across a small bay where Watercress Creek is a dark thrust of open water, there is a light in the home of Sibyll Yug, village matriarch. I hear a door open, and I hear her talking, perhaps to her cat. The ducks hear her, and now they stir about. She sets a table for them, too.

6:00 a.m. Tooling along again, I pass Blue Pool and stop on the shore of New Pool. From a thick grove of tall spruce, a screech owl whimpers. Then it gets hold of itself and claims territorial rights in a series of melodious trills. A mouse hears the owl, too, and it is a black streak across the snow before disappearing to where it has eaten out tunnels to create a snow-buried city of many streets.

6:15 a.m. I ease down on the hand throttle, and the Gray Ghost moves quietly among the spruce down a narrow, winding trail. I hear mourning dove wings against the branches as the birds flee, startled from their roosts. A cottontail is a swiftly moving shadow coming straight toward me. I turn on the headlights and it stops so suddenly it kicks up snow. It waits until the Gray Ghost is upon it before diving beneath a spruce skirt. I turn off the lights and wait for my eyes to adjust before proceeding.

6:30 a.m. On the road bridge that spans Watercress Creek, I face the Gray Ghost south and wait. The sky is pale as paper now. Light filters between the trees, and bits of bottom vegetation move on the creek's current, so I know a muskrat is feeding somewhere upstream. A passing reflection in the creek tells me a bird is through roosting for the night.

6:45 a.m. I am getting cold sitting so still, but resist the temptation to move when a long, dark shadow comes at me from beneath a spruce clump. It is a mink, and when it winds me, it stops about fifteen feet away. I wait. So does the mink. I turn on the Gray Ghost's lights. It is a big mink, almost black and obviously a buck. With the light in its eyes, it turns its head from side to side as if in bewilderment. But, as is typical of mink, it exhibits no fear, even when I rattle the brake pedal. From now until early spring, he will travel some hundreds of miles in ever-widening circles, looking for willing females. He will lose weight, get a few fresh scars quarreling with rival bucks, and likely be glad when it is finally over and all there is left to worry about is his neglected appetite. I turn out the lights and he swims the creek and disappears in a brush pile.

7:00 a.m. The Gray Ghost grinds up the hill to where bees are in winter quarters. Topping out, I park in a clearing. Now I can see the sun's rays above the treetops. I hear the kitchen door of my home open and then close, and so I put the Gray Ghost into neutral, release the brake, and coast down the hill.

7:15 a.m. The house is warm. Breakfast tastes good. Frosty morning.

⋙ *Edge of the Hereafter* ⋘

January narrows perimeters, and wild ones, so plentiful during the halcyon days of green grass, have experienced such population losses that, from the anonymity of overabundance, the remaining survivors begin to emerge as individuals. The big-city dweller, moving about the crowds of nameless faces, knows about this when on moving to a village he gets to know everybody in town. When there were a hundred cotton-tails, we could not distinguish one from the other. Now, likely they number a dozen or fifteen.

So, they get names, and two are referred to as the Prickly Ash rabbits. The prickly ash is protection from attack. Hawk and fox, knowing about the thorns, settle for mice, and the Prickly Ash rabbits scrounge out a living by eating the bark of any digestible plant within the confines of their nigh-impenetrable fortress. Then there is the Pine rabbit, which hides for protection against enemies and cold beneath conifer skirts, for-aging only as far as the ironwood tree for catkins, which droop low as the snow. A particularly hardy individual is the Watercress Creek rabbit. It lives right on the ice of a desultory tributary to the main stream beneath an overhang of red dogwood. If its quarters are less than comfortable, its pantry contains all manner of bankside greens, where forty-eight-degree spring water keeps the snow away and the soil soft.

Then the Cattail Patch rabbits: five cattail patches, five Cattail Patch rabbits. Only a weasel or a mink is likely to catch them in such heavy cover, but since food is scarce in any cattail patch, they must risk night-time forays across less friendly terrain. Brush Pile rabbits are always eating their own homes. There are at least three brush piles, and each houses at least one and sometimes two cottontails.

There is one Sugar Bush rabbit. Though his home is short on protec-tive cover, plenty of maple shoots provide sweet eating. Then we have the Fence Line rabbit, Briar Patch rabbit, Spruce Grove rabbit, and three House rabbits. All except the House rabbits, which hang around the back door waiting for handouts, live right on the edge of the Hereafter. One deep snow can lift them above the fuel that feeds their furnaces.

⋙ *Winter Passion* ⋘

Though it may seem the cold heart of January would ice down any passion, know that already the foxes and coyotes are running in pairs, and the great horned owls are mating. The fox barks, and the coyote announces his intentions in a scattering of yelps threaded together by a thin howl. Most impressive is the great horned owl's deliberate wooing: "To-who-woo-o-o-oo, woo-o." Far away, another owl takes up the chant, and perhaps a third, a rival, announces that there will be a considerable clacking of predacious bills, ruffling of feathers and show of talons before the pairing has been decided, before the mating takes place.

To come silently to a midnight forest under the light sent out from a star a million years ago, and to hear the owls talk of mixing creative juices during a brief joining so that there may be eggs and owlets, is to come as close as any will ever get to the core of the universe. Standing in the intense cold, listening to the lovers chant, an egotistical man may feel that only he and the gods are witness to such rites. But there are a thousand ears — mouse, shrew, tree sparrow, goldfinch, otter, mink, muskrat, jay, weasel, snow bunting, redpoll, siskin, porcupine — all understanding with primordial instinct that which a man only hazily comprehends.

⋙ *Time of Truce* ⋘

Just as catastrophic visitations, man-made or of the natural order, dissolve differences and put friends and enemies into the same camp, so all birds declare a January truce. The interminable bickering, the feather-pulling assaults for territory, mates and food, are forgotten. Like forlorn miscreants in a Salvation Army chow line, they do not jostle, and even the raucous blue jay patiently awaits a turn at the bird feeder.

Juncos, which only last month spent most of daylight performing unbelievable aerial maneuvers in a war that ended for one or another in a window pane crash, now scratch side by side to uncover seeds the last snow has covered. Cock cardinals stack up among the tortured branches of a hawthorn to take turns dipping down for sunflower seeds. Even red-headed woodpeckers, usually so arrogant in their sharply pieced suits of red and black and white, feed peaceably alongside a grackle detained by a wing injury when its squadron went south. The grackle, a razor-sharp blade concealed along the roof of its beak, makes no threatening gesture, nor does the woodpecker point its stiletto, except in the direction of the food. So perhaps it is no idle assumption that when the shadow of world-wide catastrophe threatens extinction, humans will at last become friends.

But let spring come, and the cold that congealed the warlike aspirations of the feathered ones warms, and once again the heated battles begin. Then robin chases robin, jays route all except the grackles, and a cock cardinal dies in an explosion of red feathers against the chrome bumper of a parked auto. Peace will have to wait until another January presents a common adversary, and cold, like a sword, hangs again by a thread above every neck.

⫸ *Places of Giant Steps* ⫷

The raptures of country living have captivated this generation. Today's cities, often characterized as filthy and crime-ridden, are losing people as never before. Dry rot, spreading from downtown, leaves behind the specter of empty buildings, their broken windows offering little hint of the days when they looked down on streets vibrant with life.

Businesses are following the people, locating factories in industrial parks. Department stores and bookstores, restaurants and theaters, hotels and motels locate in, or cluster around, shopping centers accessible to the families who have opted for a cottage on a country lane or a colonial house on a lazy village square.

City, thy name has become anathema. Your once-shining storefronts are heavily draped and boarded. In many areas, only the imprisoned poor stand waiting for traffic lights to change. Only the gutter runners, clutching their brown-bagged bottles, shuffle past. On once-important streets, the chic shops have closed; where gentlemen would buy diamonds for their ladies, a sorrowing woman hocks her wedding ring for money to buy a ring of bologna. High-rise office buildings still stand proud, but they empty on signal, and workers flee as far as their wallets will allow, until the morning alarm sends them back in bumper-to-bumper traffic. Even zoos have deserted the boulevard parks for country acres, and libraries, universities and museums are losing customers to satellite schools, mini-museums and suburban libraries.

But it was not always thus. Cities were proud places, exciting havens, refuges from the drudgery and monotony of an isolated rural existence.

Then, even if escape was not possible, the city was the dream world of most every country boy and girl, the enchanted land, a place of happy shops, blazing lights, glare and glitter, fun and noise and, above all, opportunity. Contrary to popular notion, the greatest number of city-bound migrants did not make their move when World War I boys decided nothing could keep them down on the farm (after they'd seen Paree). In fact, it came years before the Kaiser shook his fist at the world.

The crucial decades were much earlier, from 1840 to 1870. At no time in history did such a large segment of America's population gravitate to the cities. In 1840, the census registered a 63.7 percent increase in urban dwellers as compared to 1830. In 1850, there was a startling 92.1 percent increase, and even in 1860, with the Civil War about to explode, the increase was 75.4 percent.

The publishing industry, according to an article by New York City educator Adrienne Siegel in the *Journal of Popular Culture*, became quickly "alert to the needs of supplying a mass market with cheap books," churning out an extraordinary number of novels that presented a hungry readership with information about the burgeoning urban centers of America. Writing in 1869, Junius Henri Browne described the city as a place of "saints and sinners, mendicants and millionaires, priests and poets, courtesans and chiffoniers, burglars and boot-blacks ... "

It was a place, according to Ms. Siegel, "always varying, always new, every day and every hour. The city seemed to enlarge the mind, sharpen the faculties and quicken the wit."

Even George C. Foster, a critic of urban society, admitted in 1849: "A great city is the highest result of human civilization. Here the soul ... has put forth its most wonderful energies — energies developed to their utmost power and excited to their highest state of activity by constant contact with our souls, each emulating, impelling, stimulating, rivaling, outdoing the others ... It is only in a large city, where some hundreds of thousands combine their various powers, that the human mind can effectively stamp itself on everything by which it is surrounded."

What Foster wrote more than a hundred years ago is as true today as it was then. No matter how much we may need the land to refresh and revitalize our sagging spirits, we need — and must preserve and rebuild — the great cities, every man's true university, the only place civilization can take giant strides.

⇒⇒ *Dumb Animals?* ⇐⇐

Since I have libeled my animal friends by listing a few of the dumb things they do, it is only fair to turn the coin for a look at the other side.

Let me tell you about a quarter-horse mare named Joker. There was no gate she could not ultimately open, unless it was padlocked or nailed shut. Then there was a German short-haired pointer named Rainey, who, on needing to relieve himself during the night, would come to my bedside and, with his nose, lift my hand and let it fall until I awakened and let him outside. There was a tame crow who could steal an earring, sometimes without even disturbing its owner, who had fallen asleep on a lawn chair.

One blue jay always won my game of find-the-peanut, whether hidden in a pants pocket or under a stone. And if some foxes and some mink were easily trapped, there have been others who upset my boyhood equilibrium by continually stealing the bait without disturbing the trap. Even the quarrelsome and seemingly stupid English sparrow adapts to adversity with an inventiveness bordering on animal genius.

But forgetting such birds as have learned to use tools (twigs) to pry insects out of holes, the everyday variety of wild and domestic animal is among the most fastidious of creatures, cunningly and convincingly neater, cleaner and better organized than most humans. Take the gate opener, Joker. She never fouled any part of her grassy pasture by recklessly broadcasting "horse apples" instead piling them in an out-of-the-way fence corner. Rainey was a fanatic in matters of cleanliness. Even as an old dog, after having worked from sunrise to sunset on quail or pheasant, grouse or ducks, he would groom every inch of his body with his tongue before falling asleep. Many a night I flopped exhausted on a motel bed without even washing my hands, and hours later I would awaken to hear the old dog still cleaning the grime accumulated during the hunt.

Ever see a messy wild bird nest? You haven't, because after every delivery of food to the fledglings, the parent picks up the deposits and carries them away. Maybe raccoons do wash everything when water is available because, as some scientists insist, they "taste" with the sensitive palms of their hand-like feet. Ever see a nest of dirty puppies, kittens, coyotes, wolves, muskrats? Of course you haven't. Animals keep their young squeaking clean, which is more than can be said of some human mothers.

Watch a flicker, wings akimbo, sprawled on an anthill. Picking up insects, the flicker rubs them over its body to obtain enough ant acid to discourage lice. What is more, animals groom each other in hard-to-get-at-places. And large hawks, at the risk of being vulnerable to predator attack, thoroughly soak themselves while bathing and must remain grounded until their feathers dry.

Did I say "dumb animals"? Yes, I guess I did, and it is true that one opossum came to the same live trap fifteen times without having learned of its hazards. So how come the opossum outlived the dinosaur? Maybe it has something to do with knowing precisely when to play dead. Even a dog is not about to bother an old possum "carcass," even if it is lying right across the trail.

Dumb animals? Maybe. Plastic clothespins, red, yellow and white, hanging on a line in the backyard, keep hummingbirds in a tizzy as they flit from one to the other looking for nectar from what appear to be blossoms. Down on Fish Pond, a raccoon regularly investigates the submerged head of a large, aluminum nail driven into a post supporting a pier. Night after night the masked one returns, never remembering that the nail is not a shiny minnow. Every spring, a robin (the same one?) comes to tug at a fishline trellis meant as a stairway for morning glories, despite the fact that it never succeeds in getting a single inch for nesting.

For twenty years, sparrows fly white chicken feathers to the same wren house, even though the doorway is much too small for the likes of such a bird. A grackle, minus many feathers, has had to be rescued a dozen times because it makes the same mistake of walking through the low doorway of the dog kennel, then can't find a way out. A certain mole has been carried from the basement perhaps fifty times, but still returns, though there is not one a morsel of food on the concrete floor to ensure survival.

A matronly gray squirrel, with a large scar across her neck, has been trying for five years to gnaw through the heavy sunroom door in search of nuts. Although our country place has hundreds and hundreds of trees, a pair of blue jays insist on nesting in a runty spruce within thirty feet of where a squirrel has her den in a linden. The birds spend more time protecting their eggs and fledglings from the squirrels than scavenging for food. Even though secluded nesting sites abound, a certain mallard hen sits on eggs within inches of a path where a careless foot might easily scramble her family plans.

A fat toad has acres and acres of what qualifies as ideal toad habitat, yet on being rescued insists on going back, time after time, to fall into the same window well. Almost every year, a female mink uses a den so close to the waterline that inevitably spring rains force her to move her brood as the water rises.

Every time the ancient, thirty-pound snapping turtle in Fish Pond sees a fishing bobber on the water, it takes the bait and has to have another hook extracted from its jaws. Sometimes, since the turtle is so large and powerful, the line must be cut. Somehow, the turtle always manages to get rid of the hook before being caught again. No matter how many times we remove the hornets' nest from the inner crown of the dinner bell, within a week another is being built. Now we do not bother the nest; only ring the bell and run.

A teal builds her nest so far back in a hayfield she loses her young on the way to water. A song sparrow builds her ground nest next to the nightly parade ground of the neighborhood cats, and the mourning dove builds such a fragile nest of sticks it must produce three and four clutches a year to make up for the eggs and young doves the wind blows to the ground.

But before you start feeling superior, reckon on the humans who build their homes on flood flats, on the edges of eroding cliffs, or in tinder-dry brush country. Maybe the snapping turtle is some kind of fool for getting hooked so many times, but look at the junk you have accumulated over the years and ask yourself how come you have been suckered so often into taking the bait. At least animals don't invite death by driving while drunk, smoking cigarettes, gobbling sweets or polluting their own dens or water supplies with their own wastes.

⋙ *June in January* ⋘

June in January. Only a song? Not for the Wilson snipe, which has deferred going south and lives like a king because there are no other Wilson snipe to compete with him for the worms caddis and gamerus that live among the wilted watercress where water from a bubbling spring never freezes.

Not for a colony of robins less than a mile from the ice-armored shores of Lake Superior, where winds from the warmer waters of this great inland sea meet between high hills to put a more temperate face on the floor of the deep valley. January may come right down to build icy shelves along a far northern river, but where the current tumbles so rapidly that even the cold cannot stop it long enough to build a shield, a pair of buffleheads, diminutive as ducks go, striking in black-blues and white, turn stones to gorge on snails.

Arrogant red-headed woodpeckers, warm at night in the hollows of trees, take advantage of a record mast crop and refuse to forsake the sandy, scrub oak forests to make the round trip south. Mergansers stay, and if their harbors freeze, they fly to where the wind has opened another. Lining up, they fish in practiced dives and, like a well-drilled military unit, hold ranks to corral little fishes.

Eagles, which once wintered in the Ohio Valley, stay where a Wisconsin River impoundment catapults water over rocky basins, to harvest fish seeking the ample oxygen of the tumbling, aerated waters. Little sora rails, having learned about the tunnels and hollows under ice shelves that completely hide small flowing creeks, live adequately fed and warmed, out of sight of hawk or even prowling fox. Only a man, accidentally stepping too close to the creek edge, may break an ice roof and see the dusky shore birds scuttling for other quarters.

June in January? Where heat from a bedded deer has brought a beetle topside to see if spring has come.

February

FEBRUARY IS A MOOD RATHER THAN A
MONTH. Coming to a craggy bluff swept clear of
snow, I sit among the naked boulders as a god
waiting to witness a beginning. From my pre-
Cambrian promontory, I see no signs of life. The
earth seems to be waiting, too, as it did so many
millions of years ago, for the oceans to gather, the
mountains to rise and the basic elements of life to
join. Without prior knowledge, I would never
know that among the rocks around me, and down
the wind-swept slope to the icy valley, are a billion
beginnings. For all intents and purposes, as
viewed from my high February perch, the earth is
desolate, lifeless as when, solidified at last, it first
began to cool and make a place for trilobites and
graptolites, scorpion and sea lily, spider and
ammonite, brontosaurus and frog, the mammals,
and man.

Of course, I know better. Mesmerized,
however, by what seems an interminable winter, I
am, if not content, at least resigned to await creation. For the impatient youngster who has not
yet come to enough springtimes, it is a period of
doubt, and for them I would eliminate the month
entirely, by giving fourteen days to January and
the other fourteen to March. But we are a punch-
clock people, dividing time as if it mattered. So
we measure minutes, hours and days, slaves to a
wrist watch and the calendar. Then comes the
"month of purification," dragging its heels, and
though the shortest month of the year, it seems
an interminable time.

*As viewed
from my high
February perch,
the earth is
desolate, lifeless.*

For the impatient youngster who has not yet come to enough springtimes, it is a period of doubt.

February. A suicidal month. For the despondent, it is the month that trips the trigger. For the wild society, it is the month of denouement. The plot is simple: life or death. All reserves have been spent. One more storm can bring them to their knees for the last time. Yet February has its surprises for those who will leave the dark corners of their discontent, and I have come on a subzero day to a bend in a creek to see a hovering cloud of tiny black flies. Incredible!

But the arcing sun is already two months in seasonal ascendancy, and the protected pocket warms like a heart under the burning glass of love. Cold notwithstanding, sap starts rising. Waxen willows become vivid, and maples bleed from every winter wound. Rocks retain the sun's warmth to melt surrounding snow, and in a dish or crevice of a southern slope, a snowdrop, tulip or daffodil shows green fingertips. Sometimes, too, the somber mood brightens to a white-throated sparrow's song, repeated and repeated, as if survival depended on it. The cardinal, which whistled somewhat tentatively in January, becomes more insistent.

Several times I have found eggs of stay-over ducks in the water of spring holes, though it is still weeks before nest-building time. It is no month for rave reviews. Its virtues are few. Like nights for the insomniac, these moments seem never ending. February tolls the days like muffled drums, measured to mark the funeral march. Even death is no longer surprising. Has not January provided the winter quota? So why this mongrel month? To give the year an even dozen? I will endure it, of course, but I give it short shrift. There is no point in lingering to inflict its somber monotony on the white purity of any page.

⇛ *Sparklers in the Sky* ⇚

To my brother George:

I think often of you on your far northern island miles beyond the end of the road, especially at night. Perhaps it is because, down here, even in our Wisconsin country place, there is no real night any longer. Once (can it be less than a decade ago?) I could sit in my favorite corner of what we euphemistically call the music room and, looking out the picture window, pick a certain star and reckon almost to the minute what time it was. I could know for sure that just as the star hung itself on the first branch of the white birch, or came to the top of the chestnut tree, Gwen would ask: "Want a sandwich before you go to bed?"

We still took nighttime walks then, leisurely strolls to stop at each bend in the creek to hear the water murmur, to sit on a log and watch the bat's arcing flight, to count how many bullfrogs we "owned" as each boomed about love. We even slept, sometimes, right there on the nighttime grass, until the dew was on our cheeks and the chill sent us somewhat creakily up the slope to warmer beds. Mostly, those days (of course, I should say nights) are gone. Now, even if we take a nighttime walk, it is with a downcast eye, because where are the stars to light the dim trails?

We are worried about the stars. We never even guessed how important they were until, on one of those rare nights when a superb combination of weather conditions swept back the gray veil, a surprised grandson, standing in awe, gasped, "Somebody sprinkled the sky full of sparklers."

That was when I first began thinking about how it is on your island, where the stars seem so low as to festoon the spruce on the ridge, and even hang like boat-landing lights in some of the distant bays and along the peninsulas we used to fish. An odd combination of conditions has all but eliminated our stars. On the east side it is mostly the Milwaukee glare of those high-intensity sodium vapor lights, and on the west it is the pall of minute particles which, when the wind dies, leave telltale slicks on a pond's quiet waters.

Actually, I suppose I should be less worried about my own feelings and more concerned about what the ever-increasing artificial light is doing to trees and grass and animals and even people. There are theories about how artificial light is affecting the sex ratio of wildlings and even putting a damper on their sexual activity. Some theorists conclude that what can happen to wild ones exposed to artificial light can happen to people. There are studies suggesting that the elimination of nighttime is causing all kinds of aberrations, physical and mental.

But somehow I do not buy these theories. I have New York friends who, for most of their lifetimes, have been going to bed in darkened rooms at dawn, and then rising to start their day when the neon signs blink on. And they have raised healthy families, and some are older and more rugged than I am.

Mostly, I am concerned with the stars and all those other props that nighttime once employed to make it mystical, like bats and owls, crickets and tree frogs, and leopard frogs, whose ranks have been so thinned that it is a rare night when there is volume enough for any kind of concert. And to think I once complained about the predawn chorus of bird voices. Now, there is such a diminishing music that when I awaken in the halflight (when I was young I used to call it the "holy" light) of dawn, sometimes all I hear is the far-off growl of a truck grinding up some hill. But what seems tragic to me may not seem so tragic to others, especially those too young to remember how, on all except cloudy nighttimes, the skies were always crowded with stars.

Take the rosy-cheeked young lovers, almost breathless with the excite-ment of a new snow, who came to our back door one night last winter to ask if it would be all right to wander around the place, drinking in the wintertime beauty. My first inclination was to say, "This is nothing. I remember when ... " But it was something, even if the stars were not there to add extra sheen to the whitened skirts of the spreading spruce, or to make the frost flowers on branches sparkle like thousands of dia-monds. It was something to be the first to make a track under the bending boughs of snow-burdened pines, to be a part of the magic that is silence, a soft stillness as deep as snow. Then, even if I do not live long enough, I have the feeling that these lovers are young enough to be around on some future night, when humans have scrubbed the air and shaded the glare of their artificial lights, to discover for themselves the stars that lit the skies of my life.

Anyway, George, I am sure you get what I am driving at: Do not take your nighttime for granted. At the end even of an arduous day, step out from your northern island home and, looking up, know that this is a special gift you have, a gift I once had and so little appreciated.

⫷ *Talisman* ⫸

"Damn!" I say it loud enough so I can hear myself above the motor's roar. I turn the key, step from the car, walk down off the bridge. He looks lifelike lying there, yellow legs stretched behind, crest undulating in the slight current, neck folded and tucked back in that squatting position, which so identifies the black-capped night-heron.

"Damn!" I say it again, because he has been so heroic and should have made it. I retrieve the body to examine more closely the chisel-hard beak and the slate-blue feathers of the back.

A wing injury had made him a prisoner of the north. For weeks in fall he had stood in the marsh, watching the feathery cavalcade move south. Then he waded upstream to where waters rarely freeze. After every blizzard, every hard freeze, we checked on him. Our days took on an added dimension, our lives enriched by his tenacity, by the tough, invisible will to live. And now, now just as the winter gives promise of warming ...

"Damn!"

⋙ *All this Quiet* ⋘

Long ago, when I moved my office into my home, I decided that the best way to keep the kids out of my hair was to let Gwen do it. Not that I wasn't perfectly willing to lend such moral support as might be required. But after all, my role as a writer precluded such frivolous tasks as cautioning one or another of my five sprouts against inhaling water through her nose just because "Elephants can do it."

Traditionally, writers are supposed to retire to such solitary places as an attic to court the muse. But our attic is not heated, so I had to devise other ways of guaranteeing an oasis of quiet. It immediately became obvious that I had to establish barriers. "Go ask you mother" was not enough, because the kid wouldn't have come to me in the first place if Gwen hadn't already locked herself in the bathroom.

Like all fathers, in the beginning I aimed over the head of the kids and right at Gwen. "If you want to eat," I would warn her, "you're just going to have to keep your kids corralled. I can't make a living with someone drooling over my typewriter keys."

Looking stern, Gwen would announce to one and all, "Now you're all going to have to quiet down so your father can work." Then, on the pretext of having to "get a load of wash started," she would disappear and hide in the basement. But, irony of ironies, I became so conditioned to the rustle-hustle-bustle of household noises that when the kids were in school, the silence would grow and grow until I would shout: "Gwen, are you in the kitchen?"

"Yes, Mel, I'm here."

"Well, for God's sake, make some noise. I'm going nuts!"

It got so that I would sigh with relief when I would hear the horses neigh, the dogs bark and the geese honk. It meant the kids were coming home from school. Trouble is, how do you teach children to rustle-hustle-bustle in an appropriately muted manner without a sudden solo: "Ma! Dianne hit me!"? The time came when I had to decide on the masterful approach, one thump on the head for every shout, two whacks on the bottom for every scream. So they took to whispering. I could hear them, even through closed doors: *Bzzz-bzzz-bzzz.* Were they talking about me? What were they saying? I took to listening, *Bzzz-bzzz-bzzz,* until, exasperated, I would swing the door wide and shout: "I heard what you were saying!"

They would stand there then, innocent-eyed, wondering why they should be repentant about discussing the talents of white rabbits as compared to black. But I did not grow old accidentally. When it became astonishingly clear that my survival and sanity depended entirely on my sagacity, I analyzed my predicament and realized that the psychological approach was the only one.

Surprisingly, there were some standard maneuvers, no matter how many times employed, that always worked. For example, as the sounds of battle came closer, I would cough loudly in my most authoritative tone and then wait until all eyes were fixed on me. Then I would begin, "Now, when I was kid ... " No need to finish the sentence. Within moments, the kids would be in full retreat and the house would settle down to its normal rustle-hustle-bustle.

Another surefire deterrent was to call out: "Gwen, has that mess in the garage been cleaned up yet?" Presto! Rustle-hustle-bustle. It is surprising how a kid can be made to fade away, like a chameleon, to become an indistinguishable part of the household, by merely announcing in an offhand way: "It might be to their advantage if we held a daily study hour. You know, Gwen, teach them the sort of things schools can't touch on because they are so busy with basics."

Don't worry that the younger ones might not get the message. They take their cues from the older ones. They get so they can smell trouble, and know when to steal away from any potential danger. The types of roadblocks with which you can barricade your island of tranquility are limited only by your imagination. The mere suggestion of a bath may stop a younger child. Older kids can be made to do an about-face by announcing, "You know, I think it's time we sat down and had a serious talk about ... " They will not tarry.

But, of course, out here at Little Lakes, it is all over, done, finished. Since shortly after Christmas, there have been no children, no grandchildren, just Gwen and Mel, rattling around like two seeds in a dry and hollow gourd. So, next time the kids visit, I am going to cut a recording of the rustle-hustle-bustle. Then, when they are gone again, I will have household music to soothe me while I rap out more reams of immortal prose.

⋙ *Conformity* ⋘

To pass the time, and to make sure there will be properly dried logs for the fireplace, I cut much wood in February. Then, even though I know better, I sterilize some wild and wonderful bush pantries, because there is something in my schooling that opts for radishes in a row. There is no excuse, because I do not raise trees for money, but to create a forest that will serve mouse as well as cottontail, coon as well as fox, ants as well as the chickadees that feed on their eggs. Regardless of my good intentions, I find myself uprooting seedlings meant for mice, saplings to nourish cottontails, and hollow trees of poor quality but considerable character, which house raccoons. It is lunacy. Nature knows and does better. In her primordial wisdom, she creates multipurpose forests, truly artistic and utilitarian communities for the wild society. It is a haunting conception of civilization that marches me and countless thousands towards academic diplomas that lead to lives of pea-in-the-pod consistency. The curse of conformity.

⋙ *World of Words* ⋘

A writer who does any lecturing, especially to students, sooner or later is asked, "What in your life influenced your decision to become a writer?"

Though many who pound a typewriter for a living confess that they do not know, some mention a teacher's inspiration, or list a combination of circumstances leading to the lonely life. My answer is succinct: "A broken leg." It was no ordinary broken leg, you understand. I'd already had one of those, a clean break of the tibia, suffered in an infantry charge off a chicken coop. No, this one was a "dilly" as the doctor said, just before he lifted me from abject misery to Cloud Nine with a little of the poppy's magic, morphine.

It happened six months to the day after my first tibia had snapped. I was on my way back to school after lunching at home when, racing for a bouncing ball, I charged straight into an iron hitching post in front of Richardt's Meat Market. I heard the bone crunch before going down in a daze. When my mind cleared, I quickly looked around to see if anyone had witnessed my blind foolishness. Relieved to see that no one had, I got up, only to collapse. The leg would not hold me.

Fortunately, or rather unfortunately, I was wearing what we called high tops, leather boots that came within an inch of my corduroy knickers, which ended an inch below my knees. I unlaced the boot on the broken leg, and then relaced it so tightly that I could shuffle, after a fashion, and was only a little late for school. The teacher who reigned over the fourth graders clucked disapproval of my tardiness as I managed to slide into the seat behind my desk. Of course, the leg began to swell and throb, and when I turned white and began to perspire, the teacher put down her pointer, came down the aisle, and asked me what was wrong.

"Just bumped my leg," I managed, "and it hurts a little."

She looked at the leg. "No wonder," she said. "You've laced your boot so tight you've cut off the circulation." She loosed the leather laces, and the rush of blood to the injury rattled my teeth. At that moment, I could have asked to be excused so that I could make a try for home. Why I didn't I do not know. Perhaps it was foolish and inordinate pride, because didn't men suffer in silence? Or it might have been a remark my father made when the doctor bill for the first broken leg came in the mail. Maybe it was the thought of being encumbered by another cast. Or perhaps I was already something of a perverse person, for to this day doctors do not exactly jump with joy when contemplating me as a patient.

I don't know, but when school was over, instead of trying to make it home, I crossed the street to an abandoned little white church. When no one was looking, I slithered into the crawl space beneath it and, like an animal injured unto death, curled into a ball on the dry, powdery earth to whimper softly, sometimes sigh. I suppose from time to time I slipped off the cliff of consciousness, and by the time I could persuade myself that I had no alternative except to make a try for home, darkness had mercifully come to hide my movements. At the first street light (one hung over the middle of each intersection) I crawled to the oval of pale, yellow light to unlace the boot so I might bind it tighter. There was blood this time, and when I turned down the top of the sock, I got a glimpse of bone. Considerably shaken, I laced the boot as tightly as my remaining strength permitted, and then dragged on.

In front of the meat market where I had rammed the hitching post, I went down. My grandmother's hotel was less than half a block away. With everyone at supper, none saw the miserable little kid crawling like a whipped dog in the grass along the sidewalk. I made the hotel, but could continue no farther. Collapsing on the curb, I figured my only chance was to have someone find me. Within minutes, someone did. The glare of auto headlights captured me. Then I heard my mother scream and my father shout. They had been riding around looking for me, and when I smelled my mother's hair in my face and felt her warmth, the tears came gushing. Mercifully, oblivion followed.

But what, you might ask, has all this to do with becoming a writer? Nothing, really. That came during the lengthy convalescence when the townspeople heard that the "Ellis kid" had again broken his leg, and began to inundate me with books. Propped in a bed made up for me in the parlor, and with no television and only KDKA-Pittsburgh on radio, I rode the west with Zane Grey. Then, heading north, I explored the Yukon with Jack London and Buck. Back to the equator, Edgar Rice Burroughs' Tarzan swept through jungles on networks of vine. Having exhausted Grey, London and Burroughs, I flirted with James Whitcomb Riley, Ralph Waldo Emerson, and then, because the books were there, discovered with Edgar Allan Poe the ominous rhythms of "The Raven," and the thumping heartbeat in "The Pit and the Pendulum."

I traveled with Joseph Conrad on "the ship, a fragment detached from earth" across the seas to "a flick of sunshine upon a strange shore." Though at first it was rough going, I became amazed at the daring of Charles Darwin, slipped more easily into the intrigues of Sir Arthur Conan Doyle, and eventually got a grasp on Aesop. In the beginning, I quaffed but one book a day, then two, until my eyes blurred, and mother crept down from upstairs to take the lightbulb from my lamp.

By the time I was in a walking cast, pathways had to be made between the books piled around the bed, and I had moved into a make-believe world of rhythmic sentences and magical paragraphs. For a time I had difficulty distinguishing reality from make-believe. Though I finally came down to earth, when troubled, I rode away on flights of fancy. And so everything became greater than life itself, and as my exaggerations came to be called lies, I began secretly putting them to paper so they might be dignified as fiction. Thanks to the broken leg that made a prisoner of my body, I learned to free my mind so it could roam the world of adventure.

⋙ *Winter Virtues* ⋘

Of course I will be glad when spring comes. Not because I don't like winter, but mostly because I am bored with the tired old complaints of those people who should have been born bears so they might tunnel beneath the arching roots of a fallen hemlock to sleep while nature puts on one spectacular show after another. I have never envied the man who the year around languishes on some tropical isle. He will never know the warm triumph of turning a wet back toward the leaping flames of an oak fire after battling a blizzard to rescue kids from a school bus caught fast in a waist-deep drift.

Winter has been the architect of some of my most memorable moments, one of which occurred, of all places, on the banks of Florida's Withlacoochee River. It had been a morning ritual to watch from our cabin window as a quail family came to the river edge to drink. Then, one morning, winter having slipped south during the night, there was an edge of ice and the covey of six, perplexed by the unyielding shield, stood in an amazed line, cocking first one and then another bewildered eye at the frozen water.

One finally tested the ice, and at once the other five followed, until the whole covey went slipping and sliding into the water. They managed to struggle back to shore to stand, bedraggled, like six astonished kids who had suddenly fallen through the ice of their skating pond. We thought sure they would leave it at that, but, after shaking and preening and dusting until they were dry, they all tried the ice again, and it was only the roar of laughter coming from the cabin that finally sent them scuttling back to the safety of their sedge home.

While working in New Orleans in the mid-'30s, I was surprised one day to see all business in that great city come to a shrieking and delightful halt as secretary and executive, mechanic and bartender, went outside to make snowmen, throw snowballs and fashion slides, in what one native described as the deepest snow in twenty-eight years. Nor can I forget the exhilaration the faces of the Californians who, on a certain New Year's Day, came tramping for refuge into a Malibu Beach restaurant where I was washing dishes, to escape a sleet storm that had slipped down the foothills to ice their windshields and put roses in their cheeks.

Winter a bore? Well, I suppose if you pull the shades it is. If you decide ahead of time that you hate it, there will be no magic moments of surprise when in the morning your footprints are the first to mark another day's trail from the back door to the garage. Summer has given me much pleasure, but winter has held the most exciting times: caught in the mountains of the Bob Marshall wilderness area in Montana, with nothing but a horse to get me back down the snow-covered trail to the valley; marooned on a snow-covered Saskatchewan island, waiting for the weather to break so a plane could rescue us; buffeted by an icy Lake Michigan while the late Curly Lambeau, father of the Green Bay Packers, headed the cruiser north looking for a harbor where we might risk a landing.

Winter dull? It is the good earth's challenge to shake out of our lethargy, to escape the doldrums, to come alive and give it back to the wind and the snow, blow for blow. I am glad sometimes that Eve persuaded Adam to bite the apple. I do not think I could have tolerated Eden. When I die, if I have my druthers, I think I would like to come back as a great, rangy, gray wolf so I can run my pack thirty or forty miles through the snowy forests each winter's night; so I can grow lean and hard and come to appreciate the good earth's summers of abundance.

⇛ *Tranquility in the Barn* ⇚

I doubt that words can convey to this generation the peace that calms a boy's often anxious heart when he lies down between two reclining cows and watches winter moonbeams filter through the lace of cobwebs on a barn window. All the cows, milked, fed and bedded, are off their feet, willing prisoners to the stanchions, chewing cud in soft unison. Today has ended and tomorrow is more than fifty-thousand heartbeats away. There is only warm, wonderful now, an interlude unmarred even by the persistent yearning for a flivver with which to court that special girl. The mice are there, too, above me in the loft, and so are the cats, a varying population of some dozen or more. Sometimes I hear the quick, velvet rush of the hunter's paws, or perhaps a mouse's terminal squeak, but it is less an intrusion than the sound of my own breathing.

My children might say I was spaced out. And that's not a bad description of the equanimity experienced there among perhaps thirty cud-chewing, sighing Holsteins with not a worry in the world. If there was an interruption, a break in my detachment, likely it came if the cow on my right and the cow on my left sighed simultaneously. I would, of course, be squeezed. Then it would be my turn to sigh before lapsing back to that level of consciousness where everything except just being seemed superfluous. Usually, my reverie ended when one or the other of my bedded companions decided it was time to stand. While still a novice at this very special method of mesmerization, I would lie back down as soon as the cow did. But it never worked, because once the spell was broken I could not, at least during that evening, recapture it.

Of course, it was a wintertime thing, because in summer the cows kept to the pasture. And the experience could not be shared. Two boys, each with his own two cows, even though at opposite ends of the barn, would eventually be telling lies to each other. And there were the restless nights, when the cows themselves were perturbed by impending weather, or by the bull rattling his horns against the bars in his paddock. Then, it was best to stay away.

Quiet, crystal clear and sharply cold moonlit nights seemed best. Then the barn was a warm, breathing oasis in an otherwise bleak world where snowy field followed upon snowy field. It is readily apparent that a person needs such interludes, particularly since swift planes have squeezed the world from a gigantic, mysterious, foreign globe down to the size of a basketball. Now your stoop and my stoop are but a short trip from a doorstep in Africa, even though (sadly) we do not know the family right next door.

Such is the swiftness of communication that bewilderment follows upon bewilderment as, from our easy chairs, we see bombs burst in a war on the other side of the world. So we drink in catastrophe after catastrophe until we react as if to a play staged for our leisure viewing. There appears to be no avenue of escape. We try listening to music. We try religion, meditation, isolation in a forest cabin, sex, poetry. And if sometimes these antidotes come close to timing your pulse or my pulse to the rhythmical certainty of the spheres and seasons, in the end, none have lifted me to as untroubled and as high a plane as that wintertime hour in the barn at night.

Anyone who has never stretched out in a nighttime barn might be repulsed by the thought. Likely, his or her preference would be a waterbed, perhaps a flickering candle instead of moonbeams and the odor of incense instead of the wine smell of slightly fermented silage. But to me, having sampled both environments, there is nothing quite so soothing as being sandwiched between the gently undulating sides of contented cows. As for incense? What perfume can equal the faint aroma of summer flowers pressed and dried along with the timothy hay that is my bed? That was a long, long time ago. And it did not last, because as soon as I acquired my first flivver, I was off and away chasing girls. But none had such beautiful, liquid brown eyes as those contented cows of mine.

⇒ *Emergency Plans* ⇐

Some years ago, a storm knocked down some trees across our road, and the furnace, kitchen stove, refrigerator and freezer ceased to function. Without electricity, the pump could not lift water, so taps only hissed and, after one flush, the toilets were useless. Telephone lines had gone down, too, so I could not call to ask about the extent of the damage and how soon I might expect power. Then, throughout the house, because there was no music coming from the radios, there was an almost eerie silence.

In one lightning stroke, many life supports had been withdrawn. Through the driving snow that blurred past the window, I saw a cottontail fluffed in furry insulation, blissfully eating the red shoot of a bramble, unaware that, at the moment, I envied the simplicity of its existence. At the time, there still were children at our home. After a momentary hush as they gathered their wits, they came crowding around, eager to put into operation the procedures planned for just such an emergency. At first, I said, "No, not yet. The power may come on at any time."

Well, the power did not come on, not for a long time. The children roamed from window to window, watching the fat black-and-gold grosbeaks hunched behind bird-feeder windbreaks to gorge on sunflower seeds. Noses to the glass, the children were within inches of sparrows perched like brown fluffballs in junipers, which framed the windows. But the children focused primarily on the thermometer, which, since we had a good old house, was reluctant to drop.

Outside, on another thermometer that they could see through a window, the mercury had steadily descended to five degrees, but even after an hour the temperature in the house had come down only three degrees, to sixty-five. Nevertheless, the children complained that they were cold. I sent them grumbling upstairs for sweaters, but then the youngest asked, "What about our emergency plan?"

It was enough to embolden the other two (we had three then) to take up the chant. "Yeah, what's the use of having emergency plans if we aren't going to use them?"

"There's time. There's time," I said, but when they had scattered again, my wife said, "Oh, let them. They're so anxious." So we placed logs in the fireplace, and soon flames were shooting sparks up the chimney, and waves of warmth spread into the room. The candles, strategically placed, dispelled the gloom. Owls, clowns, flowers — whatever shadowy characters childish imaginations might want — danced on the ceilings and walls. The gas lantern was lit and hung on an outside post, "Just in case," the oldest child explained, "someone without emergency plans needs help and can't find the way."

We set the camping gas stove on top of the electric stove, and the burners put up their blue flowers of flame. Soon, chili was bubbling, corn popping and snow melting in kettles. Mother hummed, and I again told about the winter of storms when my grandfather kept a rope from the barn to the house so he would not get lost going to and from his chores. Outside, the snow finally stopped, and the rays of the gas lantern lay a perfect silver circle, and the dogs came from the kennels into their runs to inquire about it.

We carried perishables from the refrigerator and buried them in the snow. We made more water for the night, and put bricks we had been saving in the basement beneath the fireplace grate so they could be wrapped in flannel to warm our beds. We shut off upstairs rooms. We opened a basement water valve slightly so the pipes would not freeze and burst. We set a half-dozen cans of canned heat on the table for whatever contingency. Then, we clicked all electric light switches to an "on" position so we would know in one great burst of illumination that the power was on.

Then, as much out of defiance as anything else, we piled on clothes and trudged up the road to assess the damage. There were two lindens uprooted, but neither had touched the electric lines into our place, so we knew the damage was somewhere beyond. After surveying the downed trees, and as the five of us turned to go back to the house, child number two shouted, "Wait!" We looked, and there, in the circle illuminated by her flashlight, far down in the crater from which the tree roots had been wrenched, a round ball of grizzly brown fur opened two sleepy, bewildered eyes.

"Well, I'll be," I said. The storm had taken the roof right off the winter den of a hibernating woodchuck.

"What'll happen to him?" the youngest asked.

"Unless we help him," I said, "he'll freeze."

"Is that because he had no 'mergency plans?"

"I suppose," I agreed. "I suppose that's what it means, and maybe it also proves there's no place left to hide, to hibernate, not anywhere, not anywhere in the world."

I don't know if my universal interpretation of the woodchuck's plight made any impact, or if the kids even understood, because at that moment my wife said, "Look! The lights are back on."

Looking up to the illuminated house on the knoll, I half expected the children to respond with a whoop of delightful triumph. But as we trudged, woodchuck wrapped in my overcoat, there was complete silence. I do not know if we were disappointed that the magical moment of challenge had passed, or if we were instinctively apprehensive that someday, as with the woodchuck, our emergency plan would be sadly inadequate.

≫ *Weep for a Tree* ≪

I wept this morning for a tree. A late February storm hurling massive clots of wet snow on the enormous branches of a towering willow toppled it. But I am not the only one who is sad. Come April, the raucous flickers will arrive to find their ancestral home is gone. Blue jays who nested there will have to look for other accommodations. A screech owl who must have come startled from his knothole doorway will likely spend tonight house hunting. Opossums who found refuge from the fox in the high branches will never find another so conveniently tall and tangled.

Chickadees who scouted the rotting places for ant eggs will have to hunt for other pantries. No longer at dawn and dusk, high where the sun always lighted limb tips first, will mourning doves gather before sallying forth to fields. Squirrels will search among the ruins for nuts cached there. Nuthatches and downy and hairy woodpeckers will have to scout out other bug-hunting places.

It is difficult to lose a pet, but much worse to lose such a gargantuan tree, because not again in our lifetime will any other sprout attain such proportions as qualify it for inspiring significance. That is the way it is with some friends. That is the way it is with some trees. That is the way it is with such associations as can never again be duplicated. That is why I wept this morning, for a tree.

⇛ *A New McGuffey* ⇚

The pathway toward a better world is cluttered with such a multitude of complex issues that we even despair of intelligently educating our children. What appears true today may be out-of-date tomorrow. The swift advances of technology keep the world in a state of flux. New environmental groups rise to meet a new threat; they are met with an avalanche of conflicting technical literature. It can boggle the minds of those not prepared to handle it. And when the mind boggles, it backs off. Bewildered, our once-concerned citizenry becomes turned off, and then boredom can spread like a cancer, killing all the good healthy tissue of true concern.

I suspect that the principal reason for our confusion is the lack of firm grounding in the elemental truths, the most basic of which, very simply stated, is that conservation means saving the earth's resources by sensible recycling processes. If that sounds like an oversimplification, it is not. It is as basic as the bedside prayers upon which a child builds a lifetime of religion. What is more, it is neither new nor revolutionary. If any over forty did not get the message when they were young, it is not because the prophets weren't preaching it, but because they were not listening.

Please note: "More has been said and done and written about the conservation of natural resources since 1920 than in all the preceding years of American history. No other federal or state enterprise excepting national defense compares with the present-day projects in conservation. State and federal governments have launched thousands of conservation projects involving the employment of millions of men and the expenditure of billions of dollars."

Written recently? Wrong! Written in 1938 in the foreword to *Conservation of Renewable Resources*, a book by the late E.M. Dahlberg, a northern Wisconsin high school principal. Many have managed to get the message. The University of Wisconsin-Stevens Point, which boasts the oldest and largest conservation curriculum in the world, is graduating so many people interested in making a career in environmental protection that many fail to find work in their chosen profession.

For these graduates, and for all the truly concerned, a plethora of books on an endless variety of ecologically oriented subjects is being published. There are also endless suggestions, tools if you will, for teachers at the elementary, high school and college level. But this very broadcast of teaching procedures lends credence to the proposition that we are floundering and even striking out like disturbed hornets ready to put the bite on the first target of opportunity.

What is lacking, what we should have, is conformity, at least on an elementary level, and this begins with a classroom primer of simple wisdom. Nowhere in all my reading have I come across an adequate beginner's book that very simply and with imagination explains that all things come from the earth, and that in the final analysis they must be returned, or the earth becomes the poorer for it. So far as I have been able to discover, there seems to be no all-inclusive, yet marvelously simple, explanation for the inter and intradependence of trees and insects and animals and birds and water and soil and minerals and man.

Even changing times would not require the revision of such a book. The elemental truths of good conservation are universal and unchangeable. Basically, what was good for the earth ten thousand years ago is good for the earth today. What is good for our planet and for people in India and Borneo is good for the earth today in Des Moines or St. Petersburg.

Now, maybe there already is such a book and it has not surfaced. Or perhaps it is on the bookshelf of some writer's mind, waiting to be assembled. Or maybe it is just lying around in the bits and pieces and parts of a great many books, only waiting for a great editor to assemble and breathe life into it. If this is not so, then perhaps a genius will come forth and write it, or maybe it will be written by a humble man of simple truths. Should it happen, time may make it as indispensable in the school's curriculum as the McGuffey Reader once was.

Then, if it is not only comprehensive and comprehensible, but inspired as well, it might find a place on the shelf alongside the Bible. Naturally, I would expect that a Ph.D. should write it. But personally, I would prefer that some housewife and mother would write it while sitting beneath an apple tree watching the tree green, seeing the bees come to the flower, and observing the fruit come ripe to the mouth of a child she once was host to in the world of her womb.

⋙ Legacy of Pets ⋘

It seems I always find something lacking in an adult who, as a child, had neither a pet nor a plant to nurture. Perhaps I only imagine that the child who never raised a dog, horse, sparrow or potted plant seems lacking in tolerance and compassion. Surely tens of thousands of children have grown into admirable human beings without ever having an animal friend. Still, I do not have to be in a room with an assembly of strangers very long before I find myself mentally sorting out the pet or plant owners from those not so privileged.

Did I say privileged? Perhaps that is the wrong word. As my little scheme of playing detective progresses, I find by the end of the evening that those who had no special non-human friends are more successful financially, more successful socially and more worldly than those who had changed litter in a cat's box or sprinkled louse powder on a canary. But I never feel the urge to throw an arm around the shoulders of a man or woman who never had a dog, cat or pet mouse when he or she was young.

Of course, I am so prejudiced that I cannot be objective. My life orbited around farm and forest animals, and my five daughters had such a menagerie of wild and tame animals that my feed bill often equaled the monthly grocery bill. I have looked for evidence to substantiate the theory that youngsters who had the close companionship of non-human friends, mostly of the feathered and furred variety, were indeed, in some indefinable way, just a little more (may I say) human.

My research, mainly among the writing of sociologists, psychiatrists, psychologists and social workers, was largely unproductive. For the most part, it was inconclusive and sometimes contradictory. One psychiatrist went so far as to contend that many youngsters, especially boys who had large animals such as dogs and horses, turned into domineering and sometimes sadistic adults who became easily outraged when opposed. I once worked for a city editor who said: "Show me a man who feeds a passel of hounds and I'll show you a wife-beater."

On the other hand, less than ten miles from where I live, a "farm" for retarded boys bases its program for progress on the care and loving of animals. There are also institutions for the physically handicapped that use animals as an incentive to get discouraged youngsters "off dead center," and thus on the road to tending not only for the animals, but themselves.

If childhood pets play a part in molding character, there must be supervision, especially during the early months. Nothing can be more harmful to animal or child than rag-doll treatment of a kitten or puppy. Equally harmful is the so-called Bambi syndrome, in which the child considers the pet a person endowed with human intelligence. Out at Little Lakes in the years gone by, while raising everything from dogs and horses to seagulls and kingfishers, there were but three rules:

I.   Always adequate, nourishing food and water at precisely the same
     time each day.

2. Adequate shelter, both clean and warm.

3. No punishment administered any pet until it had been discussed with a higher authority, mainly me.

From there on it was mostly catch-as-catch-can, and if a horse tossed a girl over its head into a wheelbarrow, thanks were first given that no serious injury was sustained, and then out came the book on breaking young stallions. If there were goslings and the wild Canada gander attacked, no sympathy was extended the child failing to carry a garbage can cover as a shield. If a raccoon got an earlobe, there would likely be some minutes of talk about how the raccoon is a wild animal, and if you still wanted to love and keep it, keep your head out of its food dish. Of course, I am oversimplifying. We have many books on the training and care of animals, and we sometimes undertook supervised training sessions (when we could afford it) using professional trainers, especially in the training of dogs and horses.

Now, whether my daughters are or will be better people because of their close association with such a wide assortment of non-human friends, I am not prepared to say. I hope they are. I see much evidence of kindliness in each. I think they are more tolerant and more compassionate, even of people, than they might have been without the menagerie. Except today, sadly, I do not know if you can count that as a plus. It could be they will all die broke because they gave what they had to those less fortunate than themselves.

⋙ *Directing Destiny* ⋘

If you live in a small town for thirty or more years, you get to know all the people. The same is true if your community is a wood lot: You get to know all the trees. You call them friends, and they are, at first. Some are good friends, but most are just ordinary friends, the kind you visit intermittently and lend a hand, should the need arise. On first moving to your tree community, you just enjoy living among them. You respond only to emergencies — an insect illness, wind bruise, lightning wound — and administer first aid.

But then, as your regard for your new friends becomes an enduring affection, you gradually become concerned about all their needs. Inevitably, you begin to resent interlopers, such as striplings that threaten the domain of resident friends. So, in righteous indignation, you massacre a passel of sassy sprouts. After that, there is no turning back. You have exercised a godly prerogative. You have destroyed life. You have killed the saplings so your friends may flourish. In man's role as Earth's dominant form of life, it is a thing of little consequence, and you attach no more significance to it than to swatting a mosquito. But it becomes significant because now the well-being of your trees becomes a pressing, personal concern. You have made a commitment. Then, inevitably one day, when a sapsucker begins drilling holes in the trunk of a basswood friend, you kill the bird.

You worry, too, about the towering blue spruce. You have a special feeling for the tree because of the way the wind hums through its needles, the way the rising sun lights its spire, the way the moon chases shadows in and out of its ruffled skirts. When the neighboring ash finally lengthens its reach so with every wind it thrashes the spruce, you kill the ash with the angry snarl of a chain saw. Thus you gradually extend the sphere of your special protection: the burr oak that may be as old as the nation; a weeping willow that billows in a bower over a blue pool; an elm so huge that it takes three people to encircle it with outstretched arms. A dozen become two dozen, and eventually you number your special tree friends in the hundreds. It does not happen overnight. Five, maybe fifteen years, all goes well until the day you stand on the hill, and all about are scores of trees that have run out of room to rise and are locked in a battle for survival.

There is an ironwood, a tree of intricate branch work, that wears spring catkins as long and as lacy as tassels on a prancing circus horse. You know it is doomed unless you can open up the area and bring it some sunlight. There is a mulberry, cafeteria for flocks of bright-feathered birds. Already, only the upper part of the tree is bearing, and soon it will feed few birds. There is a Douglas fir, branches swooping like eagles' wings. But, higher than you can reach, boughs already are dead.

There is a teenage basswood with leaves as large and as brilliant as dancing kites. It will live, but each year its leaves will become smaller and smaller until, because of the crowding, the basswood will become a grotesque caricature of what it might have been. There are several birches with bark starting as paper-white skin. They, too, will survive, but only as slender shadows of what they might have been, and their white trunks will be covered with black scars. There are box elders running as excitedly through the grove as street ruffians. They will become gnarled derelicts hanging on and on and on. So you kill the box elders. Next day you eliminate the basswood and the mulberry. Then you sacrifice half the birch population.

It is heady stuff, directing destiny. You sharpen the saw and move out. The days of peace and quiet are gone. You rule. You rule until a weeping willow, famed as a widow maker, cracks your back. For six months you must wait and watch through a window, fretting at the undisciplined, wild way your trees reach out for air, soil and water. Then you are back and, not satisfied with whipping permanent party members back into line, you plant your own spruce, cedar, pines and maples, in precise rows, rank upon rank, all pruned to identical, rigid specifications.

Now you really are godly. Not only do you have the power of life and death, now you are involved in creation. It is like being mother, father, mayor, police chief, judge and executioner, all at once. And you will have order. Every tree will grow according to your dictates. The trees will march down the hills in orderly ranks. And they will stand in the valley in precise rows. You think you are doing something unique. Except you are not, because it is being done all the time with flowers and chickens and cows and people. Inevitably, of course, another widow maker comes along, and this time it does it to you but good. But it does not matter. You had no friends left anyway.

⇛ *Annual Bonus* ⇚

I need some soil for a flower pot, so I get the pick from behind the garage door and, going down the slope, scrape away the snow and swing. The pick bounces back from the iron-hard soil, and the handle vibrates so it stings my hands and sends shock waves along my spine. I put the pick back behind the door in the garage and come to the warmth of the fireplace. Why then, I ask myself, does a man who is a writer, and could live anyplace in the world, settle for Wisconsin? Perhaps, I tell myself, it is because a world without the icy challenge of a real winter cannot inspire praise for spring. Then, if zest for the seasons languishes, perhaps soon the gusto to write goes, too. And where, in all the world, are the seasons of man and the wild society more sharply etched than by glaring heat and biting cold? There is a bonus in coming annually to the doorstep of death to await the inevitable resurrection.

March

MARCH, THE MONTH OF AGONY AND ECSTASY, brings me down the snowy slope to where I sit on a special stump, in the shelter of crowding young spruce, to watch a certain frog who has come out of the mud more than a month ahead of time. He is on a white rock across a tiny flowing stream in a stretch suit of olive green, pale as winter lichens, immobile, hardly a heartbeat. I have watched the frog each March during ten successive years, and if you say it cannot possibly be the same frog, I see no difference. Nor does the script vary, for once the sun finds the hole in the spruce canopy and focuses on the rock, the mud bottom bulges and the frog floats slowly upward to swim a lethargic twelve inches and then climb, with labored clawing, to bunch up as if sculpted from the stone.

Then we stare, but if he sees me, it is with such cold indifference that I am prompted to pass a twig close by his nostrils, but not even the transparent shields with which he protects his eyes come down. I always wait until his rock has cooled and he must plop, bulging eyes now slowly closing, to sink to where the mud will take him back, maybe to a place where butterflies hover within easy range of his lightning-like tongue and the grass stays eternally moist, or perhaps only to the soft, dark peace of oblivion. To what other world he goes down there in the mud is not important, though I marvel at such a simple accommodation to harsh reality.

What really has me losing sleep is, why such a compulsive need to warm his blood that he will

My spirits
plummet
as the
icy wind returns
to carve a
cantilevered
overhang of snow.

try a month ahead of schedule, when there are fish and raccoons and mink and men waiting for him to come alive so they may kill him? That is the burr in my brain. Is it to chase and clasp another frog and string jellied eggs? To sit half out of the water on the warmness of a rotting log glutting on flies? To dive triumphantly into the mud inches ahead of a toothy pike? To become part of a chorus that makes springtime throb? Or only to once more be warm?

When I was young, I asked the scientists, but got only structured answers concerning light reactions among all living things, and programmed chemical adjustments to temperature. These were wise answers, I suppose, except even a thermostat knows enough to turn the furnace on.

And it is not only the anxious frog because, higher on the bank behind where it hunches, each year there is a fleshy, purple, curling finger cracking earth so frozen an axe head would bounce back in ringing protest. Relative of the orchid, this skunk cabbage comes with a built-in furnace that chemically heats its core ten degrees warmer than the atmosphere to perform the resurrection miracle. So, by the time any other growing thing might be ready and tempted to compete, the cabbage already has leaves broad enough to shut out the sun. And so only mosses come sometimes, and what they take from the soil is of no consequence to the cabbage, because the mosses are such lean eaters even rock will suffice.

It is not surprising that, when I was younger, the skunk cabbage seemed like something the devil invented: purple-greens richer than royal robes, but, when crushed or plucked, a putrefaction, vile-smelling as its namesake. And it is also not surprising that, even today, on seeing the cabbage, I sometimes think of sex, probably because there was an old priest who gave me to know that rosy cheeks and scarlet lips hid such ugly things as sins are made of. Too bad beauty became suspect, but there it was, the gorgeous but stinking cabbage. Except I did not fall for it because, even as an eight-year-old, I had the feeling the old priest was trying harder to convince

On again, off again, up again, down again, back from the bright edge of ecstasy.

himself than the little girls on the left and the little boys on the right. Still, maybe one, two or several of the squirming Saturday morning captives to this day draw their shades because the colors of a sunset are too passionate.

As with the frog, I went to the scientists about the skunk cabbage. But with their ball-bearing eyes and clicking-clacking brains, it was always the same, so in the end they too often reduced my sublime miracles to simplistic chemical combinations. Then, instead of a gorgeous oriole or a fragrant orange, all I had left were letters and numbers. So, how could I become excited enough to write a poem about moonbeams on rippling waves of H_2O?

But folklore, legend! How else would I have known the skunk cabbage sheath made spring tonic for the Indians, the taproot furnished their poultices, the root hairs stopped internal hemorrhages? But woe to the Indian who stored more than four of these roots in his wigwam, because more than that number and then the snakes would come. March, though, is more than a frog and skunk cabbage. Sometimes it is a madcap dash, and the red-winged cocks of the blackbird family, always a week or two ahead of the drab, speckled hens, get caught in a blizzard and, disconsolate, hunch in their feathers among the remnants of last year's cattails, looking like a little flock of winos in old coats, gathered to mourn as their sunshine leaks off the curb from a shattered bottle. Except I waste no sympathy on the redwing cocks, or the winos for that matter, because I know the hens will come as certainly as my derelict friends will somehow get another bottle, and then the cheering will begin.

But of course, I am no more immune than the redwings, and my spirits plummet, too, as the icy wind returns to carve, with architectural genius, a cantilevered overhang of snow above the frog's white stone. Head down then, I come through the thicker spruce where the wind is having its own troubles, and here, above the sounds of the storm, comes the voice of the gentle dove, unperturbed about the cone of snow on its makeshift shelf of little sticks, even though eggs press to be laid. And whiter even than the snow (as I come up the hill), one bloodroot blossom rises in the shelter of an old ant hummock, surprising as an angel in hell.

Frog, skunk cabbage, redwings, dove, blossom. Unquestioning, resolute, fearless. And, sure enough, the wind swings around at midnight, and in the morning storm doors slam, and the children, still bed-warm and half-clad, run outside. Oblivious to softening ice stinging their toes, they point and wildly shout: "There they are!" Indeed, there they are!

Gray etchings on the horizon. Distant echoes baying from cloud to cloud. Wild, sad, glad. All day they fly, Canada geese playing the sweet flute of freedom from winter. Winter, still a lingering terror in that primeval corner of every heart. All day, assurance from a thousand throats. All day, flock after flock, gray and high-rippling pencil marks, but sometimes hedge-hopping, eyes bright above white throat scarves.

All day they fly, Canada geese playing the sweet flute of freedom from winter.

The land hears: bears still denned among hemlock roots, wasp in a log cranny, woodchuck in the dark of a grass-lined tunnel, bog-buried turtle. Perhaps even a fetus hears, and presses against vaginal doors to be on time, because the yearning does not come from the sky, but is already and always present, even in the heart and fiber of the unborn.

March, perplexing time of transition. All winter the cock cardinal preempts the hen, but now, suddenly he comes with succulent offerings. All winter she sat fluffed against the cold in the bare thornapple, waiting, and then when he finished, and if there was time before night, she ate. Now, through the window, I see he even cracks sunflower seeds, cracks corn, and worse, not only does she accept, but with wing-quivering subservience, she promises and promises and promises. Often, winter encores shorten daylight hours, and then the hen is back on gnarled limb among the thorns — love slave, waiting without protest. And no gander offers grass to his goose, and the mallard bachelor club loosely reassembles, and the shrike cock lets his hen do her own butchering, and the mergansers float with flattened crests, and the nuthatch, only yesterday a clown, is his old calm, matter-of-fact, nonchalant self.

And I come dragging mud into the house, and miss a pair of puckered lips to brush a kiss across a cheek because it is March, on again, off again, up again, down again, back from the bright edge of ecstasy.

⫸ *Down to the Sea* ⫷

Do children still sail boats? Little boats down gutters, along brooks? Fragile wood slivers rigged with toothpick masts and tissue-paper sails? When winter's snow runs in rivulets, do children still follow bits of tree bark, pretending they are canoes floating along a stream of fascinating dreams?

Do children still launch fallen branches on puddle oceans, those ships of the line on which a few of last fall's leaves still flutter like flags in their riggings of twigs? Does today's child guide a woodchip down the meandering brook, breathless when the small craft rides the riffles, and helpful with toe or stick where tangled grasses arch across and all but halt the tiny boat, and almost halt the stream's unbelievably adventurous journey to the sea?

Do children still dig canals with bare feet to float their barges? Tow a shingle on a string with its cargo of lumber (chewing gum sticks) and logs (peanuts), and such flood victims as a wet ant or two? Does today's child know how to dam a trickle with mud to raise the water, which in turn lifts the toy boat off a shoal, then watch wide-eyed when the craft goes bouncing over the waterfall the dam has created? Does today's child know about stones with which to narrow the channel? Hasten the flow? About stones with which to divert the current around a tree, into wedlock with another waterway?

Does today's child know? About islands? A splatter of mud sprinkled with pine needles? A meadow hummock, alone and brave above a stream of hill water? Or a sandy islet in midstream, rip-rapped against erosion with "throwing stones"? About harbors, bare heel carefully but firmly placed to draw water out of the current into a quiet place where toe prints form five slips for resting ships?

Does today's child know? About bridges? A twig across a pencil of current? A log across a creek? An arching wand of willow, high bridge for a wet mouse? Or about stepping-stones? High and dry and worn from walking? Watery sides whiskered green with undulating algae? Challenging passage? A place to wait midstream for boats?

Does today's child know? About tire-track streams? About canyon gorges where water gushes from culverts to cut clear down to clean gravel? Or slow and muddy swamp creeks inching through the dead grass of last year's lawns? Does a child know? About pine cone boats? Curling leaf sailing brigs? Milkweed pirogues or flat board bateaus, boats of the

Louisiana bayous? Round, long, smooth steamships from a woodpile? Deep-sea trolling boats made of whatever? Off to hunt whales? Bait sharks? Run a trap line? Hunt ducks? Catch a muskie? Explore a wilderness? Cruise exotic shores of lands around the world? Or only see a frog, sometimes? Turtle perhaps? Silver minnow? Or a sea monster: shiny muskrat down among the new green of a rising reed forest?

Does today's child know? Do you know? That the tiny stream flowing between banks of still-lingering ice is more than just the mother of an ocean? I hope so.

⫸ *Last Lean Days* ⫷

Death, master of disguise, sometimes comes softly, especially in March. Falling innocently from an ashen overcast, the first snowflakes melt, but as I have seen the snow geese come to Saskatchewan's freshly gleaned fields, the first are followed until there is such a gathering of flocks that the brown stubble turns white. But there the analogy ends, because there is no whirlwinding, as of wings, nor the clarion calls of excitement, but a vacuum of silence that deepens as the airy bolls add inch to cottony inch until the only landmarks left are black gashes of open water.

Sometime during the second night, the barometer begins to rise, and next morning, looking through a lattice of spaced fingers, I am bewildered by the brilliance, stranger to the trail with no familiar tree or bush or fence, grateful at last for the shed's remembered odors, dim retreat when I have forced open the door.

My eyes accommodate slowly, and then I see a muskrat, far from water, trying to wedge tighter between a wall and a wooden barrel, which, when he tried to eat it, suddenly delivered a miraculous trickle of corn. Now he will not even bristle, but like a dormouse hides his face, and I suppose I could have picked him up by the tail without risking a slashed wrist.

I slide a shovel under him instead, and my trail, down to the black gash where swift creek waters have been assaulting the pond, is a rude rape of an otherwise pure place of bridal white. I count seven muskrats on the ice edge when I slide the corn-fed one into the water. Hunched up, they look deceptively fat, except I know that beneath the folds of fur there is hardly tissue for another night, because they have eaten even their homes and had been scratching the banks for grass roots until the snow came.

That is the treachery of March, and finally in some other place the deer curls up and is covered, because his stomach will accept no more tree bark, and the redbird, having spent more energy than his feeding forays have produced, falls, and there is only the hint of a shadow where the soft snow caves in to cover it. And the next morning there is a tail-dragging trail, following my path from the shed, so I know the muskrat has come back to the corn.

⋙ A Boon Year ⋘

This winter we at Little Lakes have paid more than our share of the many millions of dollars in feed that Americans throw to the birds each year. There is no doubt that the season now dying has been the best bird winter in all the years we have lived here, both in numbers and bird variety. What is more, it has been the longest feeding season, starting way back during November's unseasonable cold, when northern birds such as redpolls and evening grosbeaks arrived weeks early. But even with sunflower seeds holding at fourteen dollars for fifty pounds, it has been worth it to see the whirl of blue, yellow, red, gold, all the colors orbiting the feeders in a frenzy to be first when a low pressure system threatens to send the birds scuttling ahead of windblown snow for the nearest shelter.

One reason the bird population peaked at Little Lakes is that the spruce, cedar, pine and Douglas fir have reached full maturity, offering maximum shelter during blizzards, and seeds from swollen cones on those mornings when we are late with the seed buckets. Another likely reason is that such unpredictable vagabonds as the grosbeaks, siskins, crossbills and goldfinches figured that Wisconsin was a summer resort compared to weather in other states north of the Mason-Dixon line.

Not counting the great horned owl with yellow, ball-bearing eyes, the most unusual visitor is a woodpecker. We've had plenty of red-headed woodpeckers here, especially during winters when acorns were plentiful. But as many times as we have examined this visitor at close range, we still cannot determine whether it is the red-bellied or gold-fronted woodpecker. Only the cardinals seem in short supply. We are inclined to blame the cats. A low-nesting bird, the cardinal is especially vulnerable, and this is the year of the cat. Only once before have so many cats gravitated to our shallow valley.

Not counting such year-round residents as English sparrows, starlings and chickadees, the most numerous have been evening grosbeaks, goldfinches in flocks of fifty, and at least three species of juncos. We did not keep records this year, but there were purple finches, pine siskins, cowbirds, blue jays, three varieties of nuthatches, downy and hairy wood-peckers, redpolls, titmouse and others. That is counting what we call house birds, those that whirl around the three bird feeders and two suet chunks situated for window watching.

Walk down the slope and crows rise, protesting, from the fish heads and entrails we have dumped on the ice of Fish Pond. There are pheas-ant tracks along the pond dikes, and soon the birds are visible racing through the willow brush. Then, like grenades, they rattle the branches to become airborne. There are mallards in Watercress Creek, and they stretch their necks to see if we are carrying the yellow pail of corn. And, for as many years as we can remember, there is a solitary kingfisher flying the creek.

The mourning doves are always with us. During the day, they go far afield, scouting windswept stubble and bushes for seeds. Then, when the sun touches the horizon, they come back in pairs and small flocks to rest in the last rays of sunlight, which still brighten high places, before drop-ping off into conifer cover to sleep. There are some ground sparrows, but unless they come to a feeder they are difficult to identify among the brushy shadows. Visitors drop in. Mostly they come from Lake Michigan — buffleheads, goldeneyes, mallards and, now and again, a merganser or two. They rarely tarry, and when they do it is just long enough to stoke up and move on.

Most disconcerting this winter has been the number of hawks. Often the hawk is not visible, though you know it is out there because sudden-ly the area around the house is quiet as a graveyard. Go to a window then, and where a moment ago there may have been thirty or forty birds, there is not a feather to be seen. Unless you know about the launching pads from which a hawk is most likely to start its swoop for a kill, you may have to look a long time before you spot the intruder. But if you live here, you know the hawk is likely to be in the walnut tree by the garage, in the oak on the knoll, or among the Douglas firs along the sunken garden. These are not the big sailing hawks, such as the red-shouldered, but the small, swifter species, agile in flight as the tiny sparrow hawk. Once, one of the feathered hunters (it happened so fast I could not identify it) came down a narrow cedar trail with what seemed like the speed of a bullet. It missed my head by inches.

Generally, we are inclined to feel sorry for birds that have not gone south, never realizing there are thousands of sheltered places, even in subzero weather. Out here, waterfowl prefer to hang around springs where water usually bubbles forth at forty-eight degrees. A hollow tree, an old crow's nest with a cluster of leaves, and a creek corner where rocks reflect the sun are little summer oases.

Of all the birds, those of the rail family are as summery a clan as any. Yet a creek running through the nearby Vernon Marsh each winter plays host to a rail colony. I discovered it a decade ago on breaking through the creek ice. Just above the current were roofed hollows and havens and, along the water's edge, insects enough to feed the two-score rails that raced frantically on fragile legs to get away from the clumsy lout who had broken through their roof. But if you cannot identify with rails, there is a deep and protected valley four hundred miles north, not far from Bayfield, that tempts a small robin colony to stay each winter.

⋙ *Tackle Box Mouse* ⋘

Long-tailed velvet mouse with feet as delicate as Queen Anne's white lace, looking up at me with berry-black eyes, wouldn't you be as warm in a hollow log as you are in my old fishing-tackle box, nested alongside, of all things, a wooden mouse with which I once caught fish? There is no possible way the outrageous replica could have decoyed you. But there you are, with a pink cluster of blind babies, snuggled up to this carica-ture and its dangling treble hooks, which fish are supposed to mistake for feet.

During younger days, or maybe even this morning, I would have fed you to the fish or any passing cat, except for that tooth-scarred lure, which might leer if it could know that in some inexplicable way, it has pointed up an irony. Now March is cleaning month, and the bathhouse is where we start among the fall-stored crush of folding chairs and fishing rods, life vests, flippers, oars, and the rubbish raccoons have left before their hole was boarded over.

Were it April, velvet mouse, you would go for sure, blind babies drag-ging fastened to your teats, but there is still a dirty scarf of snow wrapped around the stoop, and then there is that wooden icon, and could an Indian take the lotus from the lap of Buddha? It is too late, anyway. The children have found you. That makes you safe for sure, because they will not step on an ant or even kill the bee that stings them. But if that is assurance enough for this time, have your next litter some other place, because, stung twice, some children squash the bee, and once it starts, that wooden mouse will not save you.

And any spiders out of your cracks, get back, because here come the brooms, and when it is done, there you will be, velvet mouse, on a rusting metal island in the middle of a clean sea of boards, you and your implacable companion. Then, when you go, use the door. I will leave it open a crack, because I have nailed a tin patch over the hole you gnawed through the floor.

⋙ *Marooned* ⋘

I am sure many outdoors lovers have been marooned at one time or another, at least temporarily. But do you know of anyone who has been marooned in the basement of his own home, sprawled on a shelf among dripping bottles of root beer? During a long life, much of it spent afield, I have been marooned many times. But never was the experience as traumatic as being marooned on the basement shelf when I was a child.

By comparison, it was almost a pleasure to spend several days in the Canadian bush on a small trout lake with an Ontario photographer when the pontoon plane, which had dropped us off for a day of fishing, was grounded by weather. Contrary to expectations, all we could catch was one ten-inch trout. We ate that and fiddlehead ferns and were trying to find where we had discarded the trout entrails so we could eat them, too, when the plane returned. Another time a blizzard swamped a boat and trapped us on Basswood, one of the cluster of Lake Superior Apostle Islands. One man died before we made it back to the mainland. And another time, Gwen and I, with a Saskatchewan photographer and guide, spent anxious hours marooned on one island after another as we made our way ten miles across a far-northern Canadian lake into a gale of rain, hail and snow. When we finally made it, hungry, wet, freezing and frightened, we were just in time to meet a rescue party leaving the harbor.

There have been other incidents, too, but none as traumatic as being marooned on the basement shelf with black water all around me. Perhaps I was four, maybe five. Each spring the earthen-floor basement of our home flooded, and the water came waist-deep on an adult. My father would skid his duck-hunting skiff through the kitchen and down the cellar steps so he could paddle the boat to where the jars, crocks and bins of preserved food from the previous year were stored on shelves above the waterline. A heavy latch on the basement door was out of reach of three toddlers, of whom I was the oldest. But I could manipulate the latch with a broom handle.

One day my mother ran next door to borrow some flour. ("Your father forgot to bring home a sack of flour last night!" she complained later.) While my baby sister was tied in a highchair and my three-year-old brother was barricaded in a corner by furniture, I was left to roam. Soon I was on my way down the steps and into the boat to paddle toward the treasure of homemade root beer. Untying the boat from the steps, I got in and paddled with a board to the root beer shelf.

While trying to hold on to the shelf with one hand to steady the boat, I reached back with the other for root beer. The movement slid the little boat out from under me! With my hands on the root-beer shelf and my feet standing on the shelf below, I gave a grunt and a lunge and sent bottles flying as I slithered to safety. All was quiet then, except for the drip-drip-drip of root beer into the water below. There was not enough room to sit up, and I could feel the root beer seeping beneath me. When a trickle of root beer appeared near my face, I put out my tongue to taste it. But I could not, not in the gloom of this forbidden place.

I remember I was very cold. The water looked very black. Inadvertently, I had kicked the skiff almost all the way back to the steps. I suppose I should have wept or screamed or done something. But I did nothing. If I was afraid, I have no recollection of it. All I can remember is that I was peacefully calm, seemingly detached from my surroundings.

Footsteps above broke the spell. Then a moan, and, "Oh my God!" I heard the telephone crank, then my mother's voice asking the operator to call my father and tell him to get home right away. Footsteps on the cellar steps. My mother's face white. Her brown eyes almost black as they searched the gloomy waters.

"Over here," I said in a tiny voice.

She tried to reach the boat and, when she could not, plunged into the waist-deep water. As for my rescue, I have no recollection. All I remember is lying on the kitchen floor, my mother alternately kissing and spanking me, until my father appeared in the kitchen door, and she turned her attention to him. "You," she screamed at my father. "You, you ... if you'd only brought home the flour ... " Over and over. Only that, and my brother and sister screaming at the top of their lungs.

⋙ *Death and the Old Dog* ⋘

A dog, of all creatures, has given me second thoughts about euthanasia, the act of inducing death for reasons assumed to be merciful. To understand how I feel, you should know that my wife and I have a pact: If one of us is doomed to a vegetable existence through severe injury or illness, the other is to order the withdrawal of all artificial life supports. Now, if this does not qualify as euthanasia, it is so close that the difference seems merely a matter of semantics. Granted, many may argue that there is a vast moral and legal gulch between taking a life and just permitting that life to expire. But I have not come to argue morality or legality — only to say that, after considering the case of our old dog, I wonder if any physical condition can be considered so hopeless that we are justified in helping the sufferer through death's door.

The old dog is a German short-haired pointer who never amounted to much except as a creature who returned more love than he got, and he got much, much more than most. Brig is his name. He was, in the beginning, a cleric's dog, resident of a priest's rectory, yet a Romeo with such a roving eye and restless heart as had him howling on the doorsteps of fair maiden dogs throughout the village. When he was admitted to our kennels, he was young, and he outlived many other dogs. But then at last, death came knocking at his door. After he had spent days in a dog hospital, and after we had spent more money for medicine than we had spent on our kids for a long time, the veterinarian finally said, "Best you let him go. He's had a long life. There's nothing for him but misery now. He can't possibly last the winter."

The children, of course, greeted that news with tears that turned to anger and then obstinacy until, in the end, I threw up my hands and said, "Okay, kids, we'll keep him." Well, it was not easy. He could not have survived in the kennel; he had to be brought into the house, where his health problems caused all kinds of complications. What is more, during any alert moments, he had a penchant for chewing each boring minute away on anything within reach. He finally was relegated to the basement, and his condition worsened. His eyes weakened and he bumped into things. He had to be helped to his feet and helped outside. He had to be watched lest he wander off, get stuck in the mud or fall into a pond. He upchucked what he ate and, worst of all, was in such pain that his whimpering could tear the heart out of a man of stone. One night he was so bad that I looked to my gun rack and eyed a rifle, thinking that I could not torture him with the long ride to the veterinarian for a painless drug to ease him on his way.

But I didn't do it, and my kids kept stuffing him with painkillers and vitamins and exercising him, even though it seemed an utterly hopeless thing to do. Then, one day when winter was waning, he got up on his own, found the back door without help, and begged to get out. He stood for a long time that day in the spring sunshine, and from that moment on his recovery was nothing short of miraculous. He began putting his old dog life back together again. Almost totally blind, so deaf I think he only sensed such sounds as an auto makes by the airborne vibrations of the motor, he created a whole new and almost vigorous lifestyle using only his nose. And he did it virtually alone, asking only that we not move his water and food from their familiar places. We tried not to rearrange the lawn furniture or drop tree limbs on his many trails so there would be only a minimum of painful collisions.

In time, his eyesight became infinitely better. He lives outside again. He no longer whines with pain, and he can even run again. Last summer, the kids built a stone ramp into a pool so that on hot days he could go swimming. When tired, he came to lie down beside any lawn chair having a kid for an occupant. Then, when no one was outside to be guarded, he went around teaching young rabbits to run fast enough to escape the fox, or keeping young mourning doves up off the ground so a cat could not get them.

He had another summer, a warm, beautiful time filled to overflowing with living. And now it looks as if he will make it through the winter and, perhaps, to another, final summer. And so I look at my wife and she looks at me, and we wonder. Now that we have seen how it is with Brig, we wonder if, sometime in the future, one of us might inadvertently deprive the other of a whole, long, warm, sweet-smelling summertime.

⋙ *Darkness Before Dawn* ⋘

Sometimes she stands in sweet array,
Sometimes pink as dawning day.
Of every shade of azure made,
And oft with breath as sweet as May.
JOHN BURROUGHS

Sullen month, days and weeks without the sun. Shut-in minds have circled the first day of spring in red, expecting that then their melancholic mood will melt and, like the meadow brook, lift sparkling at last on the freshet of one more beginning. But March twenty-first is as gray as the day before. And the brook is silent under ice. Trees still stand as stark, black bones. Shouldering my own sadness, I come to where last year's leaves, prisoners of a dogwood thicket, rustle without meaning, tiresome as an endless sermon.

But I am too late. Gray days and cold nights notwithstanding, already the pink and azure hepatica petals are wilted and blown. I should have known. Protected by a fuzz resembling fur, the tiny hepatica is in such haste to bloom, it shoots up its stems before the leaves appear. Then, like a thermostat, the furry coat opens and closes with temperature changes. While I sat dispirited and almost despairing, spring had already announced itself.

So I kneel where the blossoms were, because already the leaves are fanning into traps with which to catch and hold next fall's windblown debris, to blanket the plant safely through another winter. And the leaves will survive the ice and snow, because in spring they must also serve as dancing reflectors for the sun's rays, thus warming the ground so the blossoms can hurry to unfold, to reassure a tired earth, and me, that this sullen month is as ordinary as any darkness that comes before the dawn.

⇛ *Miracle Machine* ⇚

In blaming technology for providing us with tools to destroy our own habitat, we can easily overlook thousands of conservation practices and reclamation projects which the same technology has made possible. Just as complicated and innovative as the massive machines that can cut, strip and tote an entire forest to market are the advanced methods of planting and growing those same forests in half the time required by nature.

Just as mind-boggling as the conversion of coal into electricity are the scrubbers and related contrivances to keep coal fumes from contaminating the countryside. Lest you be misled, this is no brief on the merits of the technological age. Being a rural and, if not simple, then an uncomplicated person, I would settle for the rigors of yesterday just to live in such a world as preceded the Industrial Revolution.

But, not being able to go back, and having grown too old to run off to live in a tent, I can only turn off the thermostat, flick the light switch, and indulge the primitive in me with an interlude in the shadow and shine of flames from the fireplace. Although the logs I burn are cut from trees, many of which I have planted, my city cousin should not be deprived of this somewhat primordial experience just because his logs are made by machines that compress paper. If this appears to be a compromise in my continuing resistance to such age-old inventions as even the wheel, there is a specific reason. I call it my Miracle Machine.

It has been running nonstop for more than ten thousand hours, about a year and a half. It is no larger than a football, and it requires less than two dollars' worth of electricity a month. For five months I have not even gone down to look at it or reached a hand through the hole in its shelter to see if it might be running hot. But if its unfailing mechanical performance astounds me, the impact it has made on the habitat of my two-and-a-half-acre pond is nothing short of miraculous. The pond is artificial, dug about a quarter-century ago. It is fed by springs of cold, clear, unpolluted water. By the light of the moon, it is a thing of beauty, but because of the soil chemistry of its basin, it grows a noxious weed called chara, which chokes out all other vegetation and, when exposed, has a repulsive odor. Fish live in the pond, but since it is infertile, their growth is slow. Waterfowl shun it because of a lack of food, and about every fifth or sixth winter, because of decaying chara, it freezes out and everything in the pond dies.

But that was before the Miracle Machine, a tiny compressor powered by a one-quarter-horse motor. It catapults air through a length of tubing to a sleeve-like structure spiked to the pond bottom. The air erupts from the plastic sleeve with the force of a tiny volcano. In an hour, it circulates six thousand gallons of stagnant bottom water and, in one twenty-four-hour period, releases fifty pounds of oxygen into the pond.

Those, briefly, are the technological aspects of the Miracle Machine. Biologically, the results are hard to believe. The chara has all but disappeared. The fish, nourished by a revitalized food chain of all manner of underwater midgets, are growing at an amazing rate. Plant life found in more desirable waters now grows in the shallows. Ducks visit. Some stay because, during cold times, it is the only open water available. Replete with oxygen, the water has a startling sparkle.

Somewhere, of course, massive generators are consuming resources to supply energy to operate this miracle of revitalization. But here, as in many other instances, technology is working to enhance rather than destroy the beauty and productivity of an otherwise sterile habitat.

⇛ *Sacrificial Offering* ⇚

The grackles, yellow-eyed and glistening as burnished gun metal, blow in on a south wind, raucous as the hordes of any Genghis Khan, each pair to lay nesting claims to one of the hundreds of spruce, until all the trees that surround a sparkling, spring-fed pond have been spoken for.

The cacophony unnerves even the feral cats, and excrement whitens the ground. Morning damp accentuates the acrid odors, and rain, by the time it reaches the ground, stings the eyes like ammonia. So, with black retriever and special pellet gun, I collect birds, two to a cellophane package, sacrificial offerings so that the red-shouldered hawks who nest in the dead elm may have small excuse to bring a summer thrush to their scrawny-necked kids.

If you have never crushed a fly, poisoned an ant or rat or uprooted a dandelion, or if you carry spiders outside instead of flushing them away, you may look askance at such godlike impertinence. But now the perching grackles break, without exception, each tender spire of new spring growth, so all the spruce grow only sideways, one strangling the other, until ultimately, if unchecked, there would be but a thick frosting of green, crusting a tangle of dead brush.

When egg laying starts, the shooting stops. Now the trout in the spring-fed pool, having come to anticipate the speckled eggs, rise to each splash, and they are not disappointed if we have come late to one nest and there is a fledgling instead. So the grackles leave, as if from a land accursed, and the earth, flushed by clean showers, revives. In what seems like minutes, the jewelweed has spread a thin, pale and fragile mist of green across the ground, in hope the hummingbirds will be on time, because no other winged thing can officiate at its ritual of pollination.

They will come, I know, jeweled bird to jeweled blossom, and when the tiny orange flower fades, there will be seeds to explode from a tendril pocket waiting under tension like a grenade to be triggered by child or passing dog. Then, some day, it will be March again and, never remembering the gun, the yellow-eyed grackles will be back.

⇛ *So Many Rivers* ⇚

As a boy, I envied the men whose love affairs were with the world's great rivers. Men such as Jacques Cartier, who mapped the St. Lawrence. Francisco de Orellana, explorer of South America's Amazon. Louis Joliet and Jacques Marquette, leaders of an expedition down the Mississippi. David Livingstone, who explored Africa's Zambezi. In time, of course, I had my own love affairs. But they were with rivers of little consequence, except to me.

I remember the first. It was a spring-thaw trickle meandering along a muddy wagon-wheel rut. I stood fascinated as the little river widened and deepened a channel for itself and then, quickening, broke through its wheel-rut banks into a web of tributaries. The second? A nameless ditch draining a field. Marsh marigolds sprouted in spring and cattails fattened in summer. Then, in fall, brush willow bordering the stagnant waters put up a bower of golden leaves over green frogs.

On a warm day in early summer, I saw my first spring-fed creek tumbling over stones, curling around in shadowy pools, singing and sparkling on the downhill runs, silent and somber while crossing flat meadows. So I came back often, intent on following along to see where it was going. It was nearly dark on the day I finally came to where my creek disappeared, swallowed by a large river. Then, though I was still a boy, it hit me: All my little rivers were moving toward inevitable anonymity with the sea! As often happens to the very young, the thought devastated me, and it was a long time before I could bring myself to go back to the spring-fed creek.

When I did, I moved upstream, searching for the river's source. Eventually it led me to a mysterious place of shifting shadows, a cedar bog. It was the gathering place, where waters seeped among the ancient roots of leaning trees. It was a mysterious place of whispering wings and winds, of crawling and scampering creatures, which I saw but briefly as fleeting shadows. It was the place where the waters of my spring-fed creek, by joining forces, gained strength for the journey to the sea. That was the start of a lifelong hobby following little rivers, not to their destinations, but back to their beginnings.During a lifetime of outdoor living, I have been carried downstream by many rivers to such places as Hudson Bay, through the jungles of Central America, down canyons cut in western mountain ranges, on floats ending in both oceans, and on peaceful journeys through Wisconsin farmlands, where cows lifted their heads to watch me drifting by. But no downstream journey has fascinated me as much as my continuing quest for the sources, the beginnings, of little rivers.

There must have been hundreds. Some required many return trips and took years to trace. Some revealed their source after a fifteen-minute walk.

There are still many that I must go back to if I want to walk to the place where they begin. One of the most interesting little rivers ran behind a house where I lived on Milwaukee County's western boundary. At that time, ducks came, especially in spring. There were muskrat, mink, opossum and fox, and always sparkling water gurgling through wood lots, vacationing in fields, winding around homes, hurrying under railroad trestles. I followed it north where it flirted with Elm Grove and then Wauwatosa, skipped under Highway 100, and then, before I could walk to its source, became lost in new subdivisions with barking dogs and "no trespass" signs.

There remain literally thousands of little rivers in Wisconsin begging to be explored. So what if hundreds of others have preceded you. Does that make your river exploration any less precious? Maybe you cannot explore. Well, spring is a good time to make a river of your own. The ground is soft. Water stands in puddles. A stick is all you need to start a riverbed. I do it every year, and it takes me back to the days I saw my first little river meandering along a muddy wagon-wheel rut. No other river anywhere in the world can match that kind of magic.

⇛ *Trash or Treasure?* ⇚

If living close to the good earth has taught me anything, it can best be summarized by the cliche: "Nothing is forever." It took me some living to make that admission, but once resigned to the fact that nothing is forever, I suddenly had what seemed a whole world of pleasant options. Now, if you would like to incorporate the "nothing is forever" philosophy into your lifestyle, go right ahead. But this has nothing to do with lifestyles. It has to do with trees.

Like most romanticists (and you must be a bit of one to get friendly with trees) I was a burr oak, blue spruce, umbrella elm, spreading chestnut, hard maple sort of guy. I was not about to waste my time on willow or poplar or basswood or box elder, or any of those less-than-noble species, which too often spring unwanted even from ash piles. Well, it was easy for me to be smug, even snooty. When I came to what is now my home place in southern Wisconsin, my predecessor, something of a tree snob himself, had groves of blue Colorado spruce, Douglas fir, white and red pine, soft and hard maple, already reaching for the sky. Of course, my predecessor could afford such a richly selective planting of aristocrats, because nature had already endowed the area with hickory, walnut and several species of oak, including some venerable burr oaks. And there were one hundred seventy-two (I counted them) umbrella elms, some so massive I am sure they were already there in the days of Lincoln.

So it was easy for me to look with disdain upon lesser tree species trying to invade the place. But then, things began to happen. Nineteen years ago, on the southeastern boundary of my fifteen acres, leaves on a lot-line row of elms began to wilt from Dutch elm disease. Of course, we figured our Illinois, Indiana and Ohio neighbors were just dumb about trees, and that we here in Wisconsin would stem the advance of the disease and save our elms. It took me two years to realize that I would go broke fast if I tried to save my elms. It took Milwaukee County, my next door neighbor, nineteen years and about two million dollars to come to the same conclusion.

To the point: I cut all my elms. Now add a tornado, which skirted the place and took twenty-four hard maples, roughly fifty spruce and a scattering of other species. Count also deaths from age, insects and ice attacks, and one pony horse who relished bark of even the ironwoods, and there were some pretty big holes punched into my wood lot. Almost at once, basswood, box elder, poplar, willow, Chinese elm and a host of trash trees rushed in to fill the gap. Snob that was, I counter-attacked with axe and saw, and planted such socially acceptable trees as oak, spruce and pine. Of course, my aristocrats, all slow growers, needed not months but years and years to arrive at heights that would make them invulnerable to annual rabbit, drought and ice damage, and such other hazards as the trampling attacks of horses, dogs and careless friends.

Considerably discouraged, I came one hot July to a shaded place to rest after a day of watering my aristocrats. After wiping the sweat from my brow, I lay back and was at once enveloped in a mist of dripping sweetness. Looking up to where I could hear the comforting drone of hundreds of bees, I saw the perfume was coming from yellow blossom clusters hanging in profusion from, of all species, a basswood — a trash tree that will sprout at the drop of a nutlet, or any root remnant, to provide shade in the time it takes to get a baby into kindergarten.

In minutes then, as swiftly as I might have received a spiritual visitation, I gained a wood lot philosophy that changed my attitude about trees. "Trash trees or not, let them grow," was rule number one. Within a few years, the wood lot gaps were green again. Rule number two, revolving about the premise that "nothing is forever," provided the excuse and impetus I needed to cut any tree, regardless of its social status, if it was getting in the way of the tree community as a whole.

And it worked. In fifteen years, I have some aristocratic burr oaks ten feet tall, and also some trash poplars that top out at more than thirty feet. I have second-generation elms eight to ten inches in diameter, and trash willows it takes two kids to reach around. I have new hard maple up to fifteen feet, and new basswoods already spreading enough shade for the family barbecue. So, if you live in one of those snobbish subdivisions where only spindly, aristocratic trees are planted sometimes because ordinances prohibit certain trash trees, and beauty and shade must therefore be postponed for fifty or more years, give a thought to yourself and plant some Chinese elms, basswood, box elders, poplar or even willow. You owe future generations something, but you owe yourself something, too.

I recommend trash trees also to forestry departments of big and little cities for parks and curbside trees, and to farmers, so they may have shade and beauty while their aristocrats grow. It is easy if you remember that nothing is forever, and you can cut the trash trees anytime you like. But maybe you will not want to when you see how the poplar turns the silver side of its leaves to the rain and sighs in the wind.

⋙ *Respected Adversary* ⋘

Good-by, winter. I will miss you. No matter that you hung icicles in my beard, squeezed the blood out of my fingers and froze the wind tears on my lashes, because once again we fought to a draw. We have had some good fights, you and I. Remember? The time I was maybe ten years old? When a muskrat scooted beneath a shelf of ice, and when I bellied out to look beneath, my mongrel pup jumped on my back and we both ended up in the creek? Remember? You had cooled things to near zero, and you were breathing at about forty miles per hour. In seconds, I became a walking sheet of ice facing a two-mile hike home. My mother cried harder than I did while I was being thawed out.

I suppose you thought you had me that day on Vernon Marsh when I went through at the drainage ditch, filling my waders with water, and had to break the ice with my gunstock to open a half-mile path back to dry land. I will admit you had me on the ropes the night I was lost in the Chequamegon National Forest. I could even hear you laughing in the night, although I suppose you thought I didn't know it was you, thought it was just the wind chortling through the pines. Fooled you, though, when I got some fleece from my jacket smoldering with my second-to-last match and got a brush fire going.

You did come close the day you put Bumpy, my old truck, through the ice. That was a low blow. Always the fight had been between you and me, so why did you come out swinging when I had two of my kids in the truck cab with me? I cannot forgive you for that, but I still have to respect you because, perhaps more than anyone, you stiffened my backbone enough to withstand the buffeting that life usually deals up for us mortals. I respect you, too, because except for that one time, you always were up front with me. No sneaky spring attacks using chiggers, wood ticks and mosquito squadrons. No blistering my hide by first lulling me to sleep on a summery beach under a blazing sun. No nettles, poison ivy, poison oak or saw grass baited with spears of wild asparagus, colonies of morels or clusters of wild berries.

No, you came at me head-on and howling. Anytime you surprised me it was because I had ignored your warnings and let my guard down. So, if you taught me anything, it was respect for an adversary and the discipline to deal with it. You gave me fortitude, taught me to be resolute. And, scoundrel though you may be, it probably was your savage hand that changed me from boy into man.

Not that we were going at one another all the time. We had our moments. Like the nights when the moon turned the snow blue. Mornings when the sun glistened on billions of your frost diamonds. Evenings when the backlight from the west made pure crystal of your ice sculptures. Then there were those starkly black-and-white days, quiet days when you spread the world out so far that I might see a red fox napping on a southern slope a half-mile away. There were calm days, a world hushed by snow where there were only crows talking about an owl, a passing possum, an approaching poacher, a skulking cat. (Warm-weather crows are silent shadows sneaking to and from nests; winter crows see and tell all.)

You were nice about things like that, sometimes. You would even erase yesterday's snow with a fresh fall so in one trip around our place out here at Little Lakes I would know about every living thing that moved during the night. And what a classroom when my children were little! No confusing leaves or grasses or tangles of vines to obscure the truth. No pedantic, obtuse, stylistic writing. Just good, short sentences on each page of fresh snow. Sharp dramas of life-and-death struggles written without literary flourish. You used colors sparingly. But when you used them!

Never, ever are cardinals as red as when they whistle from the top branch of a winter oak. And your sunsets! You never let your colors run together. And a muskrat swimming beneath a skin of thin glare ice: shades of old mahogany, rich as combed sable.

Of course, sometimes you had to ham it up, scaring the bejeebers out of kids by making the ice boom and the trees sound as though they were exploding; frightening housewives by letting a house settle a little so a clock drops off a wall and knickknacks clatter from an end table. Oh, you are something — evil, beautiful, lovable, treacherous. So, this year, let someone else chronicle the foibles of a fickle, frail, anemic, fancy-pants spring. As for me, I will be on the hill next December, watching for you to come sneaking from out of the cold, gray horizon. Bring along a surprise. I dare you!

⋙ *Creation* ⋘

From my seat in the balcony, I wait for the curtain to go up. After so many springtimes, it must seem almost absurd, even ridiculous, that like the frog, the skunk cabbage, the redwings, I cannot wait for that certain sunny day when the feathered orchestra, with a triumphal crescendo, announces the play is about to begin.

Regardless, I climb the brown hill, thread my way between the prickly ranks of young junipers, and sit on a frosty log, where I can get a bird's-eye, almost panoramic view to wait with childlike anticipation — an old man who has seen the same play so many times.

Gwen comes, but seldom lingers, and sometimes a child stops by. And perhaps they can afford to be so casual and risk missing the first act because, barring accident, springtime will take the stage for them another twenty, forty or even sixty times, especially for the youngest. Not that I plan on dying, but I missed a springtime once, missed the first blush of naked willows, missed the geese, never saw the pale trillium grow pink with age. Removed, remote, cold, I was years regaining the seasonal rhythm, which is such a necessary part of coming especially to winter with a heart eager and excited for adventure.

And never again do I want to be out of step, to lose the cadence. If I can skip a month of summer, winter or fall, in spring I must be in my proper seat. Along with all the millions of insects, pulsing impatiently as root or seed, pressing like bud or egg or blind squirrel within the womb, I lean forward, straining to hear the first bars of the overture. For more than ten years it has been like that, and at first Gwen would come up the hill and ask, "Are you sick?" And the children would inquire, "What's the matter with Daddy?" And callers would be told I had gone to New York. Then, if a visitor saw me in my balcony seat, Gwen would say, "Oh, he's only an old man who sometimes works for us."

Aberration? Surely not the desire to witness the greatest miracle any man of any age has ever seen. What scenario can compare? And what other stage than mine could hold such a multitude of characters, each so perfectly suited to his role? Underfoot, above my head, on twig and watery wave, I am witness to the longest-running play ever presented on any earthly stage, the continuing drama of creation.

Epilogue

I WOULD RATHER PRUNE A TREE THAN A PARAGRAPH. To pluck weeds so a row of carrots may stand supremely green against the sun gives me more satisfaction than turning a phrase. If there is joy in having written, there is positive glory in coming each evening to view such progress as my ferns have made. If it is satisfying to pick up a book I have written and to see my name and feel the cloth, it is nothing compared to the feeling of fulfillment that comes through my fingertips when I touch the leaf on a tree I have planted.

Neither in nuptial bed nor in the sometimes glory of a war have I risen to such inspiring heights of life as those that send my spirit soaring across the golden waves of canary grass in fields I have planted. Perhaps in my life I have never been so completely content as when I could come as a boy to lie on the sweet hay next to the warm cows on a sharp spring night and, in my mind's eye, see once again the glistening black furrow rolling back in a never-ending wave in front of the sharp, shiny plow point I guided across a fertile field.

I feel kinship with the earthworm, with the grub, with the black ant, born there in the loam, and I sometimes wish I might explore with them the white roots of the dandelion, or travel deep where the taproot spears for water. Ecstasy surrounds me in the rhythm of existence, and the atom of my atom is in the ant, vision of my vision in the flash of the sun.

Why this obsession with the earth? Why this necessity to touch wood, to smell resin? Why

God there in my violet? My life in the smooth turn of a stone? Is it because in the fiber of all of us there is the pulse of earth from which we have surely sprung? What other womb except earth, no matter what ephemeral fantasies we otherwise spin about our origins?

I would not argue against an Eden lost, except I live in Eden. A bird's wing reflected on a wave. Wind-shredding cloud, unfolding flower. Whirlwinding universe of stars. The world in one raindrop. Evening glow in the eye of my beloved. Heaven? After this earth, who needs a bonus?

Also from The Cabin Bookshelf

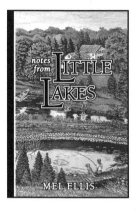

Notes From Little Lakes
Mel Ellis

Illustrated by Suzanne Ellis
Foreword by Don L. Johnson

For many years, *Milwaukee Journal* readers enjoyed "Notes From Little Lakes," in which Mel Ellis described the joys and sorrows of turning a tract of pastureland into a haven for trees, flowers and wildlife. The finest of these writings are captured here in book form. In the lore of nature and the environment, Little Lakes is as familiar and as important as Aldo Leopold's Sand County.

... of Woodsmoke and Quiet Places
Jerry Wilber

Illustrated by Terry Maciej

Jerry Wilber presents a full year's worth of daily reflections on the outdoors, and on life in the mythical North Country town of Lost Lake. Wilber's insights amuse and inspire, and along the way provide hints on how to be a better hunter, citizen, angler, camper, canoeist, cook, parent, spouse, friend. *Woodsmoke* belongs on every outdoors lover's night stand.

*These fine books are available
at your favorite bookstore.*